# WANDERING
# SOULS

# ALSO BY WAYNE KARLIN

## NOVELS:

*Crossover*

*Lost Armies*

*The Extras*

*Us*

*Prisoners*

*The Wished-For Country*

*Marble Mountain*


## NONFICTION:

*Rumors and Stones: A Journey*

*War Movies: Scenes and Out-takes*


## AS COEDITOR/CONTRIBUTOR:

*Free Fire Zone: Short Fiction by Vietnam Veterans,*
with Basil T. Paquet and Larry Rottmann

*The Other Side of Heaven: Postwar Fiction
by Vietnamese and American Writers,*
with Le Minh Khue and Truong Vu

*Truyen Ngan My Duong Dai*
(Contemporary American Short Stories),
with Ho Anh Thai

*Love After War:
Contemporary Fiction from Vietnam,*
with Ho Anh Thai

# WANDERING SOULS

### JOURNEYS
### WITH
### THE
### DEAD
### AND
### THE
### LIVING
### IN
### VIET NAM

*For Anh Hùng*
*with best wishes*

*Karlin*

## WAYNE KARLIN

Nation Books

New York

Books published by Nation Books are available at special discounts for
bulk purchases in the United States by corporations, institutions, and
other organizations. For more information, please contact the Special
Markets Department at the Perseus Books Group, 2300 Chestnut Street,
Suite 200, Philadelphia, PA 19103, or call (800) 255-1514, or e-mail
special.markets@perseusbooks.com.

Designed by Pauline Brown
Type set in 10.5-point Berkeley Book.

Library of Congress Cataloging-in-Publication Data

Karlin, Wayne.
  Wandering souls : journeys with the dead and the living in Viet Nam /
Wayne Karlin.
      p. cm.
  Includes bibliographical references and index.
  ISBN 978-1-56858-405-8 (alk. paper)
  1. Steedly, Homer, 1946- 2. Hoang, Ngoc Dam, d. 1969. 3. Vietnam
War, 1961-1975—Psychological aspects. 4. Vietnam War, 1961-1975—
Casualties. 5. Vietnam War, 1961-1975—Veterans—United States. 6.
Veterans—Mental health—United States. 7. Bereavement—Religious as-
pects—Buddhism. I. Title.
  DS559.8.P7K37 2009
  959.704'30922—dc22

                                                          2009012376

10 9 8 7 6 5 4 3 2 1

To all the wandering souls,
dead and living,
from the Viet Nam War.

# CONTENTS

(Photo insert follows page 176.)

# CHAPTER ONE

# An Encounter
# in Pleiku

On March 19, 1969, First Lieutenant Homer Steedly Jr. turned a bend in a trail in Pleiku Province and came face-to-face with a North Vietnamese soldier, his weapon slung over his shoulder.

Homer stared in astonishment. "At first it was almost sur-real. I mean, we're all in green fatigues, muddy and sweaty, and really looking like guys in the field. Here this guy comes around the corner, and he's got on a light khaki uniform, a clean light khaki pith helmet. You've seen the red Pleiku mud. You can't stay clean up there. You're tinted red. Your uniforms are red, your fingers are red, it's just—it gets everywhere. And here's this guy that's walking down the trail perfectly clean. Perfectly—not a wrinkle anywhere. I mean, not a hair out of place. I must be hallucinating, the heat's gotten to me."[1]

The soldier he was confronting was a twenty-five-year-old medic named Hoang Ngoc Dam, from the village of Thai Giang in Thai Binh Province—a fact the lieutenant would not discover for over three decades. There was no time then for more than a quick glimpse of each other. As soon as Dam saw Homer, he snatched his weapon off his shoulder and began to bring it around. Later, Homer would recall how he shouted, *"Chieu Hoi,"* the phrase he thought meant "surrender."[2] "But he continued to draw down on me," Homer says, "and then he started pulling his weapon off his shoulder. My weapon was already down at my waist, so it was ready to fire. I hollered at him, and he didn't stop. He tried to get that weapon down, and just before he got it level on me, I fired. In my total abject fear of that moment, I just cut loose and killed him instantly. I could look in his eyes, we were so close together. We were probably thirty feet apart, and then later I looked at him, and he was so young."[3]

For a time he stared at the body, dazed. He noticed more details. Not only was the young man's uniform starched, but the SKS rifle clutched in his hands still had the greasy cosmoline used as an antirust agent congealing on its bayonet hinge. Someone new to the war, Homer concluded, probably an officer; in his description of the incident in a letter home, he called the dead man a major. He was wrong on both counts. Dam, whose rank was sergeant, had already been in the war for over five years by that time; he had survived the Tet Offensive and many other major battles.

Homer bent down and went through the dead man's pockets, drawing out a notebook with a colorful picture on the front cover of a man and woman in what he took to be traditional or ancient Vietnamese dress, and on the back cover, a daily and monthly calendar grid, labeled with the English word "schedule"; a smaller black notebook; and a number of loose papers—letters, ID cards, and some sort of certificates. The spine and corners of the first notebook had been neatly reinforced with black tape.

Thirty-six years later, when I first touched that notebook, I was struck by the care Dam had taken in binding it up. He was a soldier in an army where nothing could be thrown away, nothing wasted. I thought of what the appearance of that book must have meant to Homer as he looked through it on that dark trail. Raised on small, hardscrabble farms, Homer knew the preciousness of things that could not be replaced. The way he had shot Dam was unusual: a gunfighter duel in a war in which more often than not the enemy remained faceless to the Americans, only sudden flashes of fire from the jungle, targets to be annihilated. That invisibility was frustrating to the GIs, but at least it allowed them the comfort of dehumanizing the enemy, making him into ghost, demon, target. Now to see not only the face of the man he'd killed, but also the carefully re-bound covers, the force of will that the meticulous writing and drawings inside the book revealed, confronted Homer with a mirrored and valuable humanity. He tried not to think about it. There had been no time to think, anyway. His enemy had been armed and ready to shoot him. Homer had simply been quicker. It was what could be, and was, called a good kill.

Homer sent the documents to the rear area, where he knew they'd be assessed and then burned. But later that evening he changed his mind. He contacted a friend in S-2, intelligence, and asked him to bring everything back. Homer couldn't bear to have the documents, the last evidence of the life he had taken, be destroyed.

# CHAPTER TWO

# Eyes Like
# a Mean Animal's

*Had he and I but met*
*by some old ancient inn,*
*We should have sat us down to wet*
*Right many a nipperkin*

*But ranged as infantry,*
*And staring face to face,*
*I shot at him as he at me,*
*And killed him in his place.*

*I shot him dead because—*
*Because he was my foe,*
*Just so: my foe of course he was;*
*That's clear enough; although*

*He thought he'd list, perhaps,*
*Off-hand-like—just as I—*
*Was out of work—had sold his traps—*
*No other reason why.*

*Yes; quaint and curious war is!*
*You shoot a fellow down*
*You'd treat, if met where any bar is,*
*Or help to half-a-crown.*

—"The Man He Killed" *by Thomas Hardy*

I can't think of Homer and Dam's fatal meeting without being reminded of that Thomas Hardy poem—and of Tim O'Brien's update and personalization of it in "The Man I Killed," a story chapter in *The Things They Carried.*[4] Homer's need to clutch some grief to himself by hanging onto Hoang Ngoc Dam's documents can be seen in the thoughts and actions of Tim—a character subversively created and named after himself by O'Brien—who has, like Homer and the persona in Hardy's poem, just killed an enemy soldier and cannot stop staring at the body. The description of the dead man's face is repeated, over and over, so that we understand Tim's inability to tear his eyes away, his shock and horror at what he's done. As he stares at the corpse, he creates a life story for the dead Viet Cong soldier spun from the man's frail, unsoldierly physique and the objects pulled from his body, including a photo of a young woman next to a motorcycle. He imagines the young Vietnamese as someone who loved mathematics, had gone to the university in Saigon, had fallen in love and married, had been reluctant to go to the war, but finally had—mainly because he feared disgracing his family and his village. Like Homer, who at first imagined Dam as a young officer like himself, Tim—a former university student who'd been reluctant to be drafted and had only gone to war because he feared being ostracized by his family and community—has projected his own life onto the life of the man he has killed. He has killed himself, and he refuses to stop staring at the mirror of his own corpse, to stop grieving for the loss of his own common humanity.

Later in the novel, in "Good Form,"[5] O'Brien the writer (as much a fictional character as Tim the soldier) describes the origins of "The Man I Killed," explaining that as a soldier, he could never bring himself to look at the faces of the (enemy) dead, and as a result he has been left with feelings of "faceless responsibility" and "faceless grief." But, he writes, he wants to tell his readers "why story-truth is truer sometimes than happening-truth." He is enabled by writing the story, permitting himself that wrench to the side that fiction allows, to create a young Tim who does what O'Brien did not, could not, do during the war: look into the face of the dead and see himself and mourn.[6] To re-form his own face in the mirror, he has to discover his features in the glimpsed and shadowed face of the enemy.[7]

The same need exists as well for the Vietnamese who were once our enemies. In 2007 Mike Archer, a marine veteran of the siege of Khe Sanh, read an article I'd written about Homer and Dam and asked me for some contacts in Viet Nam to help him investigate what had happened to the remains of one of his friends. Archer had written a memoir, A Patch of Ground, in which he described the death of a high school friend, Tom Mahoney, who had also gone into the marines. He was just nineteen, and photos of him reveal a heartbreakingly young face. Mahoney was ambushed and killed during the withdrawal from Hill 881, at the end of the siege. His body was dragged to the front of their position by the People's Army of Viet Nam (PAVN) troops who had killed him in order to lure other marines into an ambush when they tried to recover the body. His friends did try just that, but finally had to call in an air strike, and as a result, Mahoney's remains were never found—they were either dragged off by the North Vietnamese or obliterated.

Years later, while an American and Vietnamese MIA recovery team was searching for clues about the disposition of the body, they found in the Hanoi archives an after-action report from the five-man squad that had ambushed Mahoney. It describes the action and Mahoney: "The five-person team . . . waited for the enemy all night long. At 1400 on the following day (6 July 1968) we saw one American walking outside the entrance of the outpost. He wore a cement-colored uniform. *His face was red and his eyes were blue like a mean animal* [emphasis added]. He was looking towards Mr. Luong's team. The sounds of AK weapons roared immediately and the American fell. Mr. Luong and Mr. Long jumped out of their positions and dragged the American's body down. They placed the body in front of them to create an ambush for the other Americans coming out of their bunkers."[8] To the PAVN soldiers, it was easier to kill someone seen not only as an invader of their country, but also as a mean animal. Inhuman. Meat for bait.

Mahoney was shot in the chest. In 2005 I sat in a room in Hue, across the river from the Citadel, that crucible on which American and PAVN and NLF and ARVN troops—all the acronyms of the war—had slaughtered each other, and the inhabitants of the town, during the 1968 Tet Offensive. It was a battle in which Mahoney had fought. The poet Lam Thi My Da had been there then also, on the other side. She did not know of Thomas Mahoney, but after we met and had the inevitable cups of green tea, she told me she wanted to read one of her poems, "Khuon mat an kin" ("The Face Beneath"),[9] which was dedicated to "the American soldiers who died in the war in Viet Nam":

> *I want to be a small deer*
> *Running under the sky through green grass*
>
> *Don't make me go into the thick jungle*
> *Or I will become a fierce wolf*
>
> *Who can foresee the tricks and snares of life?*
> *Deception*
> *is disguised by sweet tongues*
>
> *I was an unwitting deer*
> *Wandering far from my field of fresh grass*

*My face was the face of a wolf*
*In deep caves, in shadows, dark and still*

*Then a call startled me awake*
*And I remembered that once my eyes*
*Had been clear, the eyes of a deer*

*At the end of the road I fell down*
*When a bullet struck my blood-filled chest*

*If you look under the wolf's skin*
*You'll find the red heart of an innocent deer*

A year later, when I read Mike's description of Tom Mahoney and saw his photo, then read the PAVN document describing his eyes "blue like a mean animal," the poem sprang into my mind with a shock of recognition and grief. My Da's poem could have been the lost voice of Thomas Mahoney, a poem coming out of the poet's recognition of how war transforms our perceptions of ourselves and of each other, out of her need to rediscover her own innocent heart by seeing beneath the skin of the wolf.

In 1993, when I first met Vietnamese writers who had been on the other side of the war, I sat across a breakfast table and looked into the eyes of a woman who had once been in the Youth Volunteers Brigade of the PAVN, one of the teenage girls who worked on the Ho Chi Minh Trails, repairing craters after our bombings, defusing or exploding unexploded bombs, and even burying the dead. The times, and some of the places, we had been in the war had overlapped, and looking at her face, I knew that if I had seen her there when I was flying as a helicopter gunner, I would have killed her. She had been a target and threat to me, the ghost under the canopy of leaves, and I had been monstrous and mechanical to her, the sky elementally reconfigured into noise and terror. Now we could suddenly see

each other's faces. We had been translated to each other; we sat
at that small table where we could look into the eyes of all we
had not known or had ignored or hated and feared, and see instead reflection and revelation. See what Homer had seen when
he once again retrieved that diary from the man he'd killed, after
it sat in thirty-six years of darkness, and opened its pages to reveal the precise drawings of a young man who had wanted to be
a healer.

It was an instant when everything came together, not just
because of where we had been in the war, but because we had
both become writers after it; we understood that the moment,
when our stories had wrapped together had embodied the latent
power of stories to save our own hearts by allowing us into the
narratives of other human beings. As Tim had done in imagination. As Homer would try to do in life. The journey I eventually
made to Viet Nam to help him return the documents to Dam's
family included plans I'd had to interview some of the Vietnamese writers I knew, veterans of the other side of the war.
Their stories, from their lives and their art, and the stories of
others, friends, other writers and veterans, or traveling companions met along the way, wove into and helped to illuminate the
entwinement of Homer's and Dam's stories, as I came to feel
they needed to do in this book.

"What stories can do," O'Brien writes, "is make things present. I can look at things I never looked at. I can attach faces to
grief and love and pity and God. I can be brave. I can make myself feel again."[10]

It was what Homer Steedly decided he needed to do. By refusing to let go of the notebooks he'd taken from Dam's body,
Homer somehow understood, though he could not put it into
words or coherent thoughts until years later, that he was hanging onto a grief that was the price of remaining human. He
needed to find and mourn what had been cut out of his heart.
He needed to find Dam's story and his own.

# PART ONE

# THE
# WAR

# CHAPTER THREE

# Bamberg

I f we pull back now from Homer and Dam, back from the terminal nexus of their meeting, we can see certain parallels emerge between them, in the places they came from and the lives they led and hoped to lead, all of which drew them to that moment when they faced each other in the jungle. Both were from small villages on midland plains; both grew up poor and worked the land: Homer, at times, behind a mule, Dam wading the paddies driving a water buffalo. Both were oldest brothers, willingly taking on the mantle of the responsible sibling, the surrogate parent. Both had parents who taught them codes of courage, custom, duty, and industry that had sustained and defined their ancestors, and both came from a tradition in which education and military service were equally sacrosanct.

The Hoang family today is certain that there was and is a spiritual connection between Dam and Homer. Even with all that has happened since, I don't know if I believe that. But each did carry in his blood the history of the hard lands from which he came; it was the tide that carried them toward each other.

Bamberg, South Carolina, has always given its sons to the nation's wars, though usually the sons have been eager enough to
give themselves, and the definition of what their nation was
sometimes shifted. The town sits astride a highway and (former)
railroad junction in the marshy scrub pine, loblolly pine, and
palmetto country of the South Carolina midlands. Its first inhabitants, the Edisto tribe of the Muskogian Nation,[1] knew it as
a cypress swamp, and the occasional alligator still lumbers
about near town, as if pulled by a dim ancestral memory of that
ancient slough. The country is blessed with an indolent beauty
best appreciated by those, like Homer, who know its secret deli-
cacies: the sway and sigh of the pines, the lush hang of Spanish
moss draped on the huge spreads of live oaks hundreds of years
old, the brush of a breeze silvering the marsh grass, shivering
the dew-jeweled filigrees of spiderwebs, touching the skin and
nostrils with the fecundity of the country. The swamps the Edistos knew were still extant when Homer Steedly was growing up;
as they did for the Edistos, they still allowed boys to hone skills
they would need as men: "I spent most of my childhood in the
country, surrounded by woods and cypress swamps, most no-
tably Lemon Swamp," Homer recalls. "I spent all my free time in
these woods and swamps hunting, fishing, and just exploring. I
became quite accomplished at stalking deer and even observed
bobcat and fox on several occasions. I learned how to move silently through the woods and keep downwind of those I sought
to locate. I ran most of the time barefoot in cut off blue jeans
with no shirt, or only a t-shirt. Often while running through the
swamps and woods I would step on snakes, but they never bit
me. Moving quietly and learning to search the environment for
shapes and movements while hunting were my strong points in
jungle warfare, as was my skill with a rifle."[2]

The first settlers in this region were the usual rural Southern
mix of English, Scots-Irish, and Huguenots, but there were also
many Swiss and Germans—and Africans, a population of slaves

the more wealthy of the emigrants brought with them when they moved south of the Edisto River. One of the descendants of those Germans, Major William Seaborn Bamberg, gave his name to the town. His grandfather, John George Bamberg, came from Germany and fought in the Revolutionary War.

But if Germany lay back in Bamberg's white history, the topography and history of the American South formed the town more powerfully, and its sons grew up the way the Edisto Indians' sons had, as expert hunters and gatherers, whether in swamp, forest, river, field, or trade, and with the need of a war to initiate and mark their comings of age. Homer's call sign in Viet Nam would be Swampfox, after the Revolutionary War hero and guerrilla fighter Francis Marion, another swamp-raised boy. When Fort Sumter was fired upon, most of the eligible white male population—the town only had 250 people then—immediately signed up to fight for the Confederacy. Capt. Isaac S. Bamberg formed a company called, unsurprisingly, the Bamberg Guards. Another Bamberg, the wonderfully named Seaborn, became a major, and his brother, Francis M. Bamberg, enlisted as a private and eventually retired as a general.

Among the other Bamberg men who enlisted at the beginning of the war was a Private Richard J. Steedly.

The Lemon Swamp today is somewhat diminished but still sprawls, dense and lush, for miles outside of Bamberg. The tight dirt trail we've followed off Hunter's Chapel Road takes us to a small clearing. If we go in further, Homer says, we'll come across breastworks set up here when a portion of Sherman's army came through on its drive south, attempting to cross the Salkehatchee River. The Union soldiers were held at bay for two days at Bamberg, at the Battle of the Rivers Bridge.[3] As we approach the clearing, the shrill chorus of the cicadas stops. There is no breeze, and the air is heavy and heated. Behind a ragged screen of pines, a few weathered gravestones, some tilted over, sentinel what once must have been a small clearing. It is the graveyard of the Hunter's Chapel Baptist Church, the building moved years ago to an area less plagued by the mosquitoes and no-see-ums that cloud around us, the latter going for the corners of our eyes. There are apparently other guardians here as well. Once, Homer tells me, he and his wife visited the graves, and when they came back down the trail, they found a small mound of rocks with some turkey vulture feathers stuck in them—a notification to them, Homer says, that this was still holy ground. Other people still visit here as well; in a slightly clearer area is a small chain-link fence enclosure, with six grave-sites in it. Homer unwraps the cord holding the gate shut, and we go inside. There are two small metal markers—the original gravestones are gone—and we squat down and read them: *Emily Elizabeth Steedly, 26 March 1841 to 20 September 1897. Capt. Richard Joseph Steedly, CSA, 18 February 1831 to 3 November 1902.* In front of the markers, a small Confederate flag has been stuck into the earth.

Homer's great-great-grandfather's military career foreshadowed the direction of Homer's own. Captain Dick (the family always called him by that name) rose through the ranks from private to become commander of Company G of the South Carolina Volunteers. He was wounded at the battle of Spotsylvania, but came home to marry Emily Elizabeth Edwards, who came from Orangeburg County. The two lived in the Hunter's Chapel community, at the edge of the swamp near where they are now buried.

Each male in the Steedly family subsequently would be given the first or middle name Richard, in honor of Captain Dick. A photograph of Homer when he was a lieutenant in Viet Nam—his head cocked to the side, thin-faced, serious, the pipe he had decided to smoke to make himself look older and wiser dangling from his mouth—could be a daguerreotype of his own ancestor or any of a hundred other Confederate soldiers, posing perhaps a little more stiffly, their collars buttoned high, their hands on the handles of the Bowie knives or pistols in their belts, looking grim, competent, and deadly. These are the typical rural southern troops, always disproportionately represented in the American military: the equivalent of the sturdy, patriotic peasantry from the hardscrabble farmlands of Thai Binh, Nam Dinh, and Nghe An in northern Viet Nam, or Quang Tri and Quang Ngai in the South. They were tough country boys who went to be slaughtered or redeemed in what they and their progeny—Homer once correcting a Yankee teacher in his high school about the name—would only call The War of Northern Aggression. They were kids like Homer, who learned how to use a rifle and stalk the woods and swamps from the time they could walk, and they were followed by other generations of warriors, whenever the reunited country gave them the chance to kill and die for it. World War I cost the tiny town twenty men killed in action, and when Homer's father went to fight in World War II, another twenty from the town were lost, as if this figure had become the accepted tithe to the god of war or the needs of the nation.

Yet Homer Steedly Sr., in spite of the family's military tradition, did not volunteer to fight in World War II. Born in 1921, he grew up on a small farm outside Bamberg, the only boy in a family of five siblings, and was his four sisters' sole provider from the time he was nine years old. His mother, Lelia, died in 1930, when she was only twenty-eight, a blow from which his father, Richard, never recovered. Soon after her death he began drinking heavily, leaving Homer to run the farm and work odd jobs to keep the family fed, clothed, and together. Richard died in 1941, just a few weeks before Pearl Harbor. A short time later Homer's draft notice arrived. He was reluctant, and worried sick to leave his sisters, but it was not in his nature or background to balk at the call to military service.

He would never speak to Homer Jr. about his war, except for a few oblique references to service as an MP and a motorcycle courier. Years later, when Homer tried to obtain information about his father's service, he learned that the records had been destroyed in the 1973 fire that devastated the National Personnel Records Office in St. Louis. The only time Homer had heard any details about what Homer Sr. did in the war was when he eavesdropped on his father's conversations with a veteran friend who came to visit. As the two sat and drank, they began to speak quietly of men in their unit who had been killed. The story that stuck in Homer Jr.'s mind was of one of his father's fellow motorcycle couriers who was decapitated by wire the Germans had strung across the road. Homer's father, who was right behind that friend, had run his motorcycle off the road as German snipers opened up on him, leaving him with head injuries that Homer later found out were the cause of the narcolepsy from which his father would suffer until his death.

By the end of the war in 1945, Homer Sr. was on occupation duty in Erlangen, Germany, not far from the original Bamberg, working as a cook for the troops stationed in an old schloss, a castle once used as a resort for high-ranking Wehrmacht officers. Homer would bring his laundry to a house in town, where a pretty eighteen-year-old named Babette Gumbmann lived. Betty, as he soon Americanized her name, was born in Uttenreuth, but her family also came originally, and perhaps auspiciously, from Bamberg: a coincidence I can imagine him using as an ice-breaking opening line, though Betty does not remember him doing so. Although he was stricken by the girl, she was not quite as taken at first by the young soldier. "After my husband's death," she said, "I came across a note in his journal noting 'first time I met Betty,' but I don't remember that day."[4]

Babette was wary of the Americans. During the war she had watched their bombs, "as big as boxcars," dropping on nearby Nuremberg. After Germany surrendered, she heard stories of local girls being raped by the invading soldiers, and for a time her family had been forced out of its home so American soldiers could be billeted there; they had left the place a filthy wreck. The war had also taken all the male members of her family. None were Nazis. Her father, a stonemason, was drafted in 1941: "They came knocking on our door at midnight and took him away," she remembers. Near the end they had received notification that he was missing in action on the Eastern front and had assumed he was dead; later they found out he had survived, and had been held in a prisoner of war camp in England. Babette's older brother did not come home. He had managed to stay out of the war until near the end, but in the desperate last days he had been drafted and almost immediately killed in action.

Now here was this slim, soft-spoken American, who kept hanging around the house, forcing her to try to use the English she had studied and hated in school, though he spoke it with an accent very different than she had been taught to use and was much harder to understand. But the GI was persistent and had a forceful personality. He told her he owned a farm back in the American Bamberg. Her girlfriends all seemed jealous, and it made her feel good to know they considered her lucky. Finally she let her heart open to him. They were married on September 5, 1945, Steedly jumping through the usual hoops the army threw in front of such couples. Homer Jr. was born several months premature, on June 7, of that same year. As soon as Homer Sr. had enough points for discharge, he returned to the South Carolinian incarnation of Bamberg, thinking he would soon send for his new family and bring them to the home and farm where he had grown up and which he now planned to live on and develop.

During his entire time in the army, Homer Sr. had been sending money home, assuming his sisters were using some of it for the upkeep of the twenty-acre farm. But the girls had had to use the money to stay alive. "Eventually," Homer Jr. recalls, "they had to sell the land to put food on the table. . . . [My father] understood their decision, but was disappointed that they had not told him about it. . . . [T]hat is why it took him over a year to get the money to send for mom and me."

When the veteran's new wife and his son finally arrived in Bamberg, the family found themselves homeless and nearly penniless. Homer Sr. was friendly with the local pharmacist, who for a time let the three of them live in a room above the drugstore.

It was all a shock to Betty. In Germany her husband had been in the wealthy, privileged class of the occupation soldier. In South Carolina, she soon found out, he was desperately poor. And in spite of its name and origin, the place in which she found herself was nothing like its namesake. Even though it had passed through war and occupation, the Germany she came from seemed to her a much less savage place than this hot, flat country, with its swamps, run-down clapboard houses, and clouds of mosquitoes tormenting her ears and eyes. The black people who seemed to make up the majority of the population (in Germany she had only seen blacks in the American army) were strange to her. She could not understand them when they spoke, and the white Americans could not understand her English. One local shopkeeper tormented and mocked her, making her repeat every sentence she said to him.

For the first years of Homer Jr.'s life, the Steedly family lived a hardscrabble existence. A girl, Nancy, was born on September 22, 1949, followed by Homer's brother, Tony, born September 17, 1950, and his youngest sister, Linda, on January 14, 1953. "We lived in several homes, most of them only partially completed and the first couple had no indoor toilet or running water," Homer recollects; the water the family used had to be hauled in buckets from the river. "Later we had both, of course, our attempt to get well water resulting in our first good money making business. We were in survival mode the first few years after Dad brought Mom and me back to this country, but with Mom's working at the sewing room [doing piecework for a local textile mill], we did OK. We had to watch our expenses, but we had enough to eat, pay medical bills, and buy the clothes us kids needed to attend school. We also benefited from lots of hand-me-down clothes from our relatives."

Much of the rest of his childhood seemed designed as well by whatever providence shapes southern boys to culminate as soldiers. The family's diet "was supplemented by the garden, vegetable planted for market, and fishing and hunting," Homer remembers. "I was given the role of providing meat with a 22 cal rifle. Dad would give me one bullet and tell me to go get some meat for supper. I quickly learned not to waste a shot, unless I was sure I could get a clean kill. I became a very good stalker and an excellent shot. I also developed the tactic of wandering through grassy fields and when I spotted a rabbit, I would run at it full speed, yelling at the top of my lungs, which would cause the rabbit to freeze for a second, during which I could catch up and fall upon it, capturing it and dispatching it with a quick blow to the back of the neck. This would save me a bullet, which I hoarded, for those days when my aim was off. We also took full advantage of the blackberry that grew wild in the woods around home."

On the weekends, the two Steedly boys would go along with their dad as helpers on the various jobs he took, and the whole family would grow vegetables—sweet corn, squash, cucumbers, tomatoes, okra, peas, butter beans, watermelon, sweet peppers, and peanuts. "All us kids hoed the weeds," Homer remembers, "picked caterpillars [off the vegetables], and harvested the crop for market. Most of the farming was on rented land and Dad and I plowed much of the crops in the early years by mule. We all worked hard, but just thought that was normal."

Bamberg today is still a small town, with a population of about 4,000. It advertises itself, with some justification, as a pleasant place to live. The school system has improved since Homer's day and now ranks in the top ten percentile of the state's eighty-six school districts. Graceful Victorian homes with wide galleries sit on either side of a wide median planted with palmettos and white and pink crepe myrtles. The median replaced the railroad tracks that once ran down the center of the town and

were the lifeline for the town's textile mill, a business that left in
the 1970s, when the union came in and most textile manufac-
ture went overseas, to Asia and eventually to Viet Nam. The two
blocks of the old town, including the pharmacy above which
Homer lived, remain, but are mostly abandoned now. The new
town center boasts a hospital, a courthouse, and a library; there
is an annual Treasure Hunt festival, and an effort has been made
to attract new businesses through the town's location near highways and its industrious workforce. The businesses are needed.
Bamberg is still a poor town; in 2005 its median annual income
was $21,736, compared to a national median of $41,994.[5] Bamberg's size and population are nearly the same now as they were
when Homer was growing up there; it is now, as it was then, almost equally divided among blacks and whites, with a slight
black majority.

The classes and the races—and the class lines were not always racial—were rigidly stratified and segregated. "There were
the public officials, judges, lawyers, Sheriff, doctors and the
like," Homer recalls. "There were also the large land owners. I
would also include the small business owners, motels, groceries,
clothing, hardware, drug stores, etc. In the middle-income
levels, I would include the smaller farms and small business
owners. The lowest income level [consisted of] those who
worked in the textile mill, sewing factory, and various service
jobs. Here you also find common laborers and farm workers.
We often found ourselves in this group, along with most of the
majority of blacks."

Today Homer considers that shared labor and his father's
example the reasons that allowed him and his siblings to escape
the easy acceptance of black inferiority that was prevalent
among the whites of the town: "The KKK was very strong. Since
we often worked in the fields side by side with the black farm
workers, often as equals, I never bought into the white superior-
ity nonsense. I was cared for by a black couple for many years
after we first moved to the country, since both parents worked.

He was a WWI veteran with only half of one lung and a third of the other left after a mustard gas attack. They were both very wise, and very loving. I considered them members of our family. The local KKK burned a cross in the driveway leading to their shack one night. I was the one who saw it and told Dad. He grabbed the shotgun and a couple of 00 Buck Shot shells filled with rock salt and took off. After several loud explosions, he came back. Years later he told of going into town later and confronting a local official (now nationally known and probably very remorseful about the entire period). Dad really chewed him out, but couldn't help but break down laughing as he left, since the individual was sitting on a pillow . . . [his] tail full of rock salt apparently."

"When I was around six or seven years old, the main street of Bamberg was dirt with wooden plank sidewalks. When it rained, the street would be ankle deep in mud. I remember one incident, where Dad and I were walking down the sidewalk to go to the barber shop, and a black woman, in her 70s jumped into the mud to get off the sidewalk so that we white men could get by. I was appalled and a little scared by the incident. Later I asked Dad about it. He said it was just the way things were. It wasn't right, but sometimes it took a long time for right to win out. He said we had to do little things until eventually everyone saw the right."

Homer and his father did not openly express affection for— or to—each other, but the two shared a deep and unarticulated bond and love whose basis was the son's almost awestruck respect for his father. "Sundays too my father got up early/and put his clothes on in the blueback cold/when with cracked hands that ached/from labor in the weekday weather made/banked fires blaze. . . . No one ever thanked him . . . what did I know, what did I know/of love's austere and lonely offices?" asks Robert Hayden in "Those Winter Sundays."[6] Hayden was himself the son of a poor workingman—in his case, in a Detroit slum—and the poem came to mind when I heard Homer speak

of his regrets about what was not said between them before his
father's death in 1986. He regretted not only not having expressed his affection more, but also that he had not at the time
realized what a remarkable man his father was: stripped of his
land, illiterate, and sometimes narcoleptic, he not only worked
the family out of poverty but lived stubbornly and courageously
according to a moral system based on his own natural sense of
justice and equality. Homer can only speculate why his father
had not been infected by the racism that was so much the order
of the world as to not even be named. Was it his experience in
the war, the labor—and social status—he shared with his black
neighbors and coworkers, or the suspicion with which his wife,
a foreigner, was first regarded? Whatever the reasons, Homer
Steedly Sr.'s color blindness also helped push the Steedlys into
financial solvency. "We planted tobacco on shares with an elderly black man for a couple of years and really struck gold,"
Homer recalls. "Sam Stevens, the nearly blind black man had
the knack for curing tobacco in wood fired barns, that resulted in
such golden yellow, leathery, leaves, that the buyers would actually get into fist fights over our bales. It was excellent cigar
rolling material and fetched a great price. The last year, the barn
caught fire and we lost the entire crop, but the previous years
made up for the loss."

The money he made from the tobacco allowed Homer Sr. to
buy tools and equipment that permitted him to branch out from
truck farming and take on construction and home repair jobs,
well-drilling, and working on well pumps. He worked twelve-
hour days, six and sometimes "six and half days a week," taking
time off only for church. Betty, who had been trained as a book-
keeper in Germany, took in clothing to do alterations and eventually got a job as a sales clerk. The family's income slowly began
to rise.

In the early 1960s, Bamberg High School was strictly segregated.
With blacks, the lowest rung of the town's social hierarchy,

missing from the even more rigid hierarchy of high school, Homer, the son of a working-class, truck, and tobacco farmer, knew where he was supposed to fit in the pecking order. But he would take neither snubs, teasing, nor bullying, nor did he give any to the good people with whom he worked shoulder to shoulder on the farm. He was determined to shine in school, and he did, something he still remembers with pride: "Bamberg High School had a graduating Class of 44 students, when I graduated in 1964. We had excellent reading, writing, and English composition courses. We also had Latin and French. We had very poor Math instruction. . . . [But] we had a course in biology and another in chemistry. I took both, but excelled in Chemistry . . . winning the regional science fair with an amateur rocketry project, that sent a 1½" steel pipe, 5' tall to an altitude of over 18,000'." The latter was another skill that would serve him well in Viet Nam.

Homer also learned that the Bohr planetary ring explanation of the atomic structure was the foundation of the universe: protons, neutrons, and electrons all circling happily around each; it all neatly fit. Then he graduated and went to Clemson, and the universe flew apart. He'd planned to attend that university since he had gone as a 4-H kid to a statewide competition on campus. But when he finally enrolled, he found his classmates and professors were talking excitedly about bosons, quarks, charmed particles, and neutrinos. He didn't know a quark from a quarterback, had no idea what they were talking about. No one at Bamberg High had mentioned that the universe had shifted, and now the former science whiz kid found himself sitting in classes where he stared dumbly at the blackboard, completely out of his depth. By September 1966 he was failing most of his subjects in the tough science major he'd chosen.

Other elemental changes were occurring in the fabric of the universe. Ground troops from the United States had been sent to Viet Nam in March 1965, but it was an event Homer little noted at the time. There was very little antiwar sentiment at

Clemson then, and when Homer signed up for Reserve Officers
Training Corps (ROTC)—at a time when other university students were demonstrating to remove reserve officer programs
and any armed forces recruiters from campus—he had no notion he "would end up in a war halfway around the planet." Perhaps whoever designed the program at Clemson had more of
an idea, as Homer's company was called the "Counter-Guerilla
Unit." But at the time Homer saw it as a way he could be patriotic, the son and progeny of soldiers entering into his ancestors'
rites, while still concentrating on his education. It was a decision that later helped him get into Officer Candidate School
when he ended up in the army, though it also ensured he would
end up in the infantry.

His grades continued to plummet. He knew that if he left
the university, he would likely be drafted, so he decided to drop
his classes for a semester, stay enrolled so the draft wouldn't get
him, and try to catch up by working on his own. He obtained
high school textbooks about the subjects he hadn't been offered
and studied them, spending his days in the university library instead of going to classes. In the evenings he browsed in the
basement archives. "Every day after supper, I would go back to
the library and read back issues of *Science Digest* and *The Scientific American*."

He also came across another set of documents that fascinated him: the transcripts of the Nuremburg War Crimes Trials:
"The murders and tortures they described scared me. I could not
believe, before reading the transcripts, that anyone could perform such deeds. One aberrant act, but systemized brutality? I
should have not been surprised, since on a lesser scale, I had often seen my own Dad stand up to the crowd in defense of others,
when basic rights were being abused." Although his mother's
family came from a town near Nuremberg, he did not, at the
time, consciously make that connection or think about what his
maternal grandfather might have been involved in, as a German
soldier in occupied Poland. Neither did he think then of any

way he could apply the horrors he was reading about to himself, though those lessons would come back to him later, when he needed them, in Viet Nam.

He was giving himself an education that had nothing to do with grades. But when he was called into the academic dean's office and told that his semester off had put him on academic probation, he decided to drop out. He was at Clemson on his parents' and his Aunt Hattie's dime—he lived in her house to save dorm fees, and his mom and dad had put their savings into his education. He could not bring himself to waste their money.

His plan was to go back to Bamberg and enlist in the army; because of his science background, he figured, he would be assigned a chemical or biological warfare specialty, which would keep him out of combat and give him time to brush up on the subjects in which he needed work; then, upon discharge, he would have the GI Bill to help him pay his own way through college. Early on the morning of October 1, 1966, he kissed Aunt Hattie good-bye and hitched back to Bamberg. He thought he knew how his parents would react, so when he got into town, he did not go straight home. Instead he went to the post office and spoke with the army recruiter. Sure, the recruiter told him, he would get into the field he wanted. But since he was not yet twenty-one, he would need his parents' permission.

The scene at home when Homer presented these plans to his parents went pretty much as he had imagined. His father was furious, his mother full of trepidation. There was no way, his father shouted, that he would sign any consent forms. Was Homer stupid enough to believe the recruiter? Didn't he see where the army needed men?

Father and son screamed at each other for a time, and then, as if embarrassed, fell silent and avoided each other until Homer went to bed. Neither was given to emotional outbursts, and they had surprised and shocked themselves and each other.

The next morning was Sunday, and when Homer awoke, his father was quiet. He asked Homer to sit down. Was Homer really set on going into the army? Homer sighed and went through his arguments again, but his father cut him off. It's a mistake, he said. But if Homer truly had his mind set on it, he would go ahead and sign the consent forms.

He had never talked about his experiences in World War II, and Betty had also rarely spoken of her own memories of that war: the falling bombs, the knocks on the door at midnight that had taken her father and brother away, the occupation. It wasn't until he was back from the war, years later, that Homer came to understand what images his parents' own experiences might have been making them see in their son's flesh when they looked at Homer that morning.

Today, Betty Steedly still lives in the neat brick ranch house on Hunter's Chapel Road that Homer and his father built in 1968, before Homer went overseas. The wood-paneled walls are hung with family photos and prints of flowers; one wall is taken up by deeply recessed, built-in shelves and a desktop and drawers built by Homer Sr. "with only hand tools," Homer tells me. The room is spotless, neat enough to be a display, yet achieves a kind of warmth without clutter. The five acres around the house are equally neat, the flower beds painstakingly weeded. "It's her German blood," Homer insists. Betty, in her eighties now, still does her own yard work. She is a slim, vigorous woman, the source of Homer's lean face and piercing blue eyes. When Homer had sent her the documents he had taken from the body of Hoang Ngoc Dam, she had treated them with the same care, neatly bundling them, putting them in the box where she kept all of Homer's letters, and eventually taking them up to the attic.

"I didn't think about them after that," she says. She points at the ceiling. "I didn't know I had a ghost in the attic for over thirty years."

# CHAPTER FOUR

# Thai Giang

*Chang tuoi tre von dong hao-kiet*
*Xep but nghien theo viec dao cung*
*Thanh lien mong tien be rong*
*Thuoc guom da quyet chang dung giac troi*

*Born to a race of heroes, you, my love*
*discard your brush and ink for tools of war*
*you vow to capture citadels for the throne*
*your sword will spare no foe of Heaven's sway.[7]*

 —THE SONG OF THE SOLDIER'S WIFE
  CHINH PHU NGAM
  BY DOAN THI DIEM FROM DAN TRAN CON
  EIGHTEENTH CENTURY

The village is about sixty kilometers southeast of Hanoi, about twenty kilometers from the provincial capital of Thai Binh province. As is true of all Vietnamese villages, it consists of a series of connected hamlets. During Dam's boyhood, the entire

community had about 3,000 people.[8] It lies in part of the original Nam Viet, the kingdom of the Viets, carved off the belly of
China by a renegade Chinese general. It is a land subject to an
almost constant state of war, its youth flocking, or levied, to the
armies the emperors raised to fight the Chinese or Mongol invaders from the north or in the Vietnamese wars of conquest
over the kingdoms of the south.

In South Carolina there was always the distant wound of
the Other War and its subsequent occupations, the more recent
repressions of poverty and racism, and the upheavals of the civil
rights movement. Dam's siblings and friends remember his
childhood as idyllic now, innocent and agrarian. But he also
grew up against a forming backdrop of starvation, occupation,
revolution, forced collectivization, and finally the war to reunify
the country, which eventually would sweep him away from the
village and into the strange landscape of the Central Highland
jungles. In Thai Giang, history pressed against a horizon picketed with the steeples of abandoned churches, reminders of
French oppression, the exodus of the province's Catholics, and
the deadly turmoil of the 1950s and land reform, when neighbor turned on neighbor.

Dam's old comrade-in-arms Pham Quang Huy, now in his
seventies, can still feel an ache of hunger, a physical squeeze of
memory in his guts; he can still remember the corpses that
piled up or floated by in the river during the great famine of
1944–1945, the first year of Dam's life. The Japanese who occupied the country during World War II and the Vichy French
who supported them confiscated the lion's share of the rice crop
for themselves, and at the same time forced the farmers of Thai
Binh and the rest of the North to destroy their other subsistence
crops of corn, potatoes, and beans and instead grow jute, cotton, oil seed, peanuts, and other plants the Japanese could use
for their war effort.[9] An estimated 2 million people starved to
death in those years, 280,000 of them in Thai Binh province.
Their skeletal corpses became the fuel of the revolution. Thou-

sands joined the Viet Minh to fight against the occupation of the country during the war and its recolonization by the French afterward.[10]

Huy was twelve when French soldiers, wearing their white pillbox kepis, first set up a command post in the village center; he joined the resistance, taking the first steps into what for him would be twenty-five years of war, and which would entwine his life with the life and death of Hoang Ngoc Dam. Because of his age then, Huy could not be a full combatant; instead, he helped lay mines in the road; ran commo—communication—wire for guerrilla units; and slipped, bluffed, or worked his way into French installations, mapping them out for the other soldiers.[11]

"None of our family ever helped the French; we all fought against them," Dam's youngest brother, Cat, says proudly. His father, Hoang Dinh Can, joined the local Viet Minh militia as well, a farmer by day and a guerrilla fighter by night; during the American war in the South he would have been called Viet Cong. Dam was old enough to help his father—he was ten by the time the French left—and he came to see his father's resistance against these foreign occupiers as a model for the course of his own life. His younger brothers and sisters still remember their father's stories about those days: "The French were trying to burn down a lot of houses, so many of the people in the village stripped the wood off their houses and threw the wood into the ponds so the French couldn't burn them," brother Luong says.[12] "Then the French killed them and raped the women. They also burned the communal shrine [a building that exists in all Vietnamese villages, filled with the ancient statues and artifacts that hold the town's guardian spirits] and now that's still called 'the burned shrine.'"

The Hoang family had been in Thai Giang as long as some of the statues in the shrine, as long as there was a Thai Giang. Generations of farmers were born in the village, their umbilical cords buried in the earth next to their homes to show their connection to the land, their bones buried in the village soil, their continuity threaded into the earth. There were three branches of the family; Dam's father, Hoang Dinh Can, belonged to the most important and largest. His mother, Pham Thi Lanh, gave birth to seven children. Dam (pronounced "Dahm") was the first-born, in 1944. He was given the name Hoang Dinh Dam, but later, during the war, he changed his middle name to "Ngoc" (Jade), for reasons the family does not know. Each year a new sibling was born: the next was also a boy, Hoang Dang Chi, fol-lowed by another boy, Hoang Huy Luong; and then a sister, Hoang Thi Tham; another brother, Hoang Dang Cat; and finally the youngest sisters, Hoang Thi Dam and Hoang Thi Tuoi.

Driving out from Hanoi to Thai Binh to interview the family, I was struck by the countless spires of Catholic churches along the horizon. Village after village is centered on its church, and the structures are startlingly French in the landscape of rice fields: arched stained-glass windows and flying buttresses, sometimes flanked by tiered pagoda towers, as if to physically demonstrate both the absorbent power of Vietnamese culture and the split in Vietnamese society that would define and direct the history of the country. When Catholic missionaries came to Viet Nam in the nineteenth century, they converted thousands among the hard-pressed villagers of the region, people exhausted by natural disasters and continual warfare, or mandarins who had lost their struggles for power. After the French colonized Indochina, many of the Vietnamese converts remained loyal to their French rulers, but many others joined the movement for independence from the foreigners. By the end of World War II in 1945, when Ho Chi Minh stood before a crowd of hundreds of thousands in Hanoi and declared the independence of Viet Nam from colonial rule (using the words of the American Dec-laration of Independence), thousands of Thai Binh Catholics, victims of starvation and occupation, were among those who rallied to his cause.[13] Nine years later, after the defeat of the

French and the supposed temporary division of the country at the Geneva conference, thousands of those same Catholics—many spurred to panic by stories and rumors planted by the legendary CIA operative Edward Lansdale[14]—fled to the South, fearing the repression of their religion and the confiscation of their lands. Their exodus was mirrored by thousands of former Viet Minh fighters and sympathizers escaping to the North in the great convulsion that drew up the sides of the war to come. The side of history the Hoang family—Buddhists, animists, and Marxists by faith—was on, was never in question. When the French left in 1954, the Hoangs believed fervently, with the Communist Party, that the Geneva accords were a travesty that left the country mutilated, cut in half, the agreement, at most, merely a cease-fire.

Homer grew up during the cold war: the all-prevalent ideological muzak in the background of his American childhood during the 1950s and early 1960s was the communist menace and the clarion call of John Fitzgerald Kennedy to halt its spread by a counter-inoculation of militant and missionary democracy. The enveloping theme of Dam's boyhood was the imperialist menace, the revolution, and the need to reunify the country through a militant and missionary Marxism. "The Revolution has given independence to one half of the country, but there still remains the other half," a People's Army private would say during the war, summing up the belief of millions. "The Revolution is going on in the South. North Vietnamese fighters must go there to fight on the people's side to free them from the yoke of American imperialism. Viet Nam is indivisible. We can't live in the North in independence and let our fellow countrymen in the South live in slavery."[15]

But in the mid-1950s, just after independence, elements in the Party put reunification on the back burner and attempted first to institutionalize the revolution and eliminate domestic enemies by collectivizing the land. Imitating Mao's programs in China, cadres were sent to villages throughout the North to

whip up local peasants into a frenzy against "rich landlords" and
"feudal elements," who were then dragged before village tri-
bunals, or simply mobs, to be criticized as enemies of the people and, too often, tortured and executed. Many were victims of
neighbors getting even for past slights or using the upheavals
for their own gain.[16] The Land Reform period is a time the
Hoang family, like many families in Viet Nam, does not speak
about; it's the excised page of its history. By 1956, when Dam
was twelve years old, Ho Chi Minh had called off the program
and apologized for its excesses, though by then thousands had
died or had been abused, humiliated, and stigmatized.[17]

The focus of the Party turned again to the reunification of
the country. By the end of the decade, the People's Army of Viet
Nam (PAVN) was sending soldiers to the South to seed the revolution there and to take charge of and fight with local forces
against the Saigon government. At the same time, it denied it
was doing so, preferring to present the resistance against the
American-sponsored Saigon government as a completely southern affair.

In Thai Giang there was no need to deny involvement: the
reunification of the country and the defeat and expulsion of
the latest invaders, the Americans now taking over from the defeated French, were the ideals that nourished Dam and his generation. In Hanoi there was a nascent peace movement urging
reconciliation with the South rather than war.[18] But Thai Giang
was far from the city. The children of Hoang Dihn Can knew
for what their father had fought. The face of foreign domination
was the face of the French rapist, murderer, and arsonist who
had tried to burn out the heart of the village, cut it from its
own history. It was the cruel and indifferent face that had
caused the starvation of millions. There was no questioning.
There were no alternatives.

By the time Dam was sixteen, five years before the United
States sent ground troops to Viet Nam, he attempted to enlist in
the army. "At that time," Luong relates, "he had gone to take a

test, an exam, to join the army, and he kept it a secret. But when my mother pressed him about it, he said he wouldn't talk about it because he was afraid it might jinx it; he didn't know if he had passed yet. In those days, it's like going to the university today where one never talks about these things because they are afraid to ruin their luck and you were as anxious to go to the army then as you are anxious to go to the university now."

After what the Vietnamese would come to call the American war started, and as it cost more and more lives, the PAVN began to rely largely on conscription for its soldiers, as did the U.S. and South Vietnamese armies. But in the period just before the war, and for several years afterward, Dam's eagerness to enlist and his worries about not being accepted were not unusual. "Nowadays," said a PAVN sergeant, "many young men lie about their age, making themselves older, so they can be accepted into the army. The morale of the young men in the North is very high. Many seventeen-year-olds volunteered and, when refused, came home crying."[19] As it was in Bamberg, in Thai Giang in the early to mid-1960s, military service was actively and even fervently sought by the generation raised on the examples of their fathers' and mothers' heroic resistance against the French and the stories of struggle against earlier foreign invaders: the thousand years of revolt against the Chinese that had led to the country's first independence in AD 938, an independence that had to be fought for again every time a new dynasty came to China and invaded Viet Nam. The necessity of resistance to foreign invaders was pressed bone-deep into Dam's perception of the world, exemplified in his father's life and in the statuettes of heroes of resistance on the family altar: Tran Hung Dao, the general who defeated the Mongol invaders; Le Luu; and the heroic Trung Sisters on their elephants, leading revolts against the Chinese.[20] Dam dreamed of subsuming and defining himself in his nation's history; he epitomized a generation that, as war veteran and author Bao Ninh describes in *The Sorrow of War*, "threw itself into the war enthusiastically, fiercely, making its own blood flow and causing the blood of others to flow in torrents."[21]

In school, Dam's teacher would often interrupt the lesson when word of a victory in the South was passed on to him, and the class would stand up and cheer the inevitable announcement of a military triumph or heroic action. Dam was one of the most enthusiastic cheerers. He joined the Communist Youth League and became a member of what was called, with great pride, the propaganda team. The family still speaks of his participation as an example of Dam's selfless assumption of civic responsibility. "In those days we had no loudspeakers," Cat says, "so he would use a piece of aluminum and roll it into a kind of semaphore and read the news of the local neighborhoods to the people. As youngsters we would watch him climb on whatever tree was the highest and then stand up there and shout the news." He was a product, the family feels, of a community whose function was to produce such young people. Even years later, at Dam's funeral, his brother-in-law Hoang Minh Dieu, a veteran himself, felt it proper to "thank the Commune's People and Party—who had made our brother Hoang Ngoc Dam a brave soldier."

He was a poster child. Yet some family memories go beyond the anecdotes demonstrating his political purity to reveal something of what in Hoang Ngoc Dam is still loved by the people who remember him. His sister Hoang Thi Tuoi was born in 1961, the last and youngest child. She suffered from a skin condition that covered her body in boils and rashes, which caused others to shy away from touching her. "I don't remember anything," Tuoi says, "because I was too small then. I just know that my mother had to go from hospital to hospital, and an uncle told my siblings that if they did not take good care of me then I would die." But Cat recalls Dam's reaction, during a short leave after he had gone into the army: "Tuoi is the last child in the family, and everybody loved her the most, including my brother

Dam. When she got that disease, my brother had just learned some medical treatments in the army, and he came back home and bathed Tuoi with herbs, according to what he'd learned, as we all stood around and looked. He told us what leaves to use to cure that disease, how to bathe her, and what medicine to use. . . . [W]hen Dam studied medicine, the only person in the family he had a chance to use his knowledge for was our youngest sister. He loved that girl, and took care of her, even though my sister cried and did not want to be bathed. He boiled a big pot of water with a lot of leaves, and he told others what to do."

What the family also remembers about Dam was the quality that would strike Homer deeply when he confronted Dam: his neatness and cleanliness in the middle of a filthy jungle . . . and what it said about him. "We were very poor," Cat says, "so I never understood how Dam got a white suit, but he wore it whenever he went out. And he studied very hard. We did not have paper, so we would take used paper and soak it in lime-water and use it again as scrap paper. Dam always kept his books in order, and he was very careful, he was neat from his hair to his way of walking, to his clothes. We did not have many clothes, but his clothes always looked pressed, even though we did not have an iron."

The Hoang family today is prosperous; its kids studying engineering, literature, and medicine, its tile-roofed houses are made of concrete; inside TVs and computers sit in rooms next to traditional family altars. When Dam was growing up, the village homes were thatch-roofed, and the scarcity Cat referred to went unnoticed unless it moved into hunger. It was the normal condition of life, of Dam's life, as were the political upheavals that moved through the village in the same way as locusts and storms, sometimes disastrously, but always passing, leaving something eternal and abiding. Dam's childhood is still remembered by the family through the golden haze with which one wants to remember the dead and the past, with a sense of nostalgia for what they now see as a solidarity and clarity of purpose absent in the more complicated tangles of peace.

Dam attended the village school. When he came home in the evening he would help his father work the paddy fields. In his free time he played soccer with his friends, using a ball made from rolled-up dried banana leaves. Life still centered, more than anything, on the rice growing all around him, the mud it grew from caked on his legs and hands. The war was somewhere past the edge of the fields, always waiting, but nebulous as the shimmer of heat beyond the vast silences of the paddies.

# CHAPTER FIVE

# Map
# Shifts

There was the diminutive, somewhat chubby-faced junior college dropout they called a brown boot. The name referred to the old boots the army had in World War II—meaning a lifer in the worst sense of that word, which did not just mean career soldier, but rather someone who had latched onto the rules and regs as if they gave him an authority he could not otherwise claim; they were what he had instead of a personality or genuine leadership ability. The other officer candidates in the 53rd Company at Fort Benning, former enlisted men who, like Homer, had applied to OCS and were smart or driven enough to get in, thought the man was something of a prig; Homer remembers he seemed competent, but had a kind of bullying quality. His fellow candidate (5 feet, 4 inches in his socks) only got things done by screaming at the top of his lungs, as if volume could stand in for height, his face red with what seemed a disproportionate and somehow unseemly rage. A martinet. Later, in the war, his own men would despise him for his erratic style of leadership; at times he'd try to ingratiate himself, kiss their asses, have them call him by his nickname, Rusty. At other

times, when they would snicker or laugh, he'd fly into one of
his rages. He was the guy who perpetually did not get the joke
and was angry that it might be about him. It usually was. People
tended to put him quickly out of their minds. Even after what
he did in Viet Nam made his name known to most of the country, his fellow former candidates had to search their memories
for him, as if looking for pieces of a puzzle. The neighbor
squinting into the lens of the news camera, saying how nobody
noticed the serial killer next door; he always was neat and quiet
and kept his lawn well cropped. Before the army, he'd been a
cook for a time and moved cars through a car wash. As the war
demanded more bodies, he'd been notified by his draft board
that his status was being reevaluated, and decided to beat them
to it by enlisting, though he'd tried to enlist once before, and
had been rejected because he was tone-deaf. But the army's
standards had relaxed; there was a shortage of men. He seemed
characterized by another kind of tone deafness as well, a lack of
nuances in how he perceived the world. "All orders are legal,"
the candidate would say later. "The soldier's job is to carry out
any order given to him to the best of his ability."[22] He had never
read about Nuremberg.

The army almost didn't take Homer—he weighed ninety-four
pounds at his enlistment physical—but he went outside the
exam room, drank water until his belly was full, and went back
in again. He was still two pounds under the acceptable weight,
but the doctor, shaking his head, told him that if he wanted it
that bad, he could have it. He had also failed the Officer Candidate School entrance exam the first time (you're being too honest, the officer in charge had told him after the initial interview),
but he took it again and after he passed did very well during the
twenty-three weeks of officer training. After graduating and receiving his commission as a second lieutenant, while many of his
classmates went straight to Viet Nam, Homer remained in South
Carolina, at Fort Jackson, where he had done his own basic

training as an enlisted man. The army felt he would be most valuable there, both because of his marksmanship—he was initially assigned as officer-in-charge of the rifle range—and because he knew how to find his way through swamps and forests and navigate by map, something the army was finding its soldiers in Viet Nam often could not do. Homer knew from his boyhood how to find his way in tangled landscapes and had honed that skill with remarkable effectiveness during the formalized training he received in OCS. He was tasked to write up a protocol for a course in map reading and land navigation for the Department of the Army. When it was approved, he set up a training course at Fort Jackson and trained the instructors.

The year was 1968. The ground war he would soon join had been going on for three years. There were other ways that the army was not teaching soldiers how to navigate in the confusing terrain that the war had become. The political goal of supporting an anticommunist government by winning the hearts and minds of the population was drowning in the blood of that population, the result of the military strategy of attrition—body count as a gauge of victory—in a war in which civilians and enemy combatants were often mixed.[23] It was a situation Neal Sheehan describes American advisor John Paul Vann as prophesizing—and warning against—just before American ground troops had been introduced into the conflict. "The Viet Cong troops were so intermingled with the peasantry that the Saigon troops had difficulty distinguishing friend from foe. 'Think,' Vann said, 'how much more difficult it would be for Americans.' The American soldier would soon start to see the whole rural population as the enemy. The Army and the Marine Corps would create a bloody morass into which they and the Vietnamese peasantry would sink. 'We'd end up shooting everything—men, women, kids, and the buffaloes,' Vann said."[24]

John Paul Vann's prophecy became reality on March 16, 1968, in the hamlet of Tu Cung, in the village of My Lai 4 (the official army designation). Homer's tone-deaf OCS classmate,

William Laws "Rusty" Calley, acting on what he and most of his
men believed were the instructions of his brigade commander,
ordered his platoon to commit hundreds of murders.[25] After
two hours of killing, the lieutenant smacked a Buddhist monk
in the jaw with his rifle butt when the man didn't answer his
questions. Then he saw that a child of about two years old, which
had somehow freed itself from the arms of its dead mother, had
begun crawling out of a ditch filled with the bodies of the people shot by Calley and his platoon. Calley stopped questioning
the monk, reached down casually, threw the child back into the
ditch, and shot it. His face was expressionless, people would remember. He turned to his men and ordered them to herd more
of the villagers into the ditch and shoot them, and when some
didn't obey, he trained his own weapon on them. After four
hours, when they stopped for a lunch break, Calley and the rest
of his company had butchered over 500 women, old men, and
children, all civilians.[26]

Unlike many of his classmates, Homer did remember Calley years later. His fellow candidate's actions surprised and horrified him. The war he fought in the Central Highlands against
the regular forces of the People's Army of Viet Nam was not the
guerrilla war of the lowlands where Calley had been, and where
the Viet Cong swam in and were indistinguishable from the sea
of the people. "I didn't walk in Calley's shoes," Homer says. "So
it is hard for me to judge him. But I can judge his actions, and
they were totally wrong."

Would he have done what Calley did if he were at My Lai?
It is "a comforting fantasy that our own character would hold
steady under the most extreme pressure of dreadful events,"
trauma psychiatrist Dr. Jonathan Shay writes. To have avoided
committing war crimes is a matter of what he labels "moral
luck," quoting a veteran in his therapy group who said, "I was
just lucky [not to have committed atrocities against civilians],
that's all. There were never any civilians up where I was."[27]
What you do, Shay implies, depends on where you are. Yet

Homer was certain he would never, under any circumstances, have shot unarmed civilians, nor would he have allowed his men to do so, no matter what the combat environment. He did not walk in Calley's boots through the rice paddies and sullen, deadly villages of Quang Ngai. But all the men who were at My Lai were under the same "extreme pressure of dreadful events," and not all of them reacted the same way. Some participated willingly, emotionlessly or happily or psychotically shooting, scalping, raping, and mutilating. Others did so reluctantly, some of them weeping, convinced that they had to follow orders. Others tried to save villagers, defying officers, noncoms, and peers and refusing to shoot; one helicopter crew trained their guns on American troops in order to save villagers huddled in a bunker, waiting to die. The diversity of their responses contradicts Shay's idea of moral luck. What you do depends not on where you are but on what you bring with you to that place—something Homer would prove later in Viet Nam when the education he had dug out from the subterranean vaults of the university, his late-night reading into the equations and balances not covered in his math and science courses, and the way he was able to place his father's moral courage in that context—would make him certain what to do when he witnessed the abuse of a captured man who wore the uniform of his enemy.

Calley is often described by what he was not. He was a blank on which the war could write its most basic and brutal premises without danger of being challenged. Its silent cadences and his own wrapped around each other. *If it's dead and it's Vietnamese, it's VC. Body count is victory. Body count is good. I must obey so that I will be obeyed. So I will be taller. I'm hot. I'm pissed off. My men despise me. My commanding officer thinks I'm a joke. These insects are maddening. These gooks are maddening. They're killing us. They're all alike. They're insects. They live in hootches. They don't own cars. I'm a god. I'm just doing what I was told to do. The soldier's job is to carry out any order given him to the best of his ability.*

What if Calley had had Homer's father as a model, to put a counter-cadence of decency into his head? But it's a useless question: the army does not issue fathers. What if he had read the Nuremberg transcripts? What if he had had a day of training in the Laws of Land Warfare instead of one hour? Two days? What if it had been delivered seriously, taught effectively and with respect?

The army, seeing its soldiers could not find their way by compass in the jungle, had ordered Homer to set up a training course. But there was little effort to show soldiers how to use a moral compass to navigate a morass of pressures and choices too confusing to be traversed by luck alone. They had to rely on what they already knew. And that was not enough for Calley and many others.

The war was altering our definition of ourselves, forcing us to look in its distant and blood-smeared mirror and see what our surrogate reflections were doing in our name. The country was as roiled and split as the three groups of soldiers at My Lai: we can do no evil; we can do no good; who the hell are we? One month before the murder spree at My Lai, on February 8, 1968, coming home from Fort Jackson, Homer drove into another massacre as he passed through Orangeburg, South Carolina, on US 301. As he got close to the campus of South Carolina State University, the traffic ahead of him slowed and then stopped, and he saw an armored personnel carrier blocking the highway. Highway patrol officers with rifles were stopping and searching every vehicle. At the university 200 students, most of them black, had been protesting a segregated bowling alley. The local police, taunted by the crowd, opened fire and killed two university students and a high school student and injured twenty-seven others. Homer heard the rifle fire from his car window. Where was he? In 1968, it sometimes seemed to him that map reading and land navigation just didn't work. The country had shifted out from under the maps.

In June, while Homer was still at Fort Jackson, it shifted even further when Robert Kennedy was shot dead in California. The murder shook him badly, reinforcing the sense of hopelessness he'd felt since the Orangeburg killings and Martin Luther King's assassination that April. He didn't understand the war, but the sense he'd tried to cultivate that the country was progressing inevitably toward its own better nature, the stubborn and natural sense of justice he'd seen in his father, was shattered by the deaths of the men who had embodied that movement to him. The neat certainty of the Bohr planetary explanation had once again flown apart into chaos; he no longer recognized the country he was being shipped overseas to defend.

By August 13, he was in Viet Nam.

# CHAPTER SIX

# "Of the Two of Us, Who Is More Sorrowful?"

As he waited to see if the army would take him, Dam became interested in Pham Thi Minh, a pretty girl of seventeen with a sense of humor he liked. He often found himself working with her in the fields of Doai Hamlet, their section of Thai Giang, and she helped him prepare his "broadcasts" from the trees. They were both in the Youth Union, the communist organization for young people. Thrown together, by their own design, in youth group activities, they would take long walks, speaking quietly about the future, although both knew what lay across the path to it. There was no question of their being intimate, and if not for Dam's status as a would-be recruit, even their courtship would have been frowned upon. The two young people formed an easy, teasing relationship. His friends recall Dam smiling when he told of going to Minh's house and pretending to sleep as she kept piling blankets and clothing on him, until he had to break into laughter. "At that time, courtship was very simple and very romantic," Cat says. But Minh's family at first objected to the match; they gave Dam a very hard time. "They just wanted to challenge him to see how tough he was," his sister Tham says. "There was still much feudal behavior here. It was what people did in those days."[28]

Finally, the notification that he'd been accepted into the army came through. He immediately pressed his proposal to Minh again, and this time her family agreed. They were married on December 26, 1963, by the head of the commune, and following the ceremony there was a small celebration in the Hoang house. A neighbor brought over a record player, the only one in the hamlet, and the celebrants played recordings of revolutionary music, or possibly "Take Me Back to Sorrento," a song by a young Italian that became inexplicably, wildly popular in Viet Nam during the war. There were many marriages rushed into during that week; all the young men who had applied to join the army had received their mobilization notices, and they and their families, with a prescient fatalism, wanted to be sure that when they left their wives would be pregnant.

Dam had been told to report to his unit in five days. But, ever the good soldier, he left a day early. Those four days were to be the extent of his married life.

"On the day of the recruitment and of saying good-bye to the young people," brother Luong remembers, "all of the young people had caught the spirit and everybody came out to cheer them on. And the commissar, the party secretary came and shook hands with each of them and then they were each given a washcloth."

Unknown to the family, Dam had already volunteered for what was called War Zone B, or simply "B"—the South.

"When Dam knew that he would go to the front, he was very happy," his sister Tham says. "He cavorted with happiness, but my mother turned her head to wipe her tears away. After he left, we folded his clothes, put them aside, and my mom would sniff them because she missed him."

Both Tham and Pham Thi Minh, now sixty-three, remember walking with Dam as he left. "I married Dam when I was only seventeen years old," Pham says. "It was four o'clock in the morning when he left. He took the knapsack; I took my conical hat and my sandals, and we walked toward Thai Binh, taking shortcuts through the paddy field, so I had to roll up my pants. When we got to the main road, I washed my legs and hands, and put my sandals back on, and then we walked. Whenever I saw cars passing by, I was scared and had to hug him. He was very caring."

> *Cung trong lai ma cung chang thay*
> *Thay xanh-xanh nhung may ngan dau*
> *Ngan dau xanh biec mot mau*
> *Long chang y thiep ai sau hon ai?*

> *You and I turned around but saw nothing*
> *Just the green of the mulberry fields*
> *The endless green of the mulberry fields.*
> *Of the two of us, who is more sorrowful?*

> —THE SONG OF THE SOLDIER'S WIFE
> CHINH PHU NGAM[29]

Tham had gone along on that walk as well. "I remember the day I came to say good-bye to him," she says. "It was very early in the morning and foggy and there was a mist on the rice stalks. We walked across the fields and then at some point we crossed a little river to get to Thai Binh, to save a little time, because if you walked it was twenty kilometers, but instead we took a little sampan across the river. I was very young then, I was ten, but I remember one thing, that he took my shoulder and he told me, 'I'm going now and either the grass will be green over me [he would lie in a grave] or my chest will be red [covered with medals],' and he said, 'the key for your success in the future is for you to go to school; please go to school'.

"We all went to say good-bye to him and we stopped at a little store; we didn't have much money so we ate a bowl of noodles—it was called a bowl of noodles without a pilot— meaning it had no meat. Then he bought a little red blanket for his brother Chi. When we got to this bridge, the old 'Bo' bridge, he told us the bus stop was here and we should go home, and we realized it was still a distance to go to the bus stop. I remember seeing him walk away; he's a short person and he had his knapsack on his back, and he turned to wave at us, and that is the image I kept in my mind of him."

> Chi lam trai dam nghin da ngua
> Gieo Thai Son nhe tua hong mao
> Gia nha deo buc chien bao
> Thet roi cau Vi ao ao gio thu

> A man will win a horse hide for his shroud—
> his life he'll drop in battle like goose down
> In war attire you leave and cross the Wei,
> cracking your whip while roars the autumn wind.[30]

A few months later, after Dam had completed his medic's training and was to go to the war zone, an accident happened that would put a strain between Pham Thi Minh and the Hoang family that still exists today. "He wrote to us from Thanh Hoa," Cat explains, "and said that his unit had allowed his wife to come and say good-bye to him before he went South. He asked her to come, but she refused to go. . . . He wrote back and said he waited a day and a night for her, but nobody came, and so he volunteered to stand guard for his friends so they could have their conjugal visits. Later I asked my sister-in-law, why didn't you go? And the simple reason was because she was embarrassed."

As he told me the story, nearly four decades after Dam's death, Cat stared at the family altar where Dam's photo stood, and to my surprise, he seemed to crumple and began to weep, his voice rising as he continued. "We tried to encourage her to go. My father even offered to go with her. But she became a disappointment to our family and because of that our relations are not good. Because what he wanted was to have a child. Others here have had a child from that day. So if she had gone that time," he nodded at the altar, at an American guest, a former enemy, sitting in front of it, and said, "on a day like this we would have his child here."

In the end, all the children of Hoang Dinh Can and Pham Thi Lanh went to what they would call the American war—or the American war came to them. Dam and Chi both died in the South, and brother Luong and youngest brother, Cat, both worked with volunteer transportation battalions in the North, driving supplies to army units, often under attack by the same kinds of American aircraft that the three sisters, remaining in the village, saw drop bombs on Thai Giang itself, at one point hitting a schoolhouse and killing many people.

When Dam walked across the fields that morning, away from Thai Giang, he did not expect to see his family or his wife until the end of the war, or, more likely, ever again. The Hoang family today does not know how many young people went South during the war, the boys to the army, the girls to the Young Volunteers, but out of that village of 3,000, 142 were never to return alive, and of the dead whose remains did make it back, only some could be identified and their names placed on their tombs.[31] Nobody knew what the exact fate of any of the other missing soldiers had been, not until thirty-five years after the end of the war, when Homer Steedly's mother remembered a packet her son had sent her from Viet Nam that she had kept carefully in the attic of her house in Bamberg.

# CHAPTER SEVEN

# "You Wish Your Buttons Were Flatter"

For Homer, the first week was a blur of impressions, a kind of reverse telescoping downward, like the characters in the movie *Incredible Voyage*, shrunk in stages until they could be sucked into a hypodermic to fulfill their function: from the huge, sprawling base at Cam Ranh Bay to the red dust of the smaller Camp Enari, Pleiku combat base in the Central Highlands, where on August 21, 1968, Homer experienced the new sensation of having someone try to kill him with high explosive, when the base was hit by twenty-one 12.7 mm rockets. "They dropped me off beside the airstrip," he remembers, "which was just a long, level piece of ground with steel planking on it. And told me walk across there, that bunker line on the other side, and that's where your unit is. So I grabbed my duffel bag and started walking, you know, diddy bopping across it, real slow because it's very hot. And, all of a sudden WHAM! Something explodes and then a couple seconds later, WHAM, WHAM! I look around, see little puffs of smoke coming towards me, and I realize they're shelling the base. And I look around and there is no place to hide, I'm in the middle of an airfield. In between the two little pieces of runway, there's a little section about three-foot wide, where there's a little drainage ditch dug to drain the airfield. And so I go and lay down flat, as flat as I can, in that. It was one of those situations where you wish your buttons were flatter. A couple of minutes go by and I don't hear anything going off, so I get up and go back over and walk over to the bunker line, and then meet my unit. And that's the way I got started in Viet Nam."[32]

Explosions, red mud, rain. It rained constantly at first, a cold drizzle that gave him both the chills and the opportunity to miss the chills when the sun came out and the temperature soared into the 90s and 100s. That was his orientation week—the right word, he thought, oriented into the Orient—but he felt anything but. A week of training, and then finally he was ejected onto a small, muddy hill, designated 1089 for its height in meters above sea level, fortified with rotting sandbag bunkers and men so caked with mud they looked as if they had turned red. They looked at him with half-lidded insolent eyes that all held the same basic question: Are you the asshole who's gonna get us killed? He had been assigned to command the 1st Platoon of B Company, 1st Battalion of the 8th Infantry Regiment, 4th Infantry Division. He had thirty-nine men in his command. He was a twenty-two-year-old country boy who still saw himself in those terms and needed to perform, to do well. The bitter memory of his inadequacy at Clemson was almost wiped out by his elevation to the status of officer and gentleman, but the test of leading these men in combat was still in front of him.

The Central Highlands where he found himself straddled two provinces on the western border of South Viet Nam—Kontum and Pleiku, under the administrative divisions of the Republic of Viet Nam; the other side called the same provinces Kontum and Gia Lai, the B3 front. The Truong Son mountain range, which ran from North Viet Nam down to the Mekong Delta, was not only a natural barrier between Viet Nam, Laos, and Cambodia, but was also an alien and forbidding world to most Vietnamese, who lived in the farming and fishing villages and cities of the coastal flatlands and rice fields or the low hill country, or on the great river deltas of the north and south: the Red River and the Mekong. Even its names were alien, un-Vietnamese: Poly Kleng and Plei Khong and Plei Ku; the ominously and, the Americans felt, accurately named Plei Trap Valley. The names were in the language of the various mountain tribal groups, the Jarai, the Bahnar, the Rengao, and the Sedang, called collectively Montagnards by the Americans, who had picked up the term from the French and brought it into the GI lexicon as Yards. They were called Moi, savages, by the Vietnamese, who for the most part saw them as loincloth-wearing, bare-breasted, crossbow-hunting primitives who carved face masks of their dead and abandoned their graves after a few months. Who else would want to live in a place where jungle-thick mountain peaks soared as high as 9,000 feet, the deep valleys cut between their steep flanks dank and fecund with tangled vegetation, often dark at midday under triple layers of treetop leaf canopies, the highest topping 150 to 200 feet? At ground level, bamboo, elephant grass, and the thick, clinging plants the Americans called wait-a-minute vines impeded movement. Trails had to be hacked through by point men, each kilometer a saga of endurance. For three months of the year it rained without ceasing; otherwise the temperature could go as high as 120°F, with 90 percent humidity, during the day, and then drop down to near freezing at night.

In 1968, when Homer arrived in the Highlands, the jungles were populated by a variety of exotic and sometimes deadly wildlife: poisonous snakes, huge pythons, tigers, and elephants, as well as the less deadly but more common leeches, fire ants, biting centipedes, and ubiquitous mosquitoes.[33] It was a place the Vietnamese troops from the North found to be as alien and sinister as both the rest of their countrymen and the American GIs did. Among them was a young medic, Hoang Ngoc Dam, who had been in the Highlands since 1966. He was attached to the 66th Regiment of the People's Army of Viet Nam, the enemy Homer would face in what Colonel Hale Knight, the commanding officer of the 1st Brigade of the 4th Infantry Division, would call "conventional warfare in an unconventional war."[34]

1 SEP 1968

*Dear Mom and Dad,*

*I got first Platoon. I have a real tough job ahead of me because my people are in bad habits . . . they got a don't care attitude. I have basically good soldiers, no kids, so I really should be able to make an excellent fighting force out of them. Our Company as a whole is the best in the Battalion and the Brigade, the Brigade commander COL Fix admits it. Our Battalion Commander "Bullet," LTC Tombaugh also depends on us, when he needs dependability and fighting guts. "Bullet" is a real sharp CO, everyone under his command really respects him and all wear a bullet on the right rear of their steel pots so all will know. The NVA [North Vietnamese Army] know the bullet trade mark and respect it as a tough fighting force. Our Company hasn't lost a person for well over a year, going on two. The NVA just doesn't like to tangle with B Company, cause we put up to much of a fight. He is always hitting A, C, and D Company, but never hardly ever us. The last time he saw us we gave him a sound defeat at Dak To without even getting one of us wounded.*

*I'll write again when I get some more time.*

*Bye for now,*

*Love,*
*Homer*

Homer's cheerful assessment in his letter of why Bravo Company had not lost any men to the NVA was both wishful, new-guy cheerleading and his way of reassuring his parents that he would be all right; in spite of what he wrote, he knew that an entire platoon from Bravo Company had been wiped out the year before. But his enthusiasm about his troops was genuine, and his men, judging quickly because their lives depended on it, saw that he was competent and fair; they could see he respected them, and they respected him enough to live up to that assumption. He didn't look any older than most of them, draftees or regulars, and he wasn't: a slim, soft-spoken, almost baby-faced officer. But they saw how tough he could be when a flipped-out long-range reconnaissance grunt, tipped over the edge by too much long-range reconnaissance, tried to stab him with a knife. Homer neatly and calmly butt-stroked the man, knocking him out. By midmonth Homer had been promoted to first lieutenant, and his company was shifted to Fire Support Base 29, another of the American outposts set on various ridgelines or hilltops all through the Plei Trap Valley in an attempt to disrupt North Viet Nam's flow of fighters and equipment to the southern battlefields. FSB 29 had been abandoned hastily and carelessly by the unit Homer and his men were replacing. The perimeter of sandbag-rimmed firing positions, claymore mines, and barbed wire surrounded an interior of filthy, collapsing, sandbag bunkers filled with dank water, piles of discarded ration cans, and feces. The whole position sat atop a nearly vertical mound of the slippery red clay, ankle deep and waist deep, which more than any other geographical feature came to signify Vietnam to the soldiers. Digging into it, it would stick to their entrenching tools until they doubled and tripled in weight and the soldiers would have to stop, take a stick, and scrape the swollen hive of mud off with a stick before they could continue. The red mud sucked off their boots, caked their bodies, and finally infiltrated their skin, the land coming into them. When they tried to scrub it out, or got the chance on R&R to lie in hot water, it would worm out of their pores in thick, spiraling curlicues.

In spite of the clay, they rebuilt the bunkers, cleaned up the positions, and set up fields of fire. Half of Homer's Bravo Company and all of Charlie Company were unable to get to the position because the rains were too heavy for the helicopters, and Homer found himself in command of sixty-six men and the Fire Support Base, until Charlie Company was finally choppered in on August 21.

At night there was only the banshee whistle of the parachute flares that silvered the constant curtain of rain; the sounds of the war—artillery, the distant pound of a machine gun all around them, the whine of a sniper round homing in on them. There was no time when they were not wet.

### 22 SEP 1968

*Dear Mom and Dad,*

*Sorry to hear about Mrs. Cora, but I'm sure glad she won't be suffering any more. Wish I could have seen her again before she died.*

*I got your letter about the APO number; 96262 is the overall code, but 96265 is 4th Div and will get mail to me quicker. I got the package and sure do appreciate those things. They helped solve a lot of little problems. That map cover you sent works just fine with the plastic tape too.*

*Send some money to the investment people, but wait until pay day check gets there, and keep about a $150 balance in the bank at all times.*

*Things finally got organized here (thank goodness!!). I know you won't believe it, cause I can't hardly, but the rucksack (pack) I carried to 29 weighed over 60 lbs., not to mention a bag of gear that was about 30 lbs. You should have seen me! I fell when we were unloading the chopper and had to take the rucksack off to get up. The 75 yards up that hill to the fire base 29 was almost straight up, and several people fell half or more (rucksack, weapon and all) down the hill several times, before we all got up. One guy hurt himself when he fell and coughed blood for awhile, but he's OK now. I've got some film of us, and the rucks look small, but they are full of explosive, ammo, etc., that's why they were so heavy. I'll send the film later. The pictures were taken in Dak To, the only level ground I've seen yet. The land out here is so thick with bamboo and woods, and elephant grass, that you have to cut your way through with a machete or else you just can't get through. When I send these people out 3 to 6 miles through that stuff in a day, they really show guts in doing it. They don't have to be coaxed or watched though, they're men and good men. Even when they can't go another step, you can't help them, cause pride won't let them accept it. You just wouldn't believe it.*

*Got to go,*

*Love,*
*Homer*

Their job was to find, interdict, and destroy any enemy moving toward the towns and larger American bases. Homer sent out four-man reconnaissance teams, the men humping those sixty- or seventy-pound rucksacks, all their weapons, and ammo, cutting and pushing their way up the jungle-thick mountains. The days were hot, the nights spent in cold rain, and there was nothing for them when they returned but old rations and shit details. By October the monsoon started tapering off, to be immediately replaced by continuous heat. "Temperatures so high now that even the dirt will blister your skin," Homer wrote in his journal. Command was shifting the companies and platoons of the 8th Infantry back and forth to the different firebases or on recon by force missions. The NVA pushed back, letting the Americans know they were still there. Homer's two B Company platoons, now by themselves after C Company was ordered to another firebase, were being probed by fire every night, snipers shooting into the perimeter, hits by B-40 rocket-propelled grenades.

Homer was becoming savvy. He'd spent his boyhood moving quietly through woods and brush, training his eyes to see the small movements and disturbances that revealed danger or game. He tried now to teach his soldiers, especially the city boys, some of those tricks. The country boys, black and white, from Alabama, Georgia, and South Carolina, he made into his scouts and point men. He knew also that what saved your life was being inside the range of your own big guns. On the new firebases to which they kept getting shifted, or on patrols, even if only to an overnight encirclement set up after a hard day's hump, Homer would call in artillery to shell the area around his perimeter, and only then send out the two-man listening posts that would provide early warning of an approaching enemy. He told the men to set up fifty yards inside where the shells had hit, so he could call in a ring of fire around them if they were attacked.

On October 13 a short-range patrol was ambushed, and Homer recorded his first man killed in action, Private First Class

Wayne Elledge, shot just as his patrol was in sight of the fire support base. The next day NVA units attempted to overrun Fire Support Base 29, the hill Homer's platoon had left on October 6. From where he and his men sat now, they could watch 29 getting hit, on one day counting more than a hundred 82mm mortars and 75mm rockets impacting inside the perimeter. As if they were watching a movie or a prophecy.

17 OCT 1968

*Dear Mom and Dad,*

*Well we moved again, this time we went to FSB-30. It's a real nice looking area. The view from up here is unbelievable. In one direction you can see for 7 or 8 "klicks" (kilometers). That is when it stops raining of course. It stopped for awhile right now. We have had rain for 24 hours constantly.*

*A plane just came over in front of us dropping Chu Hoi (give up) leaflets. As usual we are having to rebuild all the bunkers here. I've been digging with the 5 people in my group for 12 hours now, making a real bunker 12' x 21' x 6'. Some bunker, beds, table, chairs and all. It's going to take about 3,000 sand bags to cover the roof alone.*

*We are still doing OK. My skin is turning red from all the mud. It gets in the pores and you can't get it out. I had my first shower yesterday in a month. That steel pot bit just doesn't get you very clean. Sure do appreciate those packages. I have some film I'm going to send home soon. I could use 7 pack and pens again, if you can get them. Also look around and see if you can find some of the Quaker instant oat meal. It comes in a box of one serving packs. It is easy to make and sure is good in the morning, when you're wet and cold.*

*Well I have to go for now before the rain gets here again cause the pen won't write on wet paper.*

*Love,*
*Homer*

# CHAPTER EIGHT

# The Trail

We can imagine him, the enigma he is now, as he sat under the woven thatched roof of a jungle hospital, a shaft of sunlight making its way through the weave and falling on the blank page of the notebook. Perhaps he ran his finger around the golden spot on the paper, then brought the new notebook up to his face, the slight bleach smell permeating the paper bringing him back to Thai Giang, the schoolhouse, a different world. He was a different man, and now, writing his name under the picture of the surgical scissors he had drawn on the page, he kept what was precious to him of his name—the Hoang, which was family; the Dam, which was the sound he still could hear as it came from his mother's lips—but changed "Dinh" to "Ngoc" (Jade). Perhaps he simply liked the sound of it; perhaps he needed to somehow mark the metamorphosis in himself, the jade green that had seeped into his body from the alien press of the jungle around him, transformed him from the boy perched in a jacaranda tree with a make-believe bullhorn into the man he was, a healer who had seen the death waiting in everyone, that other, final metamorphosis he had seen too often. Next to him, on the earthen floor, would be the medical textbook he had borrowed from the dispensary at Hospital Cave H15, near the village of Cheo Reo. He would copy useful passages into the notebook and reproduce the anatomical drawings: the cross-sections of arms and legs and bellies and brains, the intricate parts under the skin, so neat and clean, so different from the mashed, bloody messes he had seen revealed on the bamboo slabs they used as an operating table.

When Dam began to copy the text, he chose to start his new notebook with instructions for midwifery, perhaps thinking that the Jarai and Banhar he worked with lost too many in childbirth. Perhaps each birth he assisted in Cheo Reo was a little victory, in the face of each child emerging from its mother, the briefly glimpsed face of a soldier he had lost on his operating table or in the jungle, the light going from the man's eyes and now flaring again, fleetingly aware in the eyes of the newborn, knowing Dam's face, the last face he had seen and now the first of his new life. Perhaps seeing in the face of each child also what he knew he would never have, his mind going back to the night his wife did not come to him, the creak of the beds, the whispers and groans, the sounds of the other couples making love as he walked alone in the moonlight, outside the tents, assuming already the duty he had taken on himself, the guardian of the promise of life.

The day Dam walked away from Thai Giang, taking the shortcut through the rice fields with his bride and sister, was the beginning of a thousand-mile journey that would take him finally to Gia Lai and his encounter with Homer. On that first day he and the other young men from Thai Giang laughed and sang, filled with the excitement of leaving home and the adventure that awaited them, the opportunity they felt they had been given for an instant transition into adulthood or immortality.

They mustered in Thai Binh, where they were issued green cotton uniforms with plastic buttons, webbed cotton belts, sun helmets—made not of pith, as the Americans assumed, but rather of pressed cardboard covered with green cloth—and Chinese green canvas boots. For many of them it was the first time they had completely encased their feet and ankles. They were given backpacks of dark green cotton and chest pouches with three large pockets in front to hold the thirty-round banana-clip magazines they would eventually carry.[35] As soon as they were dressed, they were also given a taste of what the next years would bring, when they were marched by night fifty kilometers to the larger town of Nam Dinh. The march didn't faze them—they were tough farm boys—but the boots did, and before long many had taken them off and slung them over their necks by their laces. At Nam Dinh trucks were waiting for them, and they clambered aboard, still excited. They were driven through Hanoi at night. For many of Dam's comrades, as for Dam himself, it was their first time in the fabled capital, and they peered out through the canvas flaps of the truck, hoping to see an electric lightbulb; all they had ever had in the villages were kerosene lamps. The truck convoy roared out of Hanoi, over the Red River, heading northwest, and perhaps Dam glimpsed that river in the dawn, when the light hitting the water reveals the origin of its name.[36]

They headed toward another name that he had heard in his classrooms, read in his textbooks, and heard spoken by veterans, with no elaboration, as if just saying the name was enough. Dien Bien Phu, where the famous last stand of the French had taken place, was now a training base for the People's Army.

Their first night at the famous base, and from then on, the recruits were fed sticky rice with their meals. Dam hated sticky rice. He wrote home to his mother, his first complaint about the army, and she cried, remembering how she could never get him to eat such rice when he was a child, and thinking how hungry he must be in that place thick with foreign ghosts.

The training he received was similar to the training any army gives its recruits. He and his comrades learned how to judge distances; how to field strip, clean, aim, and shoot their weapons—AK-47s, K-45s, or the Chinese SKS rifle, with its folding bayonet that Dam would have in his hands, newly issued, when he met Homer. They learned how to use grenades and set mines and booby traps, and were introduced to enemy weapons, ordnance, and mines. They did not receive any special training in jungle warfare; the emphasis was on giving them enough stamina and know-how to survive the trek South. They hiked and ran over the rugged mountains around Dien Bien Phu, where many of their fathers and grandfathers had fought; the place itself was a lesson in the inevitability of victory. They had to carry loads of up to sixty pounds, sometimes rocks put into their knapsacks, and undergo other physical conditioning, all designed to develop their legs and stamina. The rest of what they needed to know would come from on-the-job training, during which, it was assumed, their rugged peasant background would help them prevail.[37]

At night, after a long day's training, they were given political indoctrination lectures: why we fight. Sometimes the speaker was a somewhat older man Dam knew from the village, Pham Quang Huy, who had joined the regular army in 1959 and now was the political officer of the unit. It was an important position. Political officers had to be Communist Party members, and their rank structure was separate from (and above) the rank structure of any unit's military cadre. Although the regular military officers and noncoms would plan and execute operations, they would do so according to strategic decisions made by the political cadre, and their plans always had to be approved by that cadre.

Some soldiers found the lectures and speeches boring, others found them inspiring, and some resented the political officers' power to interfere in the minutest parts of their daily activities. A poem found in a diary, translated by Bruce Weigl and Thanh T. Nguyen in *Poems from Captured Documents*,[38] reveals the resentment of one soldier, apparently annoyed with how closely everything he did was monitored:

> *They talk nonsense and wonder*
> *why those who eat so little shit so big*
> *If I had more teeth, I would eat a village of frogs.*
> *I would eat a meal of rotten food* .
> *And see if they'd still want to watch*

There is no indication that Huy was the kind of officer who would monitor his men's bowel movements and inspire such poetry. His conversations today reveal a true affection for the men he was with, and even though he has absolutely no doubts about the justice of and necessity for the war, he still allows an edge of criticism, a soldier's resentment of rear-area commanders willing to spend troops recklessly, into his remarks when he speaks of the number of lives he believes were unnecessarily lost because of the tactics used during the Tet Offensive. But that would be years in the future; while they were in training camp, he took an avuncular interest in Dam, whom he had known since childhood, and to whom he was related by marriage.

Dam had been at the training camp for a month when the unit was ordered to Laos, to begin, he assumed, a trek to the southern battlefield via the Truong Son Trails. He crossed the border with Huy and his unit, but shortly thereafter he was ordered back and told he would receive additional training as a medic in Thanh Hoa, the southernmost province in North Viet Nam. The family was somewhat surprised when he wrote the news to them. "We had no knowledge of medicine at that point, in my family," Cat said. "It wasn't until Laos that [Huy and Dam] were separated and Dam went to Thanh Hoa to receive his training." The medical training he got was fairly rudimentary, basic first aid techniques. But the fact that he had been chosen for the job apparently affected him deeply. He was the boy whose last words to his sister urged her to get an education; he had, he thought, put his own education on hold for the duration of the war, and now he was being given a chance to study a profession that suited both his need to serve and his drive for self-perfection.

It was from Thanh Hoa that Dam sent for his wife to join him, to have one night together before he would go, finally, to the war.

After 1965 the North Vietnamese no longer felt the need to disguise the fact that their troops were fighting in the South, but in 1964, when Dam again crossed over the Laotian border, his ID and personal papers were taken away, and his uniform was replaced with the black cotton, pajamalike peasant clothing the Viet Cong wore. His first stop in Laos was in the town of Techephone, south of the Demilitarized Zone (DMZ), already parallel to the border of South Viet Nam. From there he would leave friendly territory and enter the jungle.

What Americans would call the Ho Chi Minh Trail and what Dam knew as the Truong Son Trails was really a network— the main trails numbered like highways—running down the north-south spine of the Truong Son Mountains. The trails were sometimes narrow footpaths, sometimes the wide lanes seen by the American soldiers in the Plei Trap Valley, and were used for truck and armored vehicle transport as well as for foot soldiers. Whenever possible the trails ran under the sheltering canopy of the jungle; otherwise they might have branch- and leaf-woven camouflage lattices arched over them. Wooden bridges were often built just inches under the surface of streams so they would be invisible from the air.

Some of the system was inside South Viet Nam, but most of it was located in Laos and Cambodia. As soon as he came onto the trails, Dam came under the control of the 559th Command Group, the unit responsible for getting troops to the war, constructing new routes, maintaining the existing routes, and protecting the trails from air attack. The group's cadre divided the infiltrating soldiers into platoon- or company-sized groups. Dam, assigned to such a group, found himself stepping into a world that was as alien to the farm boy from Thai Giang as it was to the farm boy from Bamberg. The conditions of the trails echoed the conditions Homer would describe as typical of the Central Highlands: constant dampness and constant heat, followed by freezing nights, leeches, clouds of mosquitoes, biting ants, poisonous centipedes, and snakes. And there was always the problem of the Americans. If soldiers infiltrating down the trails were spotted or detected by the sensors the Americans dropped along it, they would be bombed and strafed, and they were often sprayed with the chemical defoliants used to strip away the jungle cover.

Guides, sometimes the girls from the Young Volunteers, sometimes from the communication and scout outfits, and sometimes from among the tribal minorities, led Dam and his group along the torturous and at times treacherous trails. In his rucksack he carried an extra uniform and a couple of pairs of underwear, some rubber-tire Ho Chi Minh sandals, a small entrenching tool, and a tent coated with tar on one side to keep out rain. He also had a week's worth of rations, and, as a medic, carried more than the usual number of antimalarial pills—the mosquitoes that plagued the marchers were all carriers—and battle dressings, along with his weapon and three magazines. He camped at way stations, set approximately one day's march apart; if he made it to a station, he set up his tent or used it as a hammock strung between two trees; if he was too exhausted, he just rolled up in it.[39]

It was a hump.

It would have taken him fifty days or more to finally arrive in the southern part of what he considered the soon-to-be undivided country of Viet Nam.

# CHAPTER NINE

# One
# Week

H omer fell into the routine of the war. The platoon humped their sixty- or seventy- or eighty-pound loads, carrying the whole rattling, flesh-cutting, chafing panoply of rucksacks, canteens, grenades, ammunition, and weapons up the slippery, steep slopes of the mountains; hacking through thick bamboo; wading through razor-sharp elephant grass that left hands and faces bleeding, the cuts drawing more mosquitoes, clusters of leeches swelling from whatever flesh they could crawl onto. They set up ambushes, trying to interdict the trails the NVA had been using and cratered the larger roads the enemy had hacked through the jungle for the trucks and equipment they were infiltrating into or through the highlands. The soldiers could feel the enemy building up around them, like a sensation on their skin. The size of the roads the NVA was hacking out of the jungle in the Plei Trap Valley northwest of Pleiku was an ominous sign; roads that big were not being built just to infiltrate troops. Helicopter crew chief Ron Carey, of the 119th Assault Helicopter Company, described landing in a crater on one trail as big as the two-lane country roads he was used to at home; it had been completely invisible from above the jungle canopy.[40]

They searched the jungle for signs of the NVA. Too often they acted as bait; the enemy was located when it hit them. Vines clutched at the men's arms and legs to delay or trip them; sometimes they would fall with a clatter of equipment. Clouds of mosquitoes buzzed around their heads and settled into their ears and on whatever skin was exposed. Their sweat poured over and around the bumps of insect bites that covered their skin and made them itch more fiercely; scratching them led easily to suppurating infections. Heat rash prickled their shoulders and chests and crotches like someone was driving hot needles further into their flesh with each step or rub of their packs. The triple-canopy layers of the trees enveloped them in a steamy, green-stained gloom. "Day after day, same thing," recounts Tom Lacombe, whose unit, Bravo Company, 3rd Battalion, 12th Infantry, moved in that same area, "dawn to dusk, one foot in front of the other, lean over, try and catch your breath, shift the load, hope for a time-out."[41] At night Homer and his men pulled off the leeches, wrapped themselves in their ponchos, and caught a few moments of uneasy sleep. The sweat and dirt felt like a filthy crust freezing on their skin as the temperature plummeted with the darkness. Every three or five days they'd stop and find or hack out a landing zone for the helicopters to come in and resupply them; pull out the wounded; and bring mail, ammo, and rations. They got used to water, dipped out of jungle streams, that tasted like bleach from their purification tablets.

On one patrol a soldier fell backward onto some of the stumps of bamboo the point man had cut, the sharpened stake of the plant impaling him, penetrating his anus and going at least twelve inches up his colon. The medic, certain that the soldier would bleed to death if they pulled out the bamboo, injected the screaming man with morphine. It did little to stop the pain as four men held him down and another cut through the bamboo with the serrated edge of a K-bar knife, leaving most of it inside, and then placed him in a litter jury-rigged from the man's poncho and two bamboo poles. They had to haul him up the nearly vertical slope to their LZ, six men in front pulling the litter with ropes, the others lifting it in three-foot heaves, the man screaming all the way. "I still do not know where we found the strength to keep that up long enough to reach the top," Homer wrote. "At first the adrenalin helped, but that soon wore off and it was sheer will power."

Days slipped into each other, Homer remembering in his journal the most dramatic or deadly occasions, the times time lurched to a vivid halt, the railroad stations of memory during one long, hot, green week in November. The crowd of events during that week would remain stuck in his mind, too much for one week, as if the war had decided to coil all of itself into that narrow space.[42]

The men claw their way toward the ridgeline, gripping slippery roots, pulling themselves up, and then using the same roots as foot braces to get to the next point, their packs and ammo and weapons and gravity always dragging them backward. The point man has to machete-hack a path no wider than his own shoulders out of the thick undergrowth of bamboo and vines in front of and above him. He is moving upward steadily but slowly. Then he abruptly stops, causing the men behind him to crash into each other, the domino effect, some losing their grip, falling backward. Homer, in midcolumn, curses, calls up to demand an explanation. As if it were one, the single word "snake" comes back down to him. It irritates him. How can a single snake hold up the whole platoon? He is something of a snake buff; when he was a kid he had loved to catch them, feel the dry, fluid muscularity of their bodies wrapping around his arm or neck, an interest he shared with one of his men now, an Alabama boy who would bring him the snakes he found in the jungle, let him touch and handle them.

Homer climbs up to the point man, slipping and sliding back. The newly cut trail is narrow, and his men are wedging themselves against the roots they have used as footrests or clinging onto those above them, exhausted, the deep fatigue of the march settling heavily into them now that they've stopped their forward momentum. He has no choice but to go around, making his own path upward. Crawling on his knees, he finally makes it to the point man and asks him again what the hell is happening. The man shrugs eloquently and points to the slope just past his head. Twelve feet ahead of him, there is what seems to be a large log lying across the trail the point man had been cutting. When Homer peers closer, he can make out definite patterns, diamond shapes on its sides. But he dismisses the thought. The object is big as a barrel, too big around to be a snake. He knows he needs to get closer, but finds himself full of a kind of leaden weight; he is spent from the climb and can only lie there, panting.

He finds some bamboo stumps to brace against, takes a long drink from his canteen, and splashes his face and neck, panting slightly in the heat. He works his way closer, knowing what is in front of him in spite of its impossibility, but still refusing to admit it to himself. He is nearly on top of it now. At first it seems motionless, but as he watches he can see that it is constricting and relaxing almost imperceptibly, moving a fraction of an inch every few minutes. Finally, he steps over the sinuously gliding mass and then sits down just uphill from it, staring. Its head, he sees from the direction of crawl, would be to his right; the tail would be to his left, but he can see neither end of the snake, its body disappearing into the underbrush on both sides, seven feet further away in the direction of the head, five feet back toward the tail, its diameter bulging thick in either direction.

They can go back down, go around it, or kill it. He decides to tell his men to go over it, as he has done. He crosses back over the . . . what?—anaconda? python? ouroboros, circling the earth to bite its own tail?—and there is still no end of it in sight. He stays at that point, helping each of the three dozen soldiers in the patrol over the gliding body, sometimes holding their packs and rifles until they are on the other side. Each man crawls up to it, rises, crouching, and steps or leaps nimbly over, feeling the cold, scaled reptile-ness of the thing as it is briefly under him. From above, if you stripped back the top layers of the jungle canopy and watched them, say from the hatch of an observation helicopter, you would see a line of grunts in a vertical serpentine crawl themselves, bisecting the horizontal glide of the creature.

When the soldier at the very rear of the patrol finally reaches the snake trail, the man looks at the thing in front of him and freezes. There is no way he is going over it. Homer reasons, pleads, orders, threatens. The soldier presses his lips together and shakes his head. Then stay here, Homer says. Wait until the thing passes, and then try to catch up to us. Up to you. The man stares at him incredulously, as if to say, you're going to leave me here in the jungle? Come up the trail after us, if you decide to come, Homer tells him. He steps once again over the sinuous, barrel-sized body, works his way up the mountainside a little more, and then gets behind some brush and waits. He has placed the soldier between two ancient and atavistic fears: the fear of the monster in the jungle and the fear of being abandoned in the jungle where that monster lives. Fifteen minutes later, white and shaken, the man rejoins the platoon.

They were humping the Garden of Evil, Eden abandoned to the serpent, whose path they have passed without leave or acknowledgment.

The platoon stops in a saw grass clearing. Homer gets on the radio to call in a resupply helicopter and inquire about the condition of the man impaled earlier that day. As he is speaking, the Alabama soldier walks over to him, proudly holding up a thin yellow-green snake, as if he wants Homer to take it. Its arrow-shaped head and long, oval-shaped eyes make Homer uneasy. He covers the handset with his palm and tells the boy he'll take it later. He is still on the radio when another soldier comes running up, screaming that the damn snake has bitten the Alabama boy on the neck. Homer quickly calls in a medevac and starts to run over to the soldier. But the platoon medic intercepts him, shaking his head. The boy is already dead.

After the chopper leaves, a silence descends on the platoon. Supplies have been tossed out of the helicopter. No one moves to pick them up. No one speaks. Finally, a call from his commanding officer spurs Homer out of his daze. He and the men gather the supplies and have to scramble to get to their night defensive position on the ridgeline, set up their fields of fire, and send out Listening Posts on all the slopes approaching the ridge. "I got little or no sleep that night," Homer remembered later. "I kept replaying the day's events in my mind."

Thirty-five years later he wrote: "The deaths and injuries [that we] incurred under my leadership still haunt my memories. I expect they will be among the memories that flash before my eyes when I lie on my deathbed. Somehow I feel guilty for having come back alive."

Another day. The patrol is dug in on a ridgeline where they can observe the valley below. They send out ambushes and patrols; Homer calls in artillery strikes whenever they spot or hear movement. On their third day on the ridge, the company's commanding officer orders him to take out a platoon-sized patrol and check out the valley on foot. As soon as they pass the OP, the two-man observation post placed as an early warning trigger, the column is raked by a burst of AK-47 fire. They shoot back into the jungle on all sides, shredding leaves and branches. But there is no return fire. Lowering his rifle, Homer sees his medic bent over a man who had been hit by an AK-47 round. "The bullet had blown a ten inch hole out his navel region," he remembers.

"He was bleating like a horribly injured animal. Each scream a total effort, followed by another gasping inhalation and then another soul-wrenching bleat of total agony. Doc was plunging the second morphine syringe into him as I arrived. The soldier was clawing at his intestines, desperately attempting to stuff them back into his abdomen. After a few seconds more of his inhuman screaming, I asked Doc to give him another dose of morphine. Doc said that another would probably be fatal. I looked at Doc and asked him whether he thought he would survive the 30 minutes it would take to get a chopper in and fly him back to the evacuation hospital. He looked into my eyes and just gave me the syringe. I told him to check on the others, I would stay with this man. As he left, I waited for another minute or two before I administered the final syringe. He had turned chalky white from blood loss by now and his skin was very cold to the touch. Within seconds of administering the third syringe, he finally began to calm down. He said he couldn't see. I told him to just lie still, the chopper was on the way.

"After a few seconds, he whispered something, but I didn't hear what it was. I leaned over and asked him to repeat it and he said, 'Was I a good soldier?' I told him that his people back home would be real proud of him, he was a true hero. He then asked if he was going to die. I told him that I thought he might. He then said he was afraid. I told him not to worry, where he was going, things were much better and he was a good person, so he had nothing to worry about. He smiled, exhaled loudly, but without any real force, just a deflating of his lungs, and the light in his eyes faded. I reached up and closed his eye lids with my fingers just as Doc came back to report that the point man had bad shoulder and leg wounds, but would make it. My platoon sergeant said that there were blood trails leading away down the ridge and wanted to pursue them."

5 NOV 1968

*Dear Mom and Dad,*

*I got the 6 cent letter a day earlier than usual! Sent on 31 OCT; got on 4 NOV. I finally got finance straightened out and next payday I should get my full $500.00 pay check.*

*I guess things are still pretty normal here. I think I'm going to be*
*made XO (Executive Officer) pretty soon. That will be nice, no field, ex-*
*cept payday and only paper work.*

    *The company is moving again. Today we go to Dak To to spend the*
*night. Tomorrow we have a 12 kilo hike on a BDA (bomb damage assess-*
*ment) mission North of FSB-29. . . .*

    *Gotta run.*

    *Love,*
    *Homer*

He is stunned by the amount of damage. Fifty-foot craters
pock the still-smoking ground. The stink of burnt foliage and
flesh permeates everything. Most of the trees have been splintered or knocked over. On one that wasn't, the upper half of an
enemy soldier's body, pierced by the only branch still on the
blackened trunk, hangs like a grotesque Christmas ornament.
There must have been more bodies, he figures. Probably the
NVA had come back and removed them; he'd seen some of the
wooden, homemade hooks their soldiers had used to drag bodies quickly off the battlefield, denying the Americans the body
count that was used as a measuring stick of victory. Smashed
weapons, B-40 rounds, pith helmets, canteens, Ho Chi Minh
rubber sandals, and personal papers (notebooks, letters, diaries)
are littered all over the torn ground. He tells his men to police
everything up; he'll send most of the documents to S-2, intelligence. But not all, he decides. On several of his recent missions,
he'd disagreed with his commander's orders, felt it unreasonable
to send men out into dangerous areas without the recourse of
artillery support, unable to get to them in time if they were hit,
just so they could count bodies after a fire mission. He'd even
refused such orders once, but he had managed to finesse the situation by suggesting a better plan—meaning, he understood,
one that might get a bigger body count. He has half-formed am-
bitions at this point of making a career of the army, has taken
pride in his excellent evaluations, his rapid promotions. The

Bamberg country boy. But over the last weeks his primary loyalty has shifted to his men, and now he keeps back some of the documents deliberately, so he can prove the damage he has seen here, will not have to send men back, turn them into bodies, just to get a body count.

Another day. They work their way down into a deep valley, discover and blow up a cave filled with enemy ordnance, and then wire a log bridge with detcord (detonation cord), wrapped around its handrails, and explosives, figuring the NVA will send someone to investigate. Soon the Americans hear noise around them. They lie motionless behind a boulder, watching the enemy soldiers pass them—one, two, three, eight men—and then suddenly hear the engine drone of an American Forward Air Control plane passing overhead. They watch, horrified, as the NVA scatter off the trail into the bush, nearly stumbling onto the Americans. Worse, the passage of the FAC means that the B-52s will not be far behind. Homer remembers the aftermath of the B-52 strike he saw, the body impaled in the splintered tree, the craters rimmed with the bloody shreds of uniforms and equipment; the memory leaves him in a cold sweat. But there is nothing he can do now but remain perfectly still.

Finally, the North Vietnamese soldiers, chattering, looking nervously at the sky, regroup and begin walking down the trail. Homer holds his breath as they approach the bridge. They stop. One soldier, a point man, cautiously steps onto the log, while the others wait. It is a very bright day, early in the morning, and beams of sunlight penetrate down into the valley and illuminate the bridge. It is not a beautiful sight to the Americans. They are certain the light will enable the man to see the detcord. The soldier gets to the other side and then steps back onto the bridge and waves for the others to follow. Homer waits as one by one they climb onto the log and walk across, single file. There is just room for all eight of them. As soon as the point man begins to step off again, Homer pushes the detonator. "I guess we hadn't thought about the power of the explosives we had planted," he remembers. "When it went up, there was a sharp crack from the detcord ending in the boom of the C-4 and a combination of pure white and dark black smoke roiling up into the sky. The bridge was completely gone, pieces of vegetation raining down even on top of us. We stood there frozen in horror and fascination for what seemed like a long time, then I remembered the Arc Light [the bomb run] and told everyone to start back up the trail."

Homer runs back by himself to the bridge, knowing a body count will be demanded. But he can see nothing but shredded vegetation and a huge, smoking crater. The hell with it, he thinks, all eight must be dead. He hurries back to rejoin his men, who are panting now as they frantically scramble up the trail. A hundred meters from the top they drop, exhausted, unable to move, and then look up to see the FAC plane drop smoke grenades on the opposite ridge—marking the target for the B-52s. They force themselves, pushing with their last bit of willpower, to scramble to and over the ridgeline, and then lie completely spent, about thirty meters down on the opposing slope, just as the bombs start dropping.

Before he left the States, the events of that year—the Orangeburg massacre he'd witnessed, the assassinations of Martin Luther King and Robert Kennedy—had made Homer feel as if the map of the familiar had shifted under its grid, under his feet. He finds out now the way Viet Nam has of making the symbolic literal. "We felt the concussion wave first, then heard the thunder," he writes. "Just as the shock of that was beginning to sink in, the most incredible thing happened that I have ever experienced. As I lay there, the CO still trying to get me to talk to him on the radio, the ground actually moved up and down a good couple of inches, like a wave rippling across a lake. It was terrifying! I felt a momentary wave of dizziness and nausea. My eyes went out of focus. I was totally disoriented. Then it passed and I could hear the CO frantically trying to make contact. We felt many other less intense tremors, but not as bad as that first one. Everyone was dead still and totally silent."

### 9 NOV 1968

*Dear Mom and Dad,*

*Answer—I got the money order, thanks.*

*I got the cake, it sure was good. I almost had to fight for it. Seriously every time you send me something everyone goes wild over your cooking. I told them it was a combination of "German genius" and that "Southern touch."*

*I also want you to send some money to that investment company and check with Fort Jackson Federal Credit Union to see if I'm straight with them.*

*Say what's my bank account look like?*

*Our company is moving somewhere soon, that should ruin all my work and cause me to have to start all over again, this time with only a month to straighten it out and make up all the lost equipment.*

*Saw my second soldier get killed last week. His jeep hit a mine. Sure glad I'm not out there any more.*

*I'm sorry about not writing like I used to, but I just don't get a chance very often. I work all day usually and it's dark at night unless we get the generator left on, which is seldom.*

*Love,*
*Homer*

The day before he sent that letter, on November 8, 1969, First Lieutenant Homer Steedly Jr. was awarded the Combat Infantry Badge (CIB). It is the most significant badge any infantryman can get, the only badge that many see as meaningful. Other medals may or may not have been given for truly heroic actions, while equal or greater acts of courage might have gone unnoticed or ignored. Some medals were self-awarded by officers who could get away with it, and the Purple Heart only commemorated a time you had run out of luck. The CIB said simply and sufficiently that you were there, the times you were brave, the times you defecated in your pants, the times you took another breath and another step and humped on. Homer's letter does not mention that award. It says little of what he had experienced in the previous week, either. The only death mentioned, the death of the jeep driver, was put into the letter without detail, prosaically, listed after lost equipment. The jeep had run over a command-detonated mine, in front of the truck Homer and his men were in, part of a convoy taking them back to the relative safety of base camp. Homer had run through the fire of the ensuing ambush to see if he could help the driver, but when he reached him, the man was dead already, lying facedown on the side of the road. He looked untouched. Homer knelt down and rolled him over, and then almost vomited. The man felt "like a blow up doll full of water. The concussion from the land-mine had pulverized every bone in his body."

Homer didn't put any of it into that letter. He was doing what soldiers know or think they have to do: protecting his parents from the snakes in his brain. But with his homilies about cooking, his plans for investments, and his inquiries about bank accounts, he was also keeping preserved, on the space of that page, the man who had existed before those terrible alterations, a man planning for his future as if he were certain that he had one.

It was the same impulse that made Hoang Ngoc Dam so carefully guard the small notebook in which he had painstakingly drawn the course of his own hoped-for life.

# CHAPTER TEN

# "My Brother and I Will Meet Each Other"

By the end of that week in November, Homer's fourth month in Viet Nam, Dam had been in the war for five years. In Gia Lai Province, Dam was assigned to Unit 280, a provincial unit that operated under the command of the Southern National Liberation Front. His medical organization was the H67 Dispensary, which also served the regular PAVN infantry regiments in the area.

The word "dispensary" suggests clean shelves stacked with medicines, or a MASH-type facility. In reality, the PAVN hospitals were necessarily primitive, located in tunnels, caves, or log bunkers. A famous photograph shows doctors operating while literally standing ankle deep in water, in a hidden hospital in the Mekong Delta (a secret, later-to-be famous Viet Cong hospital existed in the Marble Mountain caves a mile from my helicopter base camp and our own field hospital). Dam worked out of at least two facilities that his brother Luong and brother-in-law Dieu later visited, one a concealed log bunker, about three meters by four meters, and the other simply a cave—officially designated the H-15 Hospital cave. They were both near Cheo Reo commune, north of the Mang Yang Pass, and Dam became a well-known and popular figure in the village.[43]

Medics like Dam were assigned to such a central clinic or attached to smaller fighting units, company or platoon size— or both. Some of the hospitals could be large, spread over hundreds of meters, with separate wards, each containing seventy to eighty beds (litters) in each ward, and with tunnel complexes beneath, some with surgical facilities and even X-ray machines. Although the level of medical care available to PAVN and National Liberation Front (NLF) soldiers has been compared to what was common during the American Civil War, most medical personnel were described by surviving soldiers as caring, compassionate, intelligent men and women who made do with what they had.[44] Like Dam, doctors and medics had to hand-copy, or have someone reproduce, text and illustrations from medical manuals kept back at the training camps, or at best at headquarters. Huy frequently saw Dam with the notebook that would later fall into Homer's hands. "When I saw him in the battlefield, he still had that notebook and I know he kept that book and drew in it. That was a way of self-educating himself, and he kept the notebook to draw bones and skeletons and surgical procedures. . . . [T]he documents [he was studying] came from the medical unit near Gia Lai—he was studying at the same time we were fighting."

Dam's medical kit, besides having the usual dressings, scissors, and so on, would have included aspirin; vitamins B-12, B-1, and C; and where possible, tetracycline—or the substitute for penicillin, developed from mushrooms that grew wild in the Truong Son range by famous film director Dang Nhat Minh's physician father, who was killed by an American bomb as he was finishing his research in a jungle lab.

Like many PAVN regulars assigned as "fillers" to reinforce local, southern guerrilla units, Dam served under the blue, red, and gold flag of the Viet Cong rather than the red flag of the regular People's Army—a practice that became more frequent as the NLF lost more soldiers, particularly after the Tet Offensive in 1968. (The NLF fell from 64,000 combat troops in 1966 to 25,000 by 1973.[45]) At the time Dam infiltrated to the South, there were about 60,000 PAVN troops fighting there; two years later the number had increased to 200,000. In spite of the popular American conception of the Viet Nam War as a guerrilla conflict, the bulk of the combat by that time had shifted to conventional jungle war between regular troops. Some 66,000 of the northerners were used as fillers for the Viet Cong,[46] and it appears Dam was assigned to such duty: the unit designation stamped on each of the award certificates found on his body read "Unit 280—Southern Viet Nam Liberation Army."

There were four such certificates, and they attested to the fact that Dam kept both his idealism and the studious, driven personality his family described him possessing even as a schoolboy. The earliest, dated October 20, 1965, cited his "model" performance in serving the wounded soldiers of an artillery unit, and he was named "outstanding individual soldier" for the year 1965. The second certificate, dated December 22, 1966, commended Hoang Dinh Dam (date of birth, 1-1-1944; job classification, medic; unit, surgery; hometown, Thai Giang village, Thai Binh district, Thai Binh province) for having "contributed to the building of a good unit during the first 6 months of 1966." This certificate was also issued in Gia Lai and was signed by the vice commander of Unit 280 C. The third citation was on September 1, 1967, for "accomplishments in the first 6 months of 1967."

The fourth certificate commended Dam for his accomplishments "during the general offensive and uprising of 1968" (i.e., the Tet Offensive). It was dated February 10, 1969, a little more than a month before his death. As were the other citations, it was signed by Mai Xuan Hanh. This last certificate is the first that records his name change from Hoang Dinh Dam to Hoang Ngoc (Jade) Dam.

It was also just before that crucial point in the war that Dam reunited with Pham Quang Huy. "We met, Dam and I, on the

30th day of the lunar month," Huy says, "just before the Tet offensive of 1968. That's the memory we shared together. We were to cut off Route 19, into Qui Nhon." It was a nightmarish battle, though Huy admits to no nightmares. The words he chooses to describe it are carefully chosen, still the language of the political officer, though he is clearly critical of the tactic of throwing soldiers into battle as if into a fan of whirling, sharpened blades that would be stopped when it had sliced so many bodies that the corpses clogged the machine. "The Party and the government had two strategies [for the Tet Offensive]: one was, A, take over, liberate the south, B, if you can't, hang onto it as long as possible. The reality of it was the liberation army came in and we could not hang onto all the towns, so we started to lose a lot of men."

Huy himself was badly wounded in the fighting and found himself being treated by his young mentoree. A year later, in what would be called the Post, or second Tet Offensive—the campaign in 1969 in which Dam would meet Homer—Huy was again shot in the leg and once more became Dam's patient. A fact he remembers from seeing Dam at that time may provide an answer to the mystery of Dam's uniform, beyond Dam's natural neatness. "There had been some Chinese[47] with us," Huy says. "They provided us with clean, new uniforms which we were to use when we marched into Kontum and Pleiku. We never got to do that," he says, and then smiles grimly. "Not then. But Dam always loved wearing clean clothing."

While being treated by Dam, Huy and the young medic exchanged what news they could of Thai Giang. Dam had received a letter from his mother in which she told him his younger brother Chi had gone into the army, and how worried she was about both of them. Dam gave Huy a letter that his friend managed to get sent north to the family in Thai Giang.

The family still remembers that letter well. His sister Tham, now a doctor herself, recalled how excited her parents were because Dam mentioned he would soon return to the North. "He wrote that he had some good news, that he would be promoted to the next level of his profession, but we did not know what he meant by that."

That was his last letter, Dam's younger brother Cat explains. "That letter was written at the time a decision had been made to send him to the North, to study to become a doctor, but while he was waiting, he participated in some battles and then was killed."

Within another year, Chi would also be killed in action. His family would not find out the details of his death until the 1980s.

In the letter Dam had sent home, he wrote, "Please do not worry, my brother and I will meet each other."

# CHAPTER ELEVEN

# Camp Enari and the Plei Trap

One evening in early March, at the Camp Enari BOQ Club, Homer sat and had a few beers with a fellow lieutenant, George Callan, formerly Charlie Company's S-1, administrative officer. Callan was now doing what Homer envisioned for himself: leading the company in combat, and doing it, Homer thought, in a way that reflected his own evolving leadership philosophy of doing whatever you asked your men to do and keeping as many of them alive as you could. George's brother had managed to wangle a visit to Pleiku, and that night the three young men hoisted beers and joked, but Homer could see George was preoccupied, his mind on his company. The 4th Infantry Division had just started a large operation, and Charlie Company would be in the thick of it.

Homer empathized with the other lieutenant's concern, his feelings perhaps tinged with both envy and some embarrassment. The operation, called Wayne Grey, would eventually sweep him into the most vicious combat that he would experience in his tour, but for now he had become what he called a base camp commando: in the rear with the gear where there was no fear. In late November he had received an officer's evaluation report from his CO that rated him Bravo Company's best platoon commander. Although he had only been in the field for three months, he had been tapped for the job of company executive officer (XO), a position that brought him back to the company's forward base camps at Dak To and Camp Enari (Pleiku) and made him second in command of Bravo. He was pleased by the recognition, but nevertheless had mixed feelings. It was a relief to be in the relative safety and comfort of the base camps. He had seen more than enough death; he knew the position would be a likely stepping-stone for promotion to captain and command of his own company. But he had also grown close to his men, he knew he was good at what he did, and he hated the system that took experienced commanders out of the field and replaced them with green officers to give the latter a chance to get their career tickets punched, a learning curve often paid for with the lives of their soldiers, if not their own.[48] "I had learned how things worked in infantry combat in the 4th Infantry Division," Homer says. "A young, inexperienced officer came to a platoon, and during the 60–90 days it took him to learn his job, many lives were lost, that should not have been. Then he had only 90 more days in the field, since most officers were rotated to some rear echelon job for their last six months, which meant he got scared and became too cautious, losing men as a result. Then another new officer came and the cycle started all over again. That meant that most enlisted men saw the pattern and became afraid and angry at the waste. I had bonded so tightly to my men by the time I had the chance to rotate to the rear, and I took the XO slot so that I could return to the field as often as possible to help out by taking temporary command of one of the platoons, which was presently without any officer."

The company was sending out at least two platoon-sized patrols every day, and he would accompany them, he told himself, whenever he could. He got no rush out of combat, was not particularly fond of sleeping in mud and rain or not at all, and hated leeches and mosquitoes and biting ants and getting shot at—but he knew he could save lives. It was not only a matter of superior field craft. There had also been a subtle but fundamental shift in the way he viewed the world. He'd not yet reached the point where he questioned the war itself—it was all around him; to question it would have been like questioning the existence of the atmosphere by refusing to breathe. He would still put mission first. But he would rely on his own judgment of the efficacy of the mission, the worth of its cost in lives.

He had became XO on November 13, 1968. As he'd promised himself, he took out patrols whenever he could, once to cordon off and search a village with a hastily organized platoon of rear-area clerks and cooks (one of whom, unused to the exertion, had had a heart attack). He had met George Callan on two of the Bravo Company patrols, when the platoon Homer had taken out that day was ordered to reinforce Charlie Company, George's unit. Homer had admired the lieutenant's energy and concern for his men during those long, hairy nights, had watched appreciatively as George stayed up until daylight, checking the perimeter, making sure everyone was awake. George was the kind of officer, he felt, who led by example.

By January 1969, as his company's forward support trains (troops and equipment that followed the unit like a train) area at Dak To prepared for a visit by the Inspector General in February, Homer increasingly found himself immersed in the detailed administrative work of running a company. It was a task he could at times escape through the necessary duty of driving back and forth between Pleiku and Dak To, or sometimes from Pleiku through the treacherous Mang Yang Pass to An Khe, a three- or four-hour drive over a dusty road that was often mined and always in the gun sights of PAVN or Viet Cong snipers. Usually he would insert himself and his jeep into the convoy of armed trucks that ran between both areas each day, escorted by helicopter gunships. But after awhile, impatient and reluctant to take a driver whom he would have to both trust and be responsible

for, he started making the run alone, driving pedal to the metal,
zigzagging and ducking AK-47 rounds and even B-40 rockets.
Homer's duties at base camp were myriad: accounting for equipment; answering letters from anxious parents or spouses (or
more often, creditors, and more occasionally, congressmen with
inquiries about constituents); investigating traffic accidents;
checking on allotments and promotions; prosecuting courts-
martial; and supervising administrative and support troops. He
even delivered pay to the troops in the field, traveling out to
firebases and troops in the field, sometimes with as much as
$30,000 in his rucksack. He knew that to be given the com-
mand he wanted and get back into the field, he had to be strac
(of perfect military bearing), and admonished himself in his
journal that his "biggest flaw right now is personal appearance. I
need to get my fatigues laundered and tags and insignia sewn
on, since the Colonel expects his base camp commandos to look
sharp. . . . I need to get a briefcase to keep my paperwork from
getting dirty."

He was, at age twenty-two, doing a job equivalent in civilian
life to that of executive vice president of a company employing
several hundred people, with the added fillip of being occasionally shelled and rocketed. Now that the dry season had arrived,
he was living in a bowl of red dust that was driven into every
inch of his skin whenever a helicopter took off or landed or
whenever he took off on one of his wild rides, "leaving a dust
trail a quarter mile long when there is no breeze." He was delighted at his own competence as a staff officer, but he continued
to feel the guilt of the rear-echelon soldier. His was now the prosaic business of an army's rear area, doing what it could to keep
soldiers in the field and simultaneously replicating the relationship of an army at war to its own society: the country for which
it was presumably fighting going about its business, the screams
of its sons and daughters on the battlefield distant and unheard.
It was ultimately the source of combat soldiers' contempt for

anyone who was not one of them. One cannot hate the world for going about its business. But one does.

At Camp Enari that night, drinking with George Callan and his brother, that battlefield must not have seemed too distant. Both lieutenants could hear the crackle of gunfire, the roar of outgoing artillery, the banshee wail of parachute flares: the background noise of the new operation. It was the invisible companion sitting a few stools behind them, making the hair on the backs of their necks bristle. If they turned, it would raise a glass and toast them, grinning like a skull.

On February 23, 1969, the Viet Cong and the North Vietnamese had attacked 110 targets throughout Viet Nam. American intelligence reports for the Central Highlands indicated that the People's Army was preparing to move up through the Plei Trap Valley, seize Kontum City, and hit other bases and towns throughout the province. Four days later, the 4th Infantry Division initiated Operation Wayne Grey. Its objective was to be "a spoiling attack to disrupt the enemy post-Tet offensive against Kontum by severing his line of communication into a sanctuary."[49]

The Plei Trap is located at the western edge of what were Kontum and Pleiku provinces, under the old Republic of Viet Nam divisions. It runs roughly forty miles north and south along the Cambodian border, just south of its abutment with Laos. Although not as well known as the A Shau Valley or Khe Sanh, the Plei Trap, an area of tangled, triple-canopy jungle covering massive, hunched mountains and ridgelines and deep-cut ravines, became for many American soldiers one of those places whose name was enough to evoke a complex mélange of terror, dread, anger, and waste. Years later it awakened a complex astonishment at the memory of courage and a permanent ache of grief, as if those words—Plei Trap—had been put into human language to cover all of it. The word "Trap" in the local dialect simply meant valley, but for many GIs it was a word that said it all.

Running parallel to the Cambodian border, the valley was an entry point from the Ho Chi Minh Trail into South Viet Nam and the war zone that the North Vietnamese called B-3. The 66th (a North Vietnamese regiment had about 1,500 men—the 66th had about 1,250 soldiers at the time), along with the 24th PAVN and the 40th Artillery Regiment, had moved into the area during January and February and were now deeply entrenched, preparing for their offensive.

One of the units identified by American intelligence, the K25, was an engineer battalion, expert at constructing roads through thick jungle, as well as bunker complexes, entrenchments, and abatis (interwoven log barriers) to defend those roads. "The bunkers," in Tom Lacombe's description, "were hard to spot. They amounted to about an eight-foot man-made cave, perhaps three or four feet high. The openings were a little less than two feet square."[50] The North Vietnamese had hacked a web of trail systems throughout the jungle, and a two-lane, wide dirt road for heavy vehicles along the floor of the valley that was wide enough, the American command feared, even for the use of tanks in their offensive. Lacombe recalls seeing one path that went straight up a mountainside, with wide steps cut into it to ease ascent; upon examination, the American soldiers found the steps covered with dozens of elephant tracks.[51]

Another unit that American intelligence listed among the enemy forces was H67 Dispensary, the parent unit of Medic Sergeant Hoang Ngoc Dam.

Sitting and drinking at Enari that night, the two young lieutenants knew that on the first day of the operation a 12th Infantry company had found the firebase where they had been landed by helicopter already occupied by enemy troops; the Americans had had to fight bunker to bunker in a vicious, three-hour battle. There had been other small, sharp battles as the American units were jockeyed into position, each fight adding its single- or double-digit toll to the count of the dead. George Callan's own company, on a reconnaissance in force patrol into the valley after an American air strike, had found two Russian-made 1½ ton trucks, filled with 105mm shells and more than 1,200 pounds of rice. It was not, they felt, a good sign.

Soon after, when Callan was already back in the field, Homer jotted this entry in his journal for March 3: "A/3/8th had a heavy contact and nearly got wiped out."

What those laconic remarks referred to was the beginning of the key engagement of the first phase of Wayne Grey: the battles on and around Hill 947 in the Plei Trap, which would disrupt the North Vietnamese offensive but during which two American companies were nearly destroyed. The unit Homer mentioned, Alpha Company of the 3rd Battalion, 8th Infantry, had been helicoptered into the Plei Trap to an LZ that was, inadvertently, almost on top of the headquarters of the PAVN 66th Regiment. Out of artillery range, cut off from reinforcement by the thick jungle, the company had fought off savage North Vietnamese attacks for two days on its own, losing thirty-five dead and two wounded. Alpha also had twenty missing in action, although soon Delta Company, sent in to find survivors, would discover that most of the MIAs were also dead, shot in the head after they were captured.

Helicopter crew chief Ron Carey was on one of the ships extracting the wounded and dead. "All have more than one wound," he recalls. "Many are almost naked. They have fought the fight of their lives. . . . [T]he soldiers that have died are wrapped in their ponchos and laid near the pad."[52] Meanwhile Delta, warned by the one Alpha Company prisoner they found still alive that they were surrounded by the 66th, dug in on Hill 947 and fought off the North Vietnamese for two days. By the end of the battle, only forty men in Delta were left to rejoin the rest of the 3rd Battalion. As they were evacuated by helicopter, Lieutenant John Bauer, the 4th Platoon commander, looked down. The sight remains burned into his memory. "The dead were stacked a little like cordwood. . . . Years later, when I saw the movie *Platoon,* the last scene when Charlie Sheen lifts off in the chopper and looks down was almost identical to the real crater on Hill 947. It had a chilling effect."

The battle was later touted as the reason for the eventual success of the entire operation in the Plei Trap, since it had located the main body of enemy troops and caused the NVA heavy enough casualties to thwart their offensive. "The enemy timetable for a post Tet Offensive was disrupted, and he was forced back to sanctuary," stated brigade commander Col. Hal Knight.[53] But the bloodbath on and around Hill 947 can be regarded as a successful tactical maneuver only in the sense that inserting one's head into a tiger's mouth will enable one to locate the tiger's teeth. Bauer now regards the triumphal note in the After Action Report with some bitterness:

"Operation Wayne Grey was regarded as a success. The 66th NVA had indeed been neutralized with heavy losses in men and equipment, thanks in large part to ill-fated Company A. It had stumbled almost on top of the NVA HQ and revealed its position. Company D almost suffered the same fate, but it was able to dig in on Hill 947 and survive a two-day siege. It fought its way out using gunship support and effective artillery barrages to inflict heavy enemy casualties. At that, the brigade was able to put a successful spin on Company D's near-disaster even though it sustained over 50% casualties. . . . The Company A debacle should have been prevented. The major blunder by the brigade was made at the time of the insertion of 3rd Battalion Companies A, B, C, and D. Too far spread apart, they could not support each other. It was a blunder that may have cost far more lives than brigade officers were willing to document during those two fateful March days of 1969 when their valiant Company A went down. The time has come for the story to be set straight."[54]

Since the beginning of Wayne Grey, the companies in Homer's 1st Battalion had been shifted around like pieces on a chessboard, running recon patrols and providing security for the firebases, which in early March had been throwing out a ring of protective fire around the embattled 3rd Battalion, being decimated around and on Hill 947. They were taking their own casualties, though not as many as 3rd Battalion, and they were well aware what was happening when their sister battalion's Alpha and Delta Companies were being torn to pieces. All they could do was pity their fellow soldiers and be thankful it hadn't been their turn in the meat grinder.

On March 5, however, a few days after he and Homer had shared drinks in the O Club, George Callan's Charlie Company, engaging in a reconnaissance in force along the southern road in the Plei Trap, ran into an L-shaped ambush. Pinned down, taking heavy fire from the trees and brush on three sides of their position, their situation became even more desperate when one of their machine gunners went down. The Americans were so close to the enemy gunners that they knew a helicopter extraction would be difficult or impossible. At some point Callan leapt up and tried to get the machine gun operable, so he could lay down covering fire for his men. He was killed instantly. The rest of the company, under heavy artillery fire, held out until seven in the evening, when helicopters were finally able to land in the LZ and get them out. Before they did, they counted seven enemy bodies. But two Americans, including Callan, were dead, and twelve were wounded, one of whom would die later.

George Callan's death[55] hit Homer hard. But there was no time to mourn. He put it away, on top of a growing store of grief he kept locked in his heart.

# CHAPTER TWELVE

# A Meeting Engagement

Two days before he would kill Hoang Ngoc Dam, Homer went out in the field to deliver payroll to the company, new briefcase firmly in hand. He began the day by catching a lift from Camp Enari on a helicopter flying food and ammo out to Fire Support Base 20, about twenty kilometers northwest, at the edge of the Plei Trap Valley. Homer's system was to pay the men in the rear areas at the battalion base camps first and then to make his way out to the troops at the firebases, armed only with his .45, and carrying his case filled with paperwork and MPC (Military Payment Certificates), the substitute bills issued to troops instead of real currency and, inevitably, called "funny money" by the GIs. Even though the men often would only take partial payments, letting most of their salaries either accumulate on the books or be sent home—where were they going to spend their money?—nearly everyone still took part of his pay, and Homer was conscientious about getting it to them.

The helicopter rose out of the oppressive heat that lay over the base and Pleiku like a thick blanket, and he leaned forward, feeling the blessed coolness of the wind on his face, his teeth clamped tightly around the pipe in his mouth—the pipe a new acquisition, along with the briefcase. Even at twenty-two, older than most of his men, Homer knew people thought he had a baby face; the pipe and briefcase, he hoped, would give him more gravitas. But his eyes, looking down at the thick-jungled mountains now, were not the eyes of a young man. The leaf canopies pressed down over a seething mass of vines and thorns, of leeches and misery and slippery red mud and bad memories.

Moments after the helicopter circled down to the pimple of red mud encrusted with filthy sandbagged bunkers, barbed wire, and fighting holes that was FSB 20, he was handed another opportunity to go back out into that jungle. Two squads from the company's 2nd Platoon had gone out on ambush patrols, and another platoon had been sent back to Camp Enari—he'd missed them there—to be sent out on a road reconnaissance mission. Shortly after he landed, one squad returned, and he was able to pay the men. But the other squad remained out in the field. They had detected a large number of North Vietnamese moving toward them and had held their fire, figuring they were outnumbered and outgunned. When they reported the near contact, the battalion CO contacted Captain James DeRoos, Homer's company commander, at FSB 20, and told him to send the rest of 2nd Platoon out to try to reinforce the squad that had spotted the enemy force. Homer decided to go out with them, pay the squad he'd missed, and help with the ambush.[56]

DeRoos and the platoon leader were happy to have him on the patrol. But DeRoos also told him that the platoon scheduled for the road reconnaissance mission had no officer, and the staff sergeant who was acting platoon leader was relatively inexperienced. Would Homer take on that mission also? No problem, he said.

But for now, he moved out from FSB 20 with 2nd Platoon, to rendezvous with the squad that had spotted the North Vietnamese. They were about six kilometers from the base, but it was not easy going to get to them. The jungle was dense, the terrain at times nearly vertical and slippery. When Homer and the rest of the platoon finally got to the squad's position, they decided to move away from the place where they had spotted the North Vietnamese, in case they had been spotted in return. They would set up a new ambush site.

Meanwhile, they hunkered down, waiting for sundown to reduce the chance of being detected, and then moving into their final position along a trail the North Vietnamese had cut through the jungle. As they started to dig in along both sides of the trail, the platoon leader sent out a three-man listening post a little further up, to act as an early warning system. The three had only made their way about fifty meters when an explosion and a barrage of bullets tore into them. Two of the Americans went down, severely wounded, and the other men in the platoon immediately rushed forward to their aid, pouring covering fire into the jungle. But the enemy was gone, with only some blood trails as evidence to the Americans that any of their rounds had hit. The blood trails went on for about 200 meters, but there was no other sign of the North Vietnamese. "It was just one of those situations where [the enemy] popped a claymore, fired off everything they had and then ran," Homer remembers.

The ambush was now compromised; the mission effectively over, and the patrol had two seriously wounded men to take care of. "We had to put a tourniquet on [the leg wound]; he was bleeding really bad," Homer said. "The other had gotten shot through the lung. He was in pretty critical condition because he had a sucking chest wound, and he couldn't breathe very well. In that kind of heat you need all the lung power you got."[57]

The jungle around them was too thick for a helicopter evacuation, and it was too dark to try to carry them back to the firebase. There was an area clear enough for an LZ a shorter distance away, but it was also too dangerous to try to get there during the night. Instead they dug in and waited, everyone staying on full alert, expecting the North Vietnamese would be back any moment. All night long the men had to listen to the wheezing of the wounded man, afraid the noise would draw the North Vietnamese, feeling the contradictory emotions of fear they would lose the man and terrible hope that after each breath, the next breath would never come.

But the man survived the night, and at dawn they put the wounded on improvised stretchers and carried them to the LZ, where a helicopter landed to take them to the hospital at An Khe. The mission was over. But Homer, sleepless and filthy, needed to get to the platoon going on its road recon mission; they were waiting for him back at Camp Enari. He jumped on the chopper with the wounded.

When the helicopter, low on fuel, stopped at Fire Support Base Mary Lou, Homer decided to get off and try to catch another chopper going to Enari. He stepped out of the hatch, ducking low as he always did; once he had seen a soldier decapitated when he'd saluted Homer, turned around, and stepped into the whirling blades. Filthy, covered with mud and blood, just minutes away from the killing jungle he'd just left, Homer stepped onto the relatively safe earth of a firebase with a name that sounded like a prom queen's and found himself thrust again into a life and death situation. The helicopter took off. Homer looked around. It was very quiet. He saw a group of MPs, weapons drawn, closing in on someone, a soldier holding his M-16 at ready. The soldier was heading toward Homer.

If the man who confronted Homer when he got off the helicopter knew the officer was involved with disbursing payroll, he probably would have shot him right away. He was upset that someone had screwed up his pay; his wife was not getting her allotment money. So far he had registered his dissatisfaction with the situation by killing his payroll officer and wounding his first sergeant.

He pointed his rifle at Homer's chest now. Homer's own rifle was slung infantry style, with its barrel pointing forward, toward the man's waist. His finger lay right next to the trigger. They stood in a strange prefiguration of the confrontation he would have the next day, as if the American soldier who had swung his weapon around at Homer now would transform literally into the form of his Vietnamese enemy. Homer spoke calmly to the distraught soldier, pointing out how many other rifles were leveled at him—MPs had surrounded them by this point—and telling him that if he just let the MPs take him in, he could air his grievances and everything would be OK. "As we talked," Homer recounts, "I thought that one or both of us would wind up dead before the conversation ended." Homer walked closer and closer to the man. "When I got about ten feet from him, he finally put the rifle down and raised his hands. The MPs jumped him roughly and handcuffed him. I told them to take it easy on him, because he had probably seen far too much combat, and they relaxed and quietly led him to a jeep and took him away. I continued to the helipad to try to catch a bird back to Pleiku."[58]

It was not, he thought, an auspicious way to start the day. So far it had been the kind of incident-packed, sleepless, adrenaline-charged night and day that made each Viet Nam tour seem packed with a lifetime of events and emotions. But he was not surprised at the incident. It was the second time an American soldier had pulled a weapon on Homer; the first time he had butt-stroked the man. He had also heard stories about Americans shooting other Americans, troops eliminating the, to them, fatal problem of an incompetent or overzealous officer or NCO with a bullet or a grenade, sometimes officers drawing down on their men.

He had heard that the brigade commander himself had pulled his pistol on a pilot, furious because the man's helicopter had accidentally blown dust on him as he was taking a shower—the colonel had a "no hover" rule around his headquarters tent. The chopper was coming in after a mission during which its crew had frantically been trying to drop ammunition to a unit being cut to pieces in the jungle. The gunner and crew chief, Ron Carey, who would later write about the incident, had, moments before, been hovering at treetop level, dueling with and shooting to death North Vietnamese snipers lashed to upper branches of the jungle canopy. Carey and the rest of the crew, on edge themselves, had started laughing hysterically at the furious, red-haired colonel, covered with red dirt sticking to his wet skin. It infuriated the officer more; he had started waving the gun around wildly, until Carey finally had gotten behind his own machine gun and pointed it at him. The sight of the gun barrel and Carey's finger on the trigger had calmed the man down, and he had backed off, smiling uneasily. He never mentioned the incident again, and the crew never made an official complaint; they liked the colonel, passed the incident off to combat stress.

Not long afterward Carey himself, after carrying several loads of dead soldiers—the bodies stinking, not yet zipped into body bags—back to the same Fire Support Base Mary Lou, lost it when he landed and someone entered the chopper and pulled off the poncho Carey had draped over a body. He grabbed the man by the throat and put his pistol to his head, screaming that he was going to blow his fucking head off. At the time he experienced the incident as if he were watching a stranger, "this crazy person," doing it. Later another crew chief also threatened to shoot one of the rear-area people who was taking photographs of corpses.[59]

It is not surprising that men trained and praised for their ability to kill with deadly weapons, and who are used to doing so, will reach for them in moments of great stress. It was a habit they might not lightly shake off when they come home from war, as Homer would one day discover about himself.

Finally back at Camp Enari, Homer met the platoon he was to take out on road reconnaissance. He promptly paid the men—perhaps more than ever considering it prudent to do so. Then he turned in his payroll and got some sleep.

The next morning, March 19, 1969, he was once again on a helicopter. The recon patrol was inserted at a point on Route 19, the main civilian and military artery between Pleiku and An Khe, on the west (Pleiku) side of the Mang Yang Pass, just before the road curved and meandered down into a large valley. Their orders were to ascend to the ridgeline on the southern side of the road and then follow that ridge all the way through the pass, checking for trails the enemy might use to move troops or to ambush the road. But the slope where they had been dropped off was too steep, and Homer decided to take them down the road a little further, looking for a better place to climb. He was exhausted from the events of the past days1 and nights, running on pure adrenaline and second wind.

They trudged down the road, looking at the steep slopes of the mountains pressing in on both sides of them for the easiest place to climb. The ridgeline stood about 6,000 feet above them.

It was very hot. Homer would remember that. He would be certain of that. But in later years the memory of how he had finally gotten up to that ridgeline became nebulous. It was sometimes as if the intensity of the emotions he felt that day would stir with the heat, the sting of sweat that blurred his vision, and crowd out the details and then, finally, the emotion itself. Sometimes the events of both patrols on those two days edged into each other, the soldiers in both trudging through the same jungle terrain, the ambush, the wounded men—Was that on the first patrol or the second?[60] Was it a leg wound they'd gotten the tourniquet on? He remembered the sucking chest wound. The sound of it. He remembered seeing a tall tree on the ridgeline that they could spot on. He remembered this: that when he finally ordered the patrol to start climbing, they had refused.

It was not something that had ever happened to him before. But it was 1969, a time when most soldiers had realized that their presence in Viet Nam was a holding action; the peace talks had started on January 25 in Paris, and for most GIs, their main goal had become survival. No one, in John Kerry's words, wanted to be the last man to die for a mistake. Besides, Homer was new to them; they knew he had combat experience, but not in their platoon. The men hung back, muttering to themselves. Homer knew he could appeal, threaten, or scream, but in the end, what could he do to them if they didn't go—make them grunts and send them to Viet Nam? And how would the incident look on his fitness report: What kind of officer could not get men to follow him?

In any case, his southern stubbornness was aroused. He was going up to that ridge, with or without them. The men looked at him and then looked at two other soldiers, their medic and the NCO who had been their acting platoon leader. Homer understood that if those two obeyed him—each with his own kind of moral authority—the others would follow. He began trudging up the slope, hoping both men would join him.

They did. "I looked back down line after about a hundred fifty feet or so and they were coming, one foot in front of the other," he remembered. "The thing was, I was not even the platoon leader. The NCO that was acting platoon leader because we didn't have an officer for that platoon was kind of just standing back and letting me do my thing. But it was his platoon, he was still in charge. I knew that. Everybody else knew that. So when I got this gung-ho attitude and said we gotta go do it and everybody was wanting not to, and they turned to him to see what he would say. And thank goodness he was a good NCO and he backed me up. And so we went up and did our job."

Years later, he came to see what the sergeant enabled him to do as the opposite of goodness, seeing that balking on the part of his men as an opportunity fate had given him to change the fatal outcome of that patrol, one that the man he was at that time would have found impossible to seize.

The recon patrol struggled up the jungled slope. Homer's intention was to make the ridgeline, turn left, check out the first part of it, and then retrace their steps and go on toward the eastern side of the pass. When they reached the top, they found a well-worn path running along the ridge, just the kind of trail they were supposed to check out. They began moving cautiously down it. But again there was a small rebellion: the two squads that Homer ordered to walk flank security—that is, make their way through the jungle partway down, on either side of the ridgeline trail—refused. It was a treacherous job. Besides having to hack through the foliage, they knew that flankers would take the first blow of an ambush. They were not inclined to do so. Homer again insisted, and again they finally obeyed.

The patrol, flankers out, followed the ridgeline path to a point where they could see the entire valley at the other end of the pass spread beneath them. The sight of the country, stretching out for hundreds of miles, awed the men, even in their state of exhaustion. Their war was fought under the jungle canopies, in gloom, the trees and foliage and shadow pressed around them in a visual reflection of their ignorance about where they were, where they fit into some overall diorama of the war that made sense, they presumed, they hoped, to someone. Now the country was spread out below like a map: the patchworks of fields in the valley, the spines of mountains, smoke rising, flashes here and there from distant firefights. After a few moments, Homer got the patrol turned around. He would report the existence of the trail; for now they needed to go back to the tall tree he had spotted on, descend, and check out the other side.

They were almost at the tree when he saw that the men were played out. He decided to let everyone take a short water and rest break. "We just moved a few meters off the trail on either side and dropped our packs and lay down," he recalls. "I had rear security out, but no point security, except for the point man, who was facing forward. As I walked up to the front of the column, checking on the condition of the troops, I spoke to the point man, who turned to face me."

At that moment Dam, his weapon slung over his shoulder, rounded the trail, strolling as casually as if he were on a nature hike. It was the kind of encounter called a "meeting engagement," a phrase that in other circumstances might sound like a courtship ritual, but in American infantry jargon refers to a situation in which a unit is on a reconnaissance mission and accidentally runs into the enemy. A meeting engagement: there is a sense of arbitrary fate suggested by the term, an element of surprise that in fact was true to the situation.

"Chieu hoi," Homer shouted, thinking the phrase meant surrender. But the North Vietnamese soldier continued to bring his weapon up. A second later he was on the ground, his chest stitched with Homer's bullets. "It was the first time I'd shot someone. I'd been in fire-fights, but fire-fights means I hear noise, I shoot at it. I see muzzle flashes, I shoot at it. I call artillery in on it. When I get through, we might find bodies, we might find blood trails, but I never saw someone. . . . This guy, I saw him jerk when I fired. We were close enough that, if I had been looking at his eyes I would have seen directly into his eyes. Fortunately, I wasn't looking at his face, I was looking at the weapon because I waited as long as I could and in the split second before he had it actually aimed at me, I had no choice. As far as I knew he was going to pull the trigger and then I was gone, so I had no choice. This is the first time, eyeball to eyeball, I saw someone and I pulled the trigger and I knew, beyond any doubt, I killed that person. And—it's pretty traumatic. The only thing that kept me going after that was the fact that we had to finish the job we were assigned to do, and I just immersed myself in details. I worried about my men. I didn't think about it."[61]

He did think, for only an instant, of taking the body down with them. But his patrol was on an enemy trail, in an exposed position, and he knew he had to get them down quickly, off the ridgeline. Let the enemy take care of their own. He knelt down and went through the dead soldier's pockets, extracting two small notebooks and some loose papers.

"I took his identification papers and will send them home," he wrote to his mother that night. "Please put them up somewhere for me."

# CHAPTER THIRTEEN

# "I Will Probably Not Make It Off This Hill Alive"

Afterward Homer returned to his base camp duties as XO. He tried to keep the image of the young North Vietnamese soldier he had shot out of his mind. But he still asked his friend in Battalion Intelligence not to burn the books and papers he had taken off the body. Instead he sent them home, putting 12,000 miles between them and himself, and went back to the war.

The second phase of Operation Wayne Grey had begun. After the 66th PAVN had broken itself against Hill 947 and began looking for safe havens to regroup, the operation splintered into a series of probes, ambushes, retreats, and attacks, with separate battalions, companies, platoons, and squads engaging in a series of not always connected battles and besiegements. The casualties increased, each day adding its tally of wounded and dead, more Callans, more Dams, to the obscene scoreboard of the war. Homer was still feeling that sense of relief that he did not have to be constantly out in the field, and guilt that he should be. Predictably, he was about to both get what he wanted and regret that he ever had wished for it.

In mid-March, Alpha and Charlie Companies of Homer's
battalion were sent to secure another hill about twenty kilometers south of Fire Support Base 20. They were to dig in and
fortify the hill in order to use it as a "company-sized blocking
position,"[62] sealing off the northern part of the Plei Trap road by
sending out ambushes, sweeps, and reconnaissance-in-force patrols, and calling in air and artillery strikes on any of the PAVN
units presumably trying to retreat into the sanctuary of Cambodia or Laos. The hill, as always, was called by its height in meters above sea level: 467. But the companies from Homer's
battalion that would fortify and man Hill 467 were designated
Task Force Alpha, and as was customary, it became common
parlance, among both soldiers and command, to call the hill itself by that name. [63]

By March 21, although he still remained at base camp,
Homer's Bravo Company, under Captain James DeRoos, relieved
Alpha Company on the hill and began sending out patrols. For
the first few days there was only light contact. But Alpha had
had two sharp engagements, had lost people, and had discovered well-fortified enemy bunkers before they had pulled out,
and now the soldiers sensed that the enemy was drawing
around them, in the thick jungle surrounding the Task Force
Alpha positions.

That feeling was reinforced two days after the company dug
in, when a patrol from Bravo ran into North Vietnamese only
350 meters west of the hill. Eight Americans were wounded and
two killed in the fight; the patrol had to withdraw, firing as they
went, while mortars from 467 dropped on the enemy, killing
four of them in turn. As soon as the GIs were back into their
lines, mortar shells started to fall on the hill, and the enemy was
close enough to the perimeter to shoot B-40 rocket-propelled
grenades into the base. As the mortar shells exploded, throwing
up mud and sending rocks, wood splinters, and shrapnel flying,
bullets from snipers thudded into the sandbags, the sharp crack

of the AK-47s coming from all around the perimeter. It did not seem the action of an enemy in retreat. When Captain DeRoos took out another patrol, he found dozens of well-fortified enemy bunkers concealed in heavy jungle, only about a mile and a half from 467. "We had no idea what we were getting into; intelligence was completely inadequate," DeRoos recalls. B Company engineers set explosives in some of the bunkers, but before they could be set off, the patrol was hit by a large enemy force, raked with machine gun and rifle fire, and mortared. In the chaotic fight that followed, a dozen GIs were killed, and DeRoos pulled the rest into a makeshift perimeter, while he, in the words of the citation for the Silver Star he later received for the action, "remained exposed and directed artillery support . . . [and] dragged a wounded man to safety." Tragically, three other men, still alive, were cut off and left in the confusion. One was a wounded man, PFC Prentice Hicks; the others, who had volunteered to stay with him when he went down, were PFC Frederick Herrera and a medic, Richard Roberts. When DeRoos couldn't find them, out of some impulse—to record them, to somehow take them with him—he inscribed the names of the three on one of the legs of his fatigues. It wasn't until much later that a recon patrol could get back to the top of the hill. All they found were some of Hicks's letters and the cover of a Bible that had belonged to Herrera.[64] The men were gone. Their loss still haunts DeRoos, who has kept the piece of cloth with their names on it, cut from his jungle fatigues, to this day.[65]

What the soldiers of Bravo and Charlie Companies would not find out until later was that two PAVN battalions were moving up from the south, toward Hill 467, and at least another company was in the jungle to its north, tightening around the small American force. The North Vietnamese knew that whichever way they moved, Task Force Alpha, constantly sending out patrols and ambushes and calling in artillery, would be in their way. It had to be neutralized.

During the following days Homer listened over the command
post radio at Enari or at the closer firebase at Polei Kleng, as Hill
467 was hit regularly by the enemy, the helicopters swooping in
to support the soldiers, who were receiving heavy fire from north
and south of the perimeter, where the enemy was gathering in
greater force. The North Vietnamese lobbed 60mm and 82mm
mortar shells into the small zone on top of the hill, blowing apart
sandbagged positions, splintering trees, and sending the deadly,
red-hot shards of shrapnel zinging everywhere. B-40 rocket
rounds flew at the Americans from the surrounding jungle, and
AK-47 fire cracked overhead and slammed into sandbags all
around the perimeter, shredding them. Worse, by now enemy
artillery units near or over the Laotian and Cambodian borders
had gotten the hill's coordinates and pounded it with 105mm
rounds fired from heavy artillery pieces captured from the Americans or South Vietnamese. A helicopter trying to land was rid-
dled with bullets, and more rockets zeroed in on the helicopter
pad, from west of the hill. The gunships that were trying to provide cover as medevac helicopters attempted to extract the
wounded and the dead were all hit by a storm of ground fire.

By seven in the evening on March 27, forty-four 105mm
shells had slammed into the American positions. Among the
American casualties that night was Bravo's commanding officer,
Captain James DeRoos, struck in the leg by shrapnel as he re-
peatedly ran into the open, trying to help carry wounded men
to the LZ, until he was forced onto one of the helicopters himself. The aircraft had to dodge mortar shells and small arms fire
as it took off—the enemy was that close around the hill.[66] As
soon as the chopper carrying the captain landed back at base,
Homer jumped on board for its return flight. He had been assigned to replace DeRoos. He was now, for the sin of wanting it,
company commander of Bravo Company.

From the helicopter, Task Force Alpha's embattled outpost on
the crest of Hill 467 looked grim. "Garbage from empty c-ration

cases, along with damaged or destroyed equipment, is every-where. Several of the bunkers are in need of repair. The smell of burning jungle and death hover over this place,"[67] helicopter crew chief Ron Carey remembers. The LZ was narrow, picketed by splintered trees, and Homer landed in a hail of gunfire. He ran out of the helicopter, zigzagging into a splintered collage of sights and impressions: red mud sucking his boots, muzzle flashes, green tracers flying overhead, troopers shooting back. At the company command bunker he found another lieutenant from Bravo Company, Platoon Leader Jim Keane, getting ready to lead two platoons into the thick jungle pressing around the perimeter, to try to find and fix the enemy's positions, set up ambushes, and hopefully locate some water for the beleaguered and thirsty soldiers. Homer was relieved to see Keane. The lieu-tenant had a reputation for bluntness and competence; he was also the best map reader in the company, a calm and deadly leader when he was in the field, idolized by his men. Homer agreed with his plan.

However, with Keane out doing reconnaissance, Homer only had seventeen men to defend half the hill. Charlie Com-pany, nearly at full strength, held the other half of the perimeter, but their CO had become territorial and refused to take over any of the positions on the Bravo Company side.

That morning Charlie Company sent out another recon pa-trol, trying to determine how close the enemy was to the peri-meter. It didn't take them long. The men had only gone out a few hundred meters when they were hit by a vicious onslaught of B-40 rockets and sniper fire. They pulled back, called in ar-tillery fire, and saw four NVA soldiers blown to pieces. To their shock, the enemy answered immediately with another barrage of heavy artillery shells that fell right near the patrol, but miracu-lously caused no casualties. At 2:30 in the afternoon, Charlie Company decided to try again. This time their patrol got 300 meters past the perimeter before it was bracketed by mortar shells and had to fall back; the helicopters sent in to try to take

out the PAVN spotter who must have been calling in the mortars were hit by heavy ground fire. It was clear the base was
surrounded, with Keane and his men still out in the jungle
somewhere.

The shelling continued, though one of the shells that hit
Hill 467 was not lethal. It exploded in a shower of paper that
fluttered up into the air and then drifted back down to earth.
Some of the soldiers picked up the cards; they began with a
question that may well have been in the minds of many of the
hill's defenders, though the movie-style, GI-you-die wording
made it into a kind of grim joke:

> WHO WILL BE THE LAST G.I. TO DIE IN VIET NAM?
> The criminal war of Johnson has put an end to his shameful
> presidency and Nixon is making the last step of Johnson's escala-
> tion with many extremely perfidious schemes.
>
> It is quite clear that the "unimaginable strength" of the
> United States had been unable to save Johnson from the endless
> tunnel in Viet Nam. The dirty U.S. war in Viet Nam has brought
> you no good except suffering and shame and has but won the
> hatred of the Viet Namese people.
>
> While you consider the talks in Paris hopeful for your life,
> the U.S. government still plans to prolong the war that has cost
> lots of men and money. And the American people as well as you
> must bear its consequences. So who of you will be the last G.I. to
> die in Viet Nam?
>
> You cannot have peace by saying prayers. You also can not
> seek for life in entrenched posts in cities and towns or in the re-
> pose of the puppet troops.

"Another sleepless night, everyone suffering from exhaustion,"
Homer wrote. He had jumped around the perimeter all night
himself, trying to keep his men from nodding off, his own luck
holding out. "The next morning a B-40 rocket round exploded
into the ground by a small fire I had built for destroying some

used PRC-25 batteries. I was knocked down, almost gently, by the concussion, but not hurt, all the shrapnel going behind me." He ordered his own mortars to put down a ring of shells around the perimeter, all of them falling within fifty meters of the base. The defenders' world existed within those fifty meters; everything outside it wanted to kill them. But the tactic was dangerous: to keep the shells from flying too far, the mortar men had to use only the weapon's igniter, with no powder charge, and to aim the barrels almost vertically, which meant the mortar rounds might fall too close to or even back on their own position.

The enemy shelling increased, 60mm and 82mm mortar rounds raining down on 467, and the heavy artillery over the border had the hilltop zeroed in. That day 127 105mm shells exploded within the small perimeter. One finally found Homer's position: "[We] took a direct hit, shattering Ryan's forearm, completely deafening, SSG Brucher, my only NCO above E-5 and completely deafening my left ear and creating a very loud ringing in both. I [felt I] had been kicked in the back, and [I was] drenched in Ryan's blood, so I ran in panic to the Task Force CP bunker, to get someone to see if I had been hit in the back and to let them know what had happened; then I left to find Ryan. He was running around screaming and holding his shattered elbow on the other side of our sector, going into shock rapidly.

"I ran to get our Medic, Doc Gehringer, and convinced him to leave the safety of his hole to help Ryan. Then I began my perimeter check and forced those with no overhead cover, to get out between rounds and build some sand bag protection. I returned to my position to see if a Medevac was going to make it in to pick up Ryan, but they said they couldn't risk one at that time. Later in the day, a Medevac was able to pick up Ryan, without incident."

Fog and enemy fire had been preventing the helicopters from landing, so the defenders were desperately short of linked rounds for the machine guns and, especially, water. Men were fighting with their throats swollen and parched, their heads aching from dehydration. A resupply chopper was able to get in at the same time as the Medevac, but to Homer's dismay, instead of belts of machine gun ammunition and water, the battalion commanding officer, who had personally overseen the loading of the helicopter, had sent crates of hand grenades, which were already in good supply, and, as a treat, freeze-dried rations, the kind that had to be prepared with water. Homer was furious. He described the situation in his journal: "Water critical by now. Five people in Charlie Company and one of mine now completely out of their heads from thirst. Every one of the 4 inch bamboo left standing by the incoming has a hole drilled in every segment, hoping to find a few drops of water. An enemy 105 round killed someone from Charlie Company. The death really hurt morale, because we all knew we could be next and there wasn't anything we could do to stop it. Three days without water or sleep for most of us, and it was beginning to tell in the heat. Night was no better, two serious WIA's from grenades. Mortars got the NVA, but then we had to listen to them moaning all night until they died, one by one. We had a serious attack all around the perimeter around midnight. Some even made it into the perimeter. We wound up calling in Puff the Magic Dragon, an AC-130 ship, to hose down the perimeter around midnight. With 200,000 candle power flares and mini-guns able to spit out 6,000 rounds per minute (every 4th one a red tracer) the enemy attack came to a sudden halt.

"We kept getting AK-47 fire and grenades sporadically all night. I moved around our sector, redistributing ammo and grenades, trying to keep someone awake at each position, and letting everyone know the current situation. I tried to get some sleep around 2:30 AM, but the mortar and grenades kept me from sleeping. I spent several hours digging into the hard packed red clay and rocks with my bayonet, trying to get my fox hole big enough to stretch out some and deep enough to provide some protection against shrapnel from nearby tree bursts.

I remember sitting in my fox hole for a few minutes rest around 3:00 AM and looking up to see a single bright star through the jungle canopy, and realizing for the first time, that I will probably not make it off this hill alive. It was then that I prayed."

The pattern of close calls that marked his war continued. The next day, as he was checking the perimeter, one mortar round landed ten feet behind him and blew him off his feet; another fell three feet in front of him. The 60mm round "left a hole about two hands wide, with its tail fin sitting right in the center of it, still smoking."

By now, thirst was driving men over the edge. Homer remembers: "Morgan went berserk and had to be tied up to keep him from trying to drink from a canister of diesel fuel. On most encampments, where we stayed for several nights, the supply choppers would bring us fresh water in empty ammo tubes, and Morgan truly believed, in his delirium, that the liquid in the diesel fuel ammo tube was water. There was much talk of trying to leave the hill to get water, even though it would probably be suicidal. We had heavy movement around the perimeter all morning."

Finally Jim Keane, who had been stuck in the jungle outside the perimeter, managed to get his two platoons back to the hill, bringing some canteens of creek water with him, enough to give everyone a small drink. The word also came down that they would all be extracted the next day, March 30. At noon resupply choppers were again able to land, bringing some much-needed food, water, and ammo. They performed another much-needed task as well, taking away the wounded and dead who had been stacked up near the LZ.

"The bodies smelled real bad," Homer remembers, "with flies and maggots all over them. Lying around in the 95 to 100 degree heat had them all bloated from decomposition. It made you sick when the odor first drifted your way. I was leaning back against the stack of bodies, attempting to eat some C-rations, as I waited for the supply chopper to take out the wounded and the bodies. . . . I was so exhausted from a pounding dehydration headache, that I didn't have the strength to go somewhere else and then come running back when the choppers arrived. So exhausted, in fact, that I did not even think about the significance of where I had chosen to sit down. One of my guys had to be dragged off a bird to let the wounded get on, when the first chopper landed. He was hysterical with fear, as were most of us by now. I was helping the door gunner load the bodies onto the next chopper, when the poncho blew back, revealing the guy's head, with maggots squirming in the goo that had once been his eyes. The door gunner fell to his knees and began projectile vomiting.

"One of my guys helped me get the body on the chopper and then we both dragged the door gunner back to his ride."

Another night. More mortars. More rockets. One NVA soldier worked up close enough to the perimeter to hurl in a Chinese grenade. Homer had thought that with Jim Keane back on the hill, he could get a little sleep, but the incoming made it impossible. Close to dawn, he could hear the sound of the North Vietnamese dragging off the bodies of their dead and wounded. He also heard something more ominous: the sound of digging, all around the perimeter. Convinced the enemy was preparing to overrun the hill, he called in a Spooky 22, an aircraft armed with Gatling miniguns. He requested the plane to "hose down the jungle all around the perimeter," as close as thirty meters, telling the pilot he and the men would turn on flashlights in all their foxholes to mark the perimeter with a circle of light. A curtain of bullets poured out of the aircraft, chewing up every inch of ground around them, a terrifying and welcome sight.

As the sun came up on March 30, Homer was certain he would not live through the day. "I am so exhausted now, that getting to my feet takes all my concerted will power and physical strength, then I wobble around, stumbling to maintain my balance, until I get my head clear again. The least little thing will cause me to lose my balance and fall down, and then I have to rest up and start all over again. I have a pounding dehydration headache, like most everyone else. You should remember that I am at least three days fresher than most of my men."

He soon received a classic good news/bad news radio message from headquarters. "We got word the Air Force had gotten the 105mm guns, that had been pounding us and the CA to Polei Kleng [the extraction of the company] would begin at 0900. Also got word of two reinforced NVA companies headed our way about ten klicks out."

Charlie and Bravo Companies now began what the After Action Report would describe with typical understatement as a "tactical withdrawal from their AO." As American helicopters began to swoop down onto the hill, the North Vietnamese sent a curtain of bullets up at the vulnerable aircraft, which could only land one at a time on the small landing pad. The enemy, seeing the Americans were pulling out, started pouring everything they had into the hill. Mortar shells burst around the choppers, and streams of tracers followed them out of the LZ.

Warrant Officer-1 Jack Hawkins, a pilot from the 116th Assault Helicopter Company who had grown up on a ranch in Texas, always flew with an "I'd rather be riding an Appaloosa" bumper sticker pasted on the sliding armor plate of his helicopter. Flying into 467 was a stunt that made the words on the sticker more a fervent wish than a joke. Hawkins recalls: "During the extraction of TFA, we used most of the company slicks [lighter-armed helicopters used for medical evacuation], and two sets of [helicopter gun]ships and borrowed guns from the 57th Cougars. Sometime during the early phase of extraction, Mark Garrison, one of the . . . guns made a statement over the radio that he had taken fire from the [north], from the [west], from the [south], and now he was taking fire from the [east]. [He said]: 'It looks as if the sons of bitches have us surrounded.'

"He later took some kind of heavy round under his peter [co]pilot's armored seat. One of the Cougars took several hits and I believe had his wind screen shot out. I chased one of the slicks flown by Windy after he took a spent .50 cal hit in his transmission. He landed on a firebase a couple of miles away. Bob Nilius, platoon leader of the second platoon took hits later in the day and had to return to base. To the best of my memory, nine aircraft took hits, of which several were disabled on the firebase or at Polei Kleng."

Homer was determined to get all of his men out before boarding a helicopter; in the meantime he had to keep the North Vietnamese from overrunning the hill. "Charlie Company left first," he recalled, "and I had to shift my men to cover their positions, as best I could. I got shot at several times, while moving around directing the withdrawal."

By noon everyone was off the hill except Homer, his radio operator, Sergeant Larry Hanson, Jim Keane, and the company medic, PFC Edwin Gehringer. The four could see the North Vietnamese starting to swarm the hill. Above them a helicopter started to land—and then swooped away. Robert Granger, a PFC evacuated earlier with his platoon, remembers all the men huddling anxiously around the radio at the airstrip, hearing the chopper pilots radio Homer that the NVA were in the wire, and the helicopters might not be able to get in to extract the GIs.[68]

"The last bird started in on short final, and then pulled out saying there were NVA coming in all around the perimeter and he wouldn't come in," Homer remembers. "The four of us opened up with all we could find to throw and shoot, praying nothing would hit the mortar pit full of ammo and explosives, where we had set charges to destroy all the ammo left behind on the hill. I directed a cobra gun [ship] to get an especially pesky B-40 rocket position about fifty meters out and got him, but got badly burned on the neck by hot shrapnel from the gun ship's rockets. We decided that our only chance was to make a break for it off the north side of the hill and E&E [Escape and Evade] out of the area."

That they did not have to try that desperate move was due to the bravery of WO Jack Hawkins and his crew: "Just as we started off the hill," Homer remembers, "four double deuce [the aircraft number was 422] called to say he was on his way in to get us. . . . I'm alive today, thanks to the incredible bravery of the pilots of 422."

Jack Hawkins still recalls that day vividly: "Towards the end of the extraction, Jim Hudkins and myself had been in and out three times and we were regrouping to see who still had aircraft left to fly. At that time I had not taken any hits. There were four or five of us that departed Polei Kleng to go and pick up the last two sorties. Hud said he would go in first and asked who would go in and get the final sortie. After some hesitation, I said I would. Hud got in and out without incident, and I was getting ready to go in to pick up the final four. A pair of cobras that had been working in the area had been monitoring the extraction and stated that they both had full rocket pods and did I want them to unload. The answer was a definite yes, so I held back while they fired their rockets around the hill. I had already made three trips using the same flight path and felt that I was pushing my luck on that route so tried to change my approach into the LZ. The bottom line was that being low level, I got disorientated and missed the LZ. I fooled around for a few seconds trying to find it and remarked that I was getting out and would come back in a different way. I wound up coming in again over the flare chute, the four remaining troops jumped on board and we were out. Again I was going to take a different direction out (I think it was to the south) and heard them holler no! I was already committed and accelerated as fast as I could staying low. We came out hot, and unknowingly, I took one round in one of the rotor blades. I definitely remember Homer on board but do not remember any interactions."

"There were NVA all around the perimeter and they really gave us a send off as we flew out," Homer said. "It looked like an angry anthill as we pulled out. I felt pretty good until I looked at my rifle and found bullet scars in the hand guard and magazine guide, one more through my rucksack, right through the radio, and the large crease in my steel pot."

Jack Hawkins finally landed his crippled ship and his grateful passengers at Polei Kleng. "We made it directly to Polei Kleng, where when the four unloaded, a black trooper jumped on board and gave me a hot can of beer saying I was the best. That was the greatest award I have ever received. . . . Several of us received [the]Distinguished Flying Cross for that day, but the present of a hot can of beer was better."[69]

# CHAPTER FOURTEEN

# Death
# Dance

B ack at Enari, Homer's ears rang constantly, a thin scream in
his inner ear, like a continuous auditory memory of the
shell that had landed in his fighting position and splattered him
with the blood of his two sergeants. It would linger for the rest
of his life, subverting silence.

He returned to his duties as XO, going out to the field
whenever he could, hoping to be given a line company. He had
some ambition left, but his main goal now was to protect his
men. The purpose of the war itself had become nebulous to
him. They were there to fight the enemy; it was the condition of
the universe, and it was meaningless to question it. He did not
question it. But he knew he could not rely on the brigade or the
division or the army to shield his men from fatal danger, not
even when there seemed no worthy return for their wounds or
deaths. What had been the point of the sacrifices made on Hill
467, now back in PAVN hands? He remembered the brigade's
assessment of Operation Wayne Grey as a victory. True enough,
the operation had succeeded in disrupting the planned North
Vietnamese attack on Kontum. But it was body count scoreboard

arithmetic. Perhaps 575 North Vietnamese had been killed, to 106 Americans killed. Maybe. But there had seemed no lack of North Vietnamese around Task Force Alpha, and he had come to respect their dogged courage as much as he admired the bravery of his own men. How many more, met on mountain trails or charging up the flanks of hills, would he need to kill and add to the tally, how high would he have to stack their corpses, before someone on the other side would call a finish?[70]

His own magic finish line was the twelve months of his tour, but he knew already that he could not abandon his men to a new officer, who would get more of them killed. Three months before his war year would have ended, he volunteered to extend his tour for six months. He took a thirty-day leave in the States. His body was in South Carolina, but his heart and mind were still in the Central Highlands. By the end of May 1969 he was back, in the 1st of the 8th, assigned as company commander of Headquarters Company until a field command opened up. By October he had been promoted to captain and was given command of Delta Company.

The war continued. There were no more dramatic sieges, but a series of perimeter security and civic action duties, ambushes, small engagements, and patrols melded into each other, punctuated by the deaths of his men, each another added to the body count of Those He Had Failed to Save that he kept filed somewhere in his mind, like a bill placed in the back of a drawer. Those He Had Killed in order to save his men remained in an even deeper recess. Except for one, he had not seen their faces.

Those He Had Gotten Killed he buried in the deepest depression of his heart, along with Dam. Caught in an ambush near An Khe, his men dying around him, he watched in awe as his unarmed medic, a conscientious objector, crawled time after time into the heaviest fire, taking a bullet through the shoulder and then through the buttocks, but still dragging back the wounded to safety; another of his men, a black kid from South

Philadelphia, stood up to trade machine gun fire with the NVA machine guns pinning them down, taking bullet after bullet in his body, but taking out the enemy guns. In the midst of that deadly chaos, Homer ordered men to their probable deaths in order to save the company. Their willingness to carry out his commands, even knowing how far into harm's way he was putting them, the very courage that marked them as those most worthy of life, tormented him. "Looking people in the eye and telling them to do things to keep the unit from being wiped out, all the while knowing that they will probably not come back alive, is a haunting memory. . . . I had terrible nightmares about those decisions for decades after I returned."[71]

Worse were those who died from what he knew were his mistakes, and the worst of these had occurred when he had ordered a patrol to cross a creek that the patrol leader had reported, over the radio to Homer, was filled with raging rapids. He had not believed the man, who had a reputation for sandbagging, faking his position, and had ordered him to take the patrol across. They had obeyed, and one drowned, swept away down the creek. He could never, would never, forgive himself for that death.

His war seesawed crazily between the moments he felt like an utter failure and the moments he rose to the best in himself, tapping into depths of physical and moral courage he knew he would never have reached without the terrible extremities and clarities of choice combat offered. When the need arose, he tapped also into a type of insanity others saw as bravery. In the same ambush near An Khe, his company caught in a saw grass clearing, pinned down, four of his men already dead, he found himself paralyzed with fear, sobbing until the sight of the man next to him, the top of his head blown off, made him vomit. After he watched another man lying near him get hit, he made himself rise, screaming at his men to move out of the field to the tree line, yelling into his radio for air and artillery cover and to try to contact his lead platoon, until a bullet severed the wires

to his handset. He stood and fired his .45 at the enemy like a
crazed gunfighter, the NVA bullets kicking up dirt all around
his feet. He should have died; instead, his actions spurred his
men to shoot back and move out, and he was able to retain the
presence of mind afterward to maneuver his platoons into position to come to the aid of the lead platoon, which was being cut
to pieces; call in helicopters and artillery and save their lives.

He had taken Dam's life, but later he would save the life of a
PAVN soldier, a prisoner. He had turned the man over to an
American captain, his sergeant, an American civilian interrogator, and an ARVN soldier who had come to the firebase Homer
was commanding. Moments later, one of his soldiers told him
they were torturing the prisoner on the helicopter pad. Furious,
he ran down to the area. "When I got to the pad, the 'Civilian'
had my prisoner, with his hands still tied behind his back, on
the ground, the two American soldiers standing on his upper
arms, pinning the prisoner to the ground. They had wrapped a
towel around the prisoner's head and the 'Civilian' was pouring
water from a canteen onto the towel, choking the prisoner. The
Vietnamese soldier was shouting questions."

The water boarding he was witnessing entered our national
debate about the use of "acceptable" torture after September 11,
2001. There was no debate in Homer's mind in 1969: he was
horrified. It was one of those moments when he remembered
his father facing down the Klan. "I ran up, drawing my 45 cal
pistol and chambered a round, pointing it straight at the 'Civilian' telling him to stop or I would shoot him dead on the spot.
He laughed, then started to reach for his own weapon, when a
machine gunner let out a long burst over our heads. I turned
around to see nearly a dozen of my men drawing down on the
scene."

His men, seeing him rush to the pad, had followed him
there, a sergeant bringing along the machine gunner. "The 'Civilian' brought his hands up slowly and started backing up," he recalls. Homer got the prisoner on the chopper and sent one of

his own men back with him, to make sure he arrived safely into the custody of the provost. "I assured [the captain] that if he did not arrive at the trains area, or if anything untoward happened to the prisoner on the way, every man in my unit would make it their personal mission to find and execute them all. Since I had two men going back on the chopper for sick call, I was certain they would not chance any more mischief. The 'Civilian' looking quite terrified at this point, turned and got into the helicopter. The other American soldiers and the Vietnamese soldier loaded the prisoner and the chopper started up and left, without any of them making eye contact again. . . . If my sergeant had not taken the step of backing me up, I do not know what might have happened. I know that at that moment, I definitely would not have hesitated to shoot and I would not have backed down under any circumstances."[72]

He had stepped into his father's shoes. Their disruption of a war crime that the deaths of their own friends could easily have allowed them to accept had given Homer and his men one of the war's rare opportunities for a moment of pure moral grace. Yet the rank, ease, and expertise of those men in his uniform carrying out the torture hinted disturbingly of a habitual evil that was either encouraged by some level of authority, or, at best, ignored. It was not something Homer wanted his army to do; it was not worthy of the sacrifices he had seen his own nineteen- and twenty-year-old soldiers make.

For his last two months, February to March 1970, Homer was assigned as the air officer in charge of the 1st Battalion's Tactical Operations Center, coordinating troop movements and artillery and air support. He entered a kind of zone when he clamped on the earphones. There was no room to think of anything else: "I've got five or six radios going at the same time, some times as many as two or three fire fights going on simultaneously, I'm controlling artillery, I'm controlling air support, I'm controlling Medevacs coming in, I'm controlling units. I'm doing all of this simultaneously. I would come into the tactical operations center and sit for twenty minutes and listen to the radio chatter of the person that was on duty and then all of a sudden I'd go tap him on the shoulder and grab the radios and just take up right where he left off. . . . [Y]ou do all of this in a flow of consciousness thing. I mean, it's almost like an out of body experience and time disappears completely."[73]

The calls from infantry units for support and help poured into his head, in a coordinated, fast-paced death dance. His voice, the farmer's son from Bamberg, directed multi-million-dollar aircraft, bringing down millions of dollars of ordnance, shredding flesh he could not see, deep in his sandbagged bunker, protecting flesh he could imagine. He was saving his men.

# PART TWO

# HOMECOMINGS

*There is a part of our brain that links our sensory inputs to the center where perception and awareness live. There perception of the outside world is created. If that part is damaged, we may perceive the world differently from other people. We may see the same the world you do, but perceive it differently. We may even see parts of it through our perception that do not exist in yours.*

—HOMER STEEDLY

# CHAPTER FIFTEEN

# Tiger

And finally he came home. In some ways, he knew, the war he had fought had been as clear-cut as a war could be. He and his men had killed, as he had killed Dam on that mountain trail, in order to stay alive. He had committed no atrocities, was no baby killer. He had been promoted and decorated. He had participated in the defining history of his time. He had experienced the close camaraderie of combat soldiers, had fought bravely and led competently, and had come back more or less intact. There were men who would and did consider such experiences the high-water marks of their lives. There were others who were foolish enough to envy them

"Family and friends wondered why we were so angry," wrote former marine Michael Norman. "What are you crying about? They would ask. . . . Our fathers and grandfathers had gone off to war, done their duty, come home and got on with it. What made our generation so different? As it turns out, nothing. No difference at all. When old soldiers from 'good' wars are dragged from behind the curtain of myth and sentiment and brought into the light, they too seem to smolder with choler and alienation. . . . So we were angry. Our anger was old, atavistic.

We were angry as all civilized men who have ever been sent to make murder in the name of virtue were angry. And our anger was new too. We were angry for ourselves, for our wounded, for the dead we brought home in bags."[1]

Homer careened between rage and emptiness, tried to deal with his memories and nightmares and the void he sensed inside himself in the traditional ways, but dope and alcohol weren't enough. He chased whiskey and reefer with adrenaline, throwing himself into more and more dangerous sports—skydiving, small-plane piloting, motorcycle and stock car racing, cave diving—activities in which a careless or irresponsible move could get him killed, but could get *only* him killed. The luck that had kept a mortar from exploding between his legs on Hill 467 and a hundred other times had spared his life while others died around him held out. On cave dives he would often come across the drowned bodies of other divers, but he would always find his own way out of the labyrinthine depths. He became a volunteer Underwater Rescue Team Diver, pulled corpses out of the wreckage of cars and trucks, groping blindly in pitch black water until his hands found and shaped, again and again, the flesh of the dead, the bodies of those swept away, as once a soldier had been swept away, by raging waters.

He was still in the army. For a time he was stationed in Fort Campbell, Kentucky, 500 miles from Bamberg. He would take off on Friday evening for what should have been an eight- to ten-hour drive. He would make it in five. His GT Opel, the same car he raced on stock car tracks, could go up to 150 miles an hour, and he often did, averaging 90 mph, driving two-lane roads through stretches of rain, sleet, and snow at 120 or 140. He was on the mine-strewn road from Pleiku to An Khe, dodging B-40s and sniper fire, armed now with the loaded 357 Magnum he always kept next to him on the front seat.

Once a Tennessee state trooper chased him for over twenty miles, at speeds up to 150 mph. When he finally pulled over, the trooper got out of his car with his gun drawn, and when Homer saw him coming in his side-view mirror, he was a heart-beat away from pulling out his own gun and shooting the man. He didn't move. He was in uniform, and when the trooper got to his window and saw the ribbons and Combat Infantry Badge, he told Homer he was a veteran himself, and chatted amiably, suggesting Homer come on the force if he wanted to speed, not knowing how close he had come to having his face blown off. The incident shook Homer. He remembered the two times his fellow soldiers had turned their rifles on him: the man he had knocked out with his rifle butt and the man at FSB Mary Lou who had killed his officer. More than ever, he understood them, the small fragile line that separated him from them. "Later I thought long and hard," he says, "and realizing that with my uncontrollable combat instincts, keeping the weapons might re-sult in my killing someone before I could stop myself. I sold all the weapons that same month and have not owned anything but a small single shot 22 cal varmint rifle since then. I wonder how many other vets shot by reflex and spent significant parts of their life behind bars as a result. I wonder how many died chasing that adrenalin high on the highways. Wonder how I got so lucky as to survive myself."

It was a question he would only ask himself. The main theme of his return was silence. He spoke briefly with his father, the World War II vet. "He knew [what] I was not telling anyone. Oh yeah, he definitely knew, but it was easier for him to handle not knowing the actual details, how bad it really was. In fact I talked to him for a little bit, probably two minutes, after we got back one day, and he said, 'well, I know what you went through and it doesn't matter what the details are. When you're in that level it changes you.'"

But it was the details that ate at Homer. He got rid of his guns, but his stories remained locked inside. At first his friends asked him about the war, but he could see their eyes begin to flit away from his when he told them. He shut up. "When I came back to the states, after my second tour, one of the things I quickly learned was not to talk about [the war] because people knew me, knew me to be kind and honest and religious, friends of mine and I would talk to them and tell them about some of the encounters we had and some of the things I was forced to do and it shocked them. They couldn't picture me doing that and frankly it scared them a little bit because they thought they knew me and yet the me that was talking to them right then was somebody that scared them."

Homer had returned to his native soil, but he was in a shifted universe in which everything had a different meaning to him than to the people around him. He had seen and done things that he knew the people around him did not want to know about, and because of that he knew he could never rejoin them. There were certain images burned into his brain, certain smells seared into his nostrils, certain tastes still on his tongue, and he felt they formed a wall between him and those who had not seen, felt, smelled, or heard what he had. He was afraid that difference made him monstrous. He was afraid that he would turn anyone with whom he truly shared those tastes, those sounds, those sights into himself, and there were some people he loved and wanted to protect, so he remained silent. Besides, he knew that nobody would believe him.

He might tell people, for example, about the time when one of his men out in the jungle on a listening post had been seized by a tiger, felt without any warning the terrible clamp of the animal's jaws on his skull, its hot breath and slobber encasing his face. As he was being dragged off into the trees, the soldier had had the presence of mind to bring the barrel of his M-16 up to the animal's flank and fire. The tiger, wounded, dropped him and disappeared. The GI was left with its mark: two perfect indentations on either side of his forehead. Homer could tell the story, but people would stare at him, say nothing, or worse, say, sure, they'd seen that in *Apocalypse Now,* and think he was making it up. They had the illusion, in their safe lives, that there were no beasts. They didn't understand that the tiger had come into him, Homer, into all of them, eventually, leaving its mark on them and in them and in him. *Here there be tygers,* the old maps marked unknown territory. Once, on a jungle trail, he had been the tiger.

They'd seen that movie, people said. So Homer kept his mouth shut. Sealed his lips. Swallowed it. In the ambush near An Khe he had lain in the elephant and saw grass, next to a boy who'd had the top of his head blown off, and stared into the empty pink skull-cup as the sheltering grass was being mowed down as if by a giant scythe. He knew he would die, and then he went away—the smell of the bullet-mulched grass suddenly wonderfully evocative of peaceful summer lawns, the sun warm and gentle on his face, the noise fading, then suddenly back again, deafening, and then again fading away. Inches away from his eyes he saw a line of ants carrying bits of insect corpses and pieces of a strange pink fungus to their nest, their normality, their indifferent life comforting and amazing him. He slowly felt his body, the details of his own physicality; he could even taste, feel with his tongue, a large chunk of the C-ration ham and eggs he'd had for breakfast still lodged in his cheek. He idly chewed it, and swallowed, detached from the sounds of mortars and grenades and AK-47 rounds cracking over his head. He focused again on the ants, so busy, and he glimpsed again the empty skull of the boy who had gone down near him and it came to him in a wave of bilious nausea what the strange pink chunks carried in those mandibles were, and what that glob of breakfast meat and eggs he'd felt in his cheek and swallowed really was, and he screamed, ignoring the bullets, getting on his hands and knees and projectile vomiting. He didn't tell that story. Even years later, when he wrote it, he put it in italics and red font and warned people not to look at it if they didn't want to be changed. It was the kind of story you sealed behind your lips. How could you kiss anyone again, ever, seal your mouth to the mouth of someone you loved; how would you not be afraid to let her taste what you had tasted?

He had sent the documents he'd taken from the medic's body to his mother. Enough other memories crowded into his mind afterward to allow him to forget the small pile of notebooks and papers. But his mother had lived through a war and its aftermath herself, and she understood his need to preserve what he had taken and what had been taken from him. She carefully stored the documents in a box, which she placed in the attic. They remained there for over three decades, locked away in a space of contained darkness, a physical anamnesis of the memories of the war itself that Homer locked away inside his own mind. It all stayed inside him, not to be opened until he opened.[2]

# CHAPTER SIXTEEN

# The Sorrow
# of War

I f Dam had survived, would he have been different than Homer? Every Vietnamese in the North that I asked vehemently denied that their veterans suffer from trauma. A friend describes her brother, a veteran, who for years after the war compulsively surrounded his house with trenches and booby traps, yet insists that his behavior did not stem from his combat experiences. The veterans themselves also deny the existence of post-traumatic stress disorder (PTSD) among PAVN veterans. Dam's comrade-in-arms Pham Quang Huy gave the typical two-tiered answer: "We were too busy trying to make our living after the war to be crazy. And besides, why should we be bothered when we knew we had done the right thing?" The latter remark adhered to the Party line that there could be no trauma among those who fought for a righteous cause.

I was speaking to Huy in a restaurant near his house in Thai Binh, with the writer Nguyen Qui Duc, who was helping to translate, and Hoang Minh Dieu, Dam's brother-in-law. Huy spoke very softly, and it was hard to hear him, with the usual cacophony of horns blasting in from the street outside and a local

Party official giving a speech to a large, noisy banquet in a large conference room on the floor below us. The rooms in the restaurant were set around a center courtyard where people parked their motor scooters, and the speech, broken by the obligatory microphone screeches that mark high school graduations, intruded into our conversation like official cautions. Huy said he found out about Dam's death from a nurse named Sinh a month after it occurred. Dam had been attached that day to a small reconnaissance patrol made up of local guerrillas, whose mission was to scout out other attack routes. He was apparently engaged in that activity when he ran into Homer. Later, Huy had asked others in the unit what had happened to the body, and was told that Dam had been hastily buried near the village of Plei Ng'on by some local guerrillas, along with the other three casualties. None of the bodies had been identified by name, and the grave was unmarked.

Dieu looked up sharply. "I am a veteran also," he said sternly, and then, suddenly, told us a story about ambushing an American recon patrol in May 1967, and killing all its members—a meeting engagement. He had been a member of a ten-man commando team that had spotted and stalked the Americans and then killed them when they had taken a break before ascending a hill. Afterward, they had buried the American soldiers.[3]

As he told the story, I wondered if it was a kind of brag, payback for Dam. But looking into his eyes, I could see no triumph, only pain. The kind of reciprocity he meant suddenly became clear—he was giving back these men, whom he had secreted into the earth, to their own families, as we were giving back Dam to his family. Bill Deeter, an American who works with the U.S. Remains Recovery Team, later checked out the story and found that the incident had been investigated and the remains of the patrol had been found, exactly where Dieu said they were.[4]

When Dieu read the translation of that report, like Homer, he could see the names of men he had killed. Would he see their fingers working out of the earth in his dreams? I didn't know. I knew what he would say: they were invaders. He had not come to their country; they had come to his. If the positions had been reversed, they could have killed him and not felt a thing. Why should they? And yet that memory, all the vivid details of it, had lingered in his mind all these years, part of a sense of loss, of the missing, that he connected to the loss from his own family.

How many Vietnamese names, comrades and brothers, stirred restless in the soil of Dieu's memory? The dead that haunt combat soldiers for the most part are their own dead, and there were more than enough of those in Viet Nam. Yet one was not permitted to dwell on the deaths of comrades. In an interview with Barbara Crossette of the *New York Times,* war veteran Vu Bao, author of *The Man Who Stained His Soul,* said: "Everybody had to write about the war with revolutionary optimism so that more people would send their sons. . . . When we went South, we saw a lot but kept it in our hearts. Nobody could really discuss the war then—though now everybody does, and they wonder how we could have sacrificed so many people. In the war, when we talked about how many died, we were told to write that they were wounded. But the night my own son went to the battlefield, I said to myself: 'You have to write in a different way about this war. When your son goes to the field of death, you learn how precious human life can be. That changed my way of writing.'"[5]

The denial of psychological trauma in Viet Nam could also be a matter of semantics. At times I had the impression that the people I asked may have related "trauma" to "crazy as a bedbug," like the character in Xuan Thieu's story "Please Don't Knock on My Door," a Viet Cong assassin who would knock on the doors of men and women marked for assassination because they collaborated with the Saigon government and then strangle them with his bare hands, acts that now stained his memories: "There was the choking sound of someone being strangled and the smell of spit gushing with the last breath out of the mouth, a stink that wouldn't fade away even after you'd washed your hands for three days with lemon-scented soap." After the war the former assassin would become insane, a gibbering idiot, if anyone knocked on the door of his flat.[6]

Such a reaction might seem an aberration to many Vietnamese. But author Bao Ninh's veterans, wounded in body and mind and soul, people nearly every page of his famous novel, *The Sorrow of War*. The main character, Kien, can no longer love; his days and nights are haunted by flashbacks; a truck driver still feels the way his treads would rise and then drop as he ran his tank over the heaps of bodies carpeting the highway during the assault on Saigon; veterans hang out at their own bar, drink steadily, and tell each other war stories, as if to validate their pasts; another finds the dead sitting next to him every night as he drives in the Jungle of the Screaming Souls. "Not a night goes by without them waking me up to have a talk," he explains; to him peace is "a tree that thrives only on the blood and bones of fallen comrades. . . . I'm simply a soldier like you who'll now have to live with broken dreams and with pain."[7]

In Hanoi, sitting across from Bao Ninh in a hotel café, I realized that, physically, he reminded me of O'Brien. Both men are compact, their faces not so much sharp as sharpened, their eyes bright, at times with a flare of pain, at times with a gleefully malevolent intelligence, a sardonic, challenging grunt's stare. And they both smoke like hell. We'd tried to interview Ninh in the hotel room, where we could have privacy and silence, but after ten minutes he needed a cigarette. The worst time he'd had since the war, he said, half-joking, was when he'd flown to the States and couldn't smoke for over thirteen hours. In the café, he lit up, drew in a breath, and relaxed. Bao Ninh's character, the writer Kien, spends much of his time wandering the streets of Hanoi, haunted by his memories of the war, his lost chance of love. Outside the hotel now, as in front of most hotels, street vendors were selling pirated copies of *The Sorrow of* War to tourists; along with Graham Green's *The Quiet American*, it is the most popular rip-off for the vendors. The novel has been translated into dozens of languages; it has been called the *All Quiet on the Western Front* of the Viet Nam War.

Like his character, the author fought in many of the major campaigns of the war, including in the Central Highlands where Homer, Dam, and Huy fought. His unit was one of those that entered Saigon when the city fell in April 1975. He returned to his hometown, Hanoi, after six years of war.

In the novel, Kien feels compelled to tell the stories of those he fears have fallen or been forced into silence. The North Vietnamese soldiers returning, victorious, from the war have been ordered not to talk about the terrible casualties that they took; they are told not to ever talk about the bravery of the other side, of the South Vietnamese Army. They know that these things are true, but they are told to keep silent. In some ways, I said to Ninh, it was the same for us. We were not told directly to shut up, but we soon saw nobody really wanted to hear the way it truly was.

He closed his eyes. "Yes, it was the same for the Vietnamese as it was for the Americans," he said. "No one told me, you have to shut your mouth, don't do this, don't do that, but when we came back home, you know it seemed to me that the message was that I should keep silent. And, you know, that kind of silence can be much more irritating than when you are directly told to keep silent. And you are right when you say sometime you have the truth inside you, but you feel you have no right to speak it out, and that in fact motivates you to speak it out. And I have to say that on the Vietnamese side, there were many, many true things, many truths about the Viet Nam war that were hidden."

"Was that why you became a writer, then, because so many truths were hidden?"

He nodded, lit another cigarette, and took a deep drag before answering. The muzak from the hotel loudspeakers played

"Scarborough Fair" for the tenth time, an odd vibe from the other side of the same sixties that took this man to war against us. "The literature of the war at that time couldn't be called literature," he said thoughtfully, blowing two plumes of smoke from his nostrils. "It only showed the ghost of the war, just a ghost shadow of the war. I was very bitter about Vietnamese literature at the time. . . . I felt the Vietnamese people seemed to be waking up from a long dream and they saw the truth. And the ordinary soldier, especially the war veterans also woke up from a long dream, woke up and wanted a change."[8]

The first casualty in war is not truth but the murder of one's own heart, and at bottom it is that sorrow of war of which Bao Ninh writes. Kien's memories center on the battle in his heart, and in the heart of his country, between love and death. *The Sorrow of War* is as much a love story—of failed love—as it is a war story. The pattern of Kien's life is one of rejecting love in favor of war, and part of the controversy about the novel is not only its depiction of the ways the war brutalized and traumatized both soldiers and the culture, but the implication that the war itself was a failure of imagination, a choice of death over love. Kien's first love, his high school sweetheart, Phuong, offers to make love with Kien, but he holds back. "I just think we shouldn't," he stalls. "I'll be going off to war." She doesn't insist, but tells him, "Since your father's death I've often wondered why I loved you so passionately. I'm a free spirit, a rebel out of step in these warring times. You're perfectly suited to them. . . . You loved the idea of going to war; you were headstrong, you wanted to remain pure and loyal to your ideals. I don't want to sound disdainful, but there's nothing original in all that."[9]

Kien is seduced by war. His final chance with Phuong comes when she insists on jumping on the train taking him south to his unit. Again she offers herself; again he is too frightened. Moments later the train is bombed, and in the ensuing chaos, Phuong is brutally raped by another passenger, a man Kien kills. He rejected her, and in the end the war takes her as well, forever hardens and soils both of them. Kien comes to see his prewar self—his pure love for Phuong, unstained as yet by the brutalization, hatred, murder, and moral failures that were the results of his participation in the war—as the only time in his life he was "worthy of being a lover and in love."[10]

In the opening chapter of *The Sorrow of War*, Kien is on an MIA search team, looking for the remains of the dead in the Jungle of Screaming Souls, the ghosts who "were still loose, wandering in every corner and bush in the jungle, drifting along the stream, refusing to depart for the other world." Kien imagines "the screaming souls gathered together on festival days as members of the Lost Battalion." The dead were real; they were inextricably woven into the lives of the survivors. "To Kien dead soldiers were more shadowy and yet sometimes more significant than the living. They were lonely, tranquil, and hopeful, like illusions. . . . 'If you can't identify them by name we'll be burdened by their deaths for the rest of our lives,' the head of the MIA team had said."[11]

Kien is not only haunted by the dead; he is a living ghost himself. He exists as a repository for the ghosts of his unit and his generation. At the end of the novel he disappears, leaving the manuscript he wrote to be burned by the mute woman with whom he lived, a safely silent witness who waits at the end, with "the loyalty of a reader," for Kien to reappear, to put his story together for her. The unidentified narrator tries to piece together a sequence for Kien's jumbled pages. He reads through the manuscript and physically works through its pages, the way Homer went through Dam's pockets, finding the same kind of artifacts: "Mixed among the pages I found musical scores, curriculum vitae, award certificates, a pack of cards torn and worn and dirty." Kien has left pieces of himself, pieces of his story, but he is gone. "Was he any of those ghosts, or of those remains dug up in the jungle?"[12] the narrator asks. Kien has become one of the Missing.

# CHAPTER SEVENTEEN

# Tibby

H omer stayed in the army until 1975, all in stateside berths. His career had seemed to be on the fast track; he was selected for the Infantry Officers Advance Class, a prep school for career development. But the war was still there: 12,000 miles away, but its rot was moving into the wounded corpus of the army. The pamphlets that had fallen onto his position on Hill 467 had been jokes to him and his men, with their call to defect and their query, "Who will be the last soldier to die in Viet Nam?" But by the 1970s soldiers no longer needed that question to be exploded onto their perimeters; it was exploding in their own heads, and the numbers of fraggings—men killing their own senior NCOs and officers who were too enthusiastic about putting them in harm's way—increased so much that Congress called for an investigation.[13] The racial tension that was splitting American society was also mirrored in the microcosm of the army, and the mellowness of marijuana had been replaced by the mean of heroin, the pure stuff, pure as adrenaline; a hooked vet could kill himself looking for its equivalent high back on the street, and many did: Robert Stone's *Dog Soldiers*, bringing it all back home, only home was no longer there.

Homer had lost his belief in the institution that had sustained him. An army, Jonathan Shay writes, is "a moral world that most of the participants most of the time regard as legitimate, 'natural' and personally binding. . . . When a leader destroys the legitimacy of the army's moral order by betraying 'what's right,' he inflicts manifold injuries on his men."[14] This statement applies equally to the authority that an army exists to serve and protect. Jack Kennedy admonished you to ask what you could do for your country. But you could not feature that what you did—and what was done to you—in Viet Nam was what he had in mind. There is a certain "destruction of the capability for social trust."[15] Alpha Company is not only inserted on top of an enemy regiment without support, an act of incompetence that is later unabashedly credited as the key to a victory, but then command lies about the number of casualties the company suffered as well. You and your men desperately need water and machine gun ammunition; instead, a seemingly inept or indifferent or possibly insane commander sends freeze-dried rations that have to be prepared with water. Or the enemy and the population you have been told you were there to protect are inextricably braided together, and the gauge of victory is the body count—all leading to that spoken and unspoken mantra for murder, "If it's dead and it's Vietnamese, it's Viet Cong." Or you are sent to kill and die in an unnecessary war that an administration propagates out of a fabric of lies—nonexistent attacks against destroyers, a nonexistent monolithic and menacing communism, nonexistent weapons of mass destruction—that the government either instigates, creates, or carelessly chooses to believe. "[Viet Nam] is the place where everybody finds out who they are," Stone's character Converse says to his friend Hicks in *Dog Soldiers,* as he tries to convince him to smuggle heroin back to the States. "What a bummer for the gooks," Hicks replies.[16]

As it had for Kien, the war had become for many soldiers what Robert Jay Lifton would call "an exercise in survival rather than a defense of national values" to which the soldier could not ultimately "connect his own actions with ultimately humane principles, and . . . come to feel he has performed a dirty but necessary job."[17] What was the purpose of the death and suffering of—and the killing by—Task Force Alpha in holding and then leaving Hill 467? What was its *task* in a war from which most soldiers knew America was already withdrawing, as they themselves would from that hill? What was the destination of the eternal hump under the triple canopy of the jungle? Why didn't the people they had come to save want to be saved from themselves?

"At the time," Homer says of his enlistment, "at least until I was a couple of months in country, I thought I was going to save the world from communism. I thought it was a serious threat and that if we didn't stop it, it was just going to snowball and that the next thing you know we'd have red flags flying in downtown Bamberg."

His belief had not lasted; it lost its shine in the red mud, rusted to a fragile shell in the monsoon rains. "We carried, along with our packs and rifles, the implicit convictions that the Viet Cong would be quickly beaten and that we were doing something altogether noble and good. We kept the packs and rifles; the convictions we lost,"[18] wrote Philip Caputo. Without those sustaining convictions, even if they were buried deep and only disinterred back into consciousness after the war, many could not live with the deaths they had witnessed or dealt. They could not, the psychologists would say, put them into an acceptable narrative. Some tried to don masks of normalcy that they hoped would eventually become their faces. In time, many would come to dance to the prevailing shuck and jive that the war was necessary and righteous, that except for small aberrations, it was void of atrocity, and that passage through the fire of war was ultimately an ennobling ordeal. Others went into the antiwar movement, enlisting this time in hope of redemption and in need of new certainty to replace the sense of formless loss that floated them, unmoored, through their days. Others would come to feel, at best, that they had killed only in order to survive, or they would find moral justification in the necessity of that killing to protect or avenge their friends, shifting their sense of loyalty and meaning away from the abstractions of country and cause to the flesh and blood of the brothers sharing the same sacrifices and dangers. It was a displacement that could infuse meaning and sustain sanity at the time, but it was not enough to get many through the long, isolating days and longer nights after the war. It was not enough for Homer.

In 1973 the Paris Peace talks had ended and the last major American ground units withdrew from Viet Nam. Two years later, Viet Nam had fallen or risen, depending on the lens through which one viewed history, and the American army began thinning its own ranks, looking to slough off the debris of the war and reinvent itself. Homer was given the choice of going regular army, with a twenty-year commitment, or taking $15,000 and a discharge, with the GI Bill to attend college. He went to a combat buddy, a major, who told Homer he could go back and finish the last two years of his BA program at Columbus College, in Georgia, with full pay and tuition, under an army program in which he would still officially be in the service until he got his degree. Homer says, "I was 27 years old, a Captain, on the Major's list for promotion, which would put me into competition with men 7–10 years older than I was. They were into golf, bridge, and alcohol. I was into skydiving, motorcycle and sports car racing, flying, underwater cave diving, marijuana, and was single. Your wife's and your social skills were essential to continued career development once you made Major, so I read the handwriting on the wall and got out. As messed up as I was at this time, I had no idea what I might want to do with

my life 10–20 years down the road. I opted for a college education and civilian life."[19]

At Columbus, he did not go back to the science major he
had started with, a thousand years before, at Clemson. Instead
he opted for a philosophy major, searching for some method-
ology of meaning instead of physics, celestial or otherwise. He
knew how things worked, but he knew also how things could
and would fly apart. By the time he graduated in 1975, he had
been promoted to major, and his army career was over. He had
saved up enough to go to graduate school at the University of
South Carolina in the College of Liberal Arts; he earned a master's in sociology from that institution in 1979.

Throughout all of it, he continued racing, diving—all his
on-the-edge sports. While he was still working toward his
master's, he had become fascinated by the then-new field of
computers, and had made himself an expert in the early forms
of information technology, working in the university's newly
formed computer lab. After he graduated he was hired as a pro-
grammer, and when the assistant director of the computer lab
retired, he was offered and took that position. He loved the
work, threw himself into it. Computers were a new technology,
and learning their ways permitted him to use his brain and cre-
ativity without human complications. It challenged him in some
of the ways the war had challenged him. It also allowed him to
be subsumed. "Dedication, sometimes going over the line into
fanaticism, is normal for combat veterans in the workplace,"
notes Dr. Shay.[20]

Homer needed time to disappear. He needed to fill his mind
with anything but memories. In the computer center he was an
XO again, making sure the unit ran smoothly, assigning work,
organizing, dealing with mechanical and personnel problems,
sending out his recons into hyperspace or the even trickier world
of academia, where tactical decisions were important but nobody died, not even him. It was intellectual adrenaline. Inside,

he kept himself blank. "I didn't hate, I didn't fear, I didn't love, I didn't feel joy," he said later, "I was a zombie. I was a robot. I was good, I worked with computers, and I was mechanically perfect. But I had no feelings." Like Bao Ninh's character Kien, his emotions had frozen into a defensive crouch.

The Nez Perce warrior tells how the elders "knew that my spirit would be wounded. They said I would be lonely and that I would find no comfort in family, friends, elders or spirits. I would be cut off from both beauty and pain. My dreams and visions would be dark and frightening. My days and nights would be filled with searching and not finding. I would be unable to find the connections between myself and the rest of creation. I would look forward to an early death. And I would need cleansing and healing in all these things."[21]

Lacking a smoke lodge or wise elders, Homer bought a trailer for himself, an improbably pink-colored Fleetwood singlewide (he was color-blind), in the countryside outside Columbia, about thirty miles from his workplace. The inside of the structure was dank and foul as a cave; outside was the neat, carefully kept garden of a farm boy. He was surrounded by acres of pine forest; he lived like a hermit. He was in a bunker, the stories still locked inside himself, Dam's documents still hidden away in a box in his mother's attic.

Occasionally there was a woman, though most of his relationships tended not to last. The one that did—for a year—was with a woman later diagnosed as schizophrenic. Instead he had the job, always the job, challenging enough to fill his time and his thoughts and to keep him from dwelling too much on the past. But being a workaholic was finally what allowed him, in 1991, to met Elizabeth "Tibby" Dozier, the administrative assistant for the university's Institute of Southern Studies. Her computer had died. She was not used to the new machines, hated them, and now this one was getting back at her for her bad atti-

tude. The technician Homer would usually send to deal with
that kind of problem was out that day, so he went himself. At
first Tibby didn't know how to take this tall, wiry man. "I could
sense his intensity and deep patience all at the same time," she
recalls. "His hair was very short and he had a little goatee which
gave his face a sharp look. I noticed that he would rarely look
me in the eye but concentrated totally on the computer problem. That is, until he saw my bird's nests scattered all over the
office. I had collected nests for years and some of the professors
and students would bring abandoned nests for me to add to my
collection.[22]

"Homer's eyes lit up when he saw the nests. He exclaimed,
'You love nests too?' That is when he visibly relaxed and we sat
down to talk. And talk. And talk, gradually realizing that we
had found kindred spirits in each other."

They should have represented the opposite edges of the cultural gap that the war had supposedly opened in their generation, in the country: the ex-army officer combat veteran and the
former marcher for peace and civil rights. But Tibby Dozier was
also the daughter and granddaughter and great-granddaughter
of soldiers—her paternal family's military history was as long as
its history in South Carolina, and both went as far back as the
Revolution. If there is such a thing as a southern military tradition, the Dozier men, at least their generations in the wars of
the twentieth century, were its *Junker* class. Tibby understood
the nightmares and secrets—and strengths—of soldiers, but
also the rare and careful gentleness that marked certain men
who have come back from broken places.

These were qualities she would come to recognize in
Homer because she had seen them before, in her father. *His* father, James Cordie Dozier, had won the Congressional Medal of
Honor when he was a first lieutenant, a platoon commander, in
World War I, for almost single-handedly wiping out a machine
gun nest pinning down his men; he had killed the entire machine gun crew and taken prisoner other Germans he discovered

hiding out nearby. When he returned to South Carolina, he was feted as a hero, made fund-raising speeches for the Liberty Loan being floated to pay off the expenses of the war, married Miss Margaret Tallulah Little, and eventually rose to the rank of general in the National Guard—the appointed Adjutant General of South Carolina.[23] Tibby's father, James Charles Dozier, grew up at Camp Jackson, South Carolina, where Homer would later be stationed (then Fort Jackson), a military brat, the commanding general's son. He went straight from the parade grounds of his childhood to The Citadel, graduating as a second lieutenant in 1942, and to the Pacific War, serving as a parachute artillery officer with the 11th Airborne Division and coming back to the United States with a Bronze Star and a Purple Heart. The following year he met and fell immediately in love with Betty Jean Connor. They were married in 1948; Tibby was born four years later, in Columbia, and her sister, Jean, three years after that, in 1955.

For much of the rest of her father's life, he remained, in one way or another, a soldier, at first with the South Carolina National Guard and then, in 1961, going back on active duty. The South Carolinian writer Pat Conroy has novelized parts of his own background in a military family. The protests of his doppelganger main character against the inequities and injustices of The Citadel and segregation, and against the waste of the war, are continuations of the character's and Conroy's battle against the tyrannical militarism a damaged warrior father inflicted on his family. But Tibby's father was no Santini. He was the other sort of man that sometimes comes home from wars, a gentle and strong man with a quirky sense of humor and play. In the morning he would wake his girls for school by blasting "Zarathustra," the theme from *2001: A Space Odyssey*, into their room. He taught them the essentials of fishing and poker, and other things that still remain with her. "Daddy gave me my love of reading, science fiction, movies, and a sense of the ridiculous," Tibby recalls. "He was an English major at The Citadel and taught me to love words. He taught us self-discipline. He taught us to be true to ourselves and to try to treat everyone with respect no matter who they were or what their background was. He and Mama gave us a sense of self and a deep foundation of love that has carried my sister and me through our adult lives."

James and Betty revealed another possibility that stayed with Tibby as well. She remembers her father and mother dancing together in the living room to romantic music playing on the record player, holding hands as they walked. She held their example in her mind like a rebuke during her own first marriage, when she was twenty, to an alcoholic; the relationship had dissolved after four disastrous years.

But if her father was an exemplar of the gentling that might come from war, Tibby saw some of its darker effects as well. Her mother's brother, Wally, had gone into the army after high school and fought in the infantry in Europe. "He saw the worst of war," Tibby says, "bodies nailed to poles, horrible combat experiences and returned to the U.S. a broken man. He spent the remainder of his life in a VA hospital, a gentle, kind man who still saw German soldiers hiding behind trees. My earliest memories of him involve his experiences and how my parents explained to me what had happened to Uncle Wally. So I grew up understanding what war can do to a man, how the horrors can be etched on a brain forever. I was never afraid of Uncle Wally. Even when he 'saw' the soldiers hiding outside, he would also say, 'Honey, stay close to me. I'll keep you safe.' It broke my heart."

She remembers how the family was told to just leave her uncle alone, as he sat by himself smoking endlessly, at the bottom of some dark and fetid pool of memories. He was finally committed to a state hospital, and later to the VA Hospital in Augusta, Georgia, after he had gone out on a date and started choking the girl he was with, calling her "a dirty fraulein." Searching his room later, his parents found a cache of weapons hidden under his bed. The VA wanted to cut the war out of his head with a lobotomy, but his mother, Tibby's grandmother, Nina Hinson Connor, adamantly refused. "She was a very strong

woman," Tibby says. "[My uncle] spent the remainder of his life
at the VA Hospital in Dublin, Georgia, where we all visited him
as often as possible. In his later years, he improved and was no
longer seeing enemy soldiers, but remained mentally in the
1940s. He died in 1998 and is buried in Elmwood Cemetery in
Columbia, SC in a family plot."

Tibby's parents broke the Great Santini stereotype in another way: they remained all their lives strong, liberal Demo-
crats, enthusiastic supporters of John Fitzgerald Kennedy.
Tibby remembers seeing and cheering him as he spoke in Columbia during his presidential campaign. Her father, through
his National Guard connections, knew the route Kennedy's mo-
torcade would take out of town, and he and Betty and Tibby
stood alone on the side of the road as the senator's car rode by,
her father yelling, "Hello, Jack!" Kennedy waved from the
backseat, a move that thrilled Tibby but that perhaps her
mother would recall in a few years when she learned of the assassination and saw the films from Dallas and for the first time
in her life wept in front of her daughters. When Kennedy won,
Betty pinned a "Kennedy Wins! Hooray!" card on Tibby's dress
when she went to school, an occasion that allowed Tibby to
learn that Jack Kennedy was not appreciated by everybody in
her home state.

Neither were her parents' views on the forced segregation of
the races, a given during Tibby's childhood, as it was during
Homer's. Both of their fathers described the institution and
what they thought of it—and how they dealt with it—in nearly
the same terms. Tibby says, "What began the foundation for
my views throughout life began with a conversation I had with
my father when I was only six years old. I asked 'Daddy, why do
the colored people have to sit on the back of the bus?' His response, 'Honey, there is a law that says they have to, but that
doesn't mean it's right.' What a wonderful thing to say to a
child! It showed me to look beneath the surface of things from

a young age and taught me to question the establishment. It was a moment of illumination."

It was also a lesson she was able to apply. Integration started in South Carolina in 1963. By the time Tibby enrolled in Hand Junior High School the next year, two black students were attending the school. One of them, Cheryl Frazier, was in her homeroom. Tibby was twelve years old and suffering the usual terrors at the transition from grammar school to the big kids' school. "The only other person in the room who looked as scared as me was Cheryl," she remembers. The two girls sat together, and remained friends through high school graduation, Tibby the center of "a protective circle of girls [who] surrounded Cheryl and tried to keep her from harm."

But by 1968, Tibby had found and was pushing past the limits of her parents' liberalism. The chasm that opened between them that year reflected the rift opening up all over America as the children, not of conservative parents, but of the politically liberal, took their parents' ideals to heart and to the next level. They were the Vietnamese, learning the French ideals of liberty, equality, fraternity, and then, infuriatingly, demanding they actually be implemented. In Tibby's case, it was her father's attitude toward Martin Luther King Jr., whom she admired as a great man, that plunged her into a period of disillusionment about the parents she had until then thought perfect. Colonel James Dozier, like many high-ranking National Guard officers, was the recipient of a flood of memos from J. Edgar Hoover's FBI concerning the perfidies of King. There were bitter and increasingly tense discussions about him—and about the Viet Nam War—between father and daughter, and mother and daughter; when King was assassinated, the discussion deteriorated into shouting matches. After Robert Kennedy was killed in Los Angeles, Tibby lost her belief in the system completely, paining her father, and leading to a bitterness between them that would last

until the passions of the decade had cooled down. By the time
her father passed away in 1990, of heart and kidney disease,
they had become as close to each other, or perhaps closer than,
they had been when Tibby was growing up. "Fortunately," Tibby
says, "my parents and I were able to reach a wonderful understanding and respect of each other later in life."

In high school Tibby wore a black armband against the war. Yet
in spite of her opposition, she was still a soldier's daughter, and
most of the men she dated in high school were young soldiers at
Fort Jackson, on their way to Viet Nam. She would meet them
at dances at the USO—dances Homer, also stationed at Fort
Jackson at the time, was too shy to attend.

   In 1991, after her encounter with Homer in her office, she
forgot about the tall, quiet man for awhile, and drifted into another destructive relationship, a pattern she had fallen into
since the end of her disastrous marriage. Homer was also dating
someone else, although, Tibby says, "both relationships were
terribly destructive and both of us went through major soul
changes as a result." By 1993 they had formed a friendship,
writing to and confiding in each other, but Tibby, unable to
equate consideration and understanding with her experience of
romantic relationships, did not see it as anything more.

   What began to change her mind was a fishing trip. Fishing
had always made her feel closest to her father, the two of them
sitting quietly, side by side, for hours. Now Homer invited her
to go to a place that was very special to him, a low country cypress swamp that he had known since his boyhood. He came by
to pick her up at 5:00 A.M. and was surprised when he found
Tibby ready; he regarded her as a city girl. As they drove through
the quilted low country darkness, Tibby was pleasantly surprised by his consideration when he offered to stop for coffee or
cough drops: she was a heavy smoker and had an early-morning
hacking cough. She was no longer used to men who didn't
think primarily of themselves.

They arrived as the sun was rising, the place lovely in the dawn light. "A dark water swamp filled with cypress trees where the only sounds were the morning birds filling the wild area with their songs. When we first put the boat in the water, I saw what looked like dozens of white handkerchiefs flittering through the cypress trees. As we watched in awe, beautiful white egrets flew out of the trees, over our boat circling above us. It was their lovely wings I had seen through the trees."

Bringing her here was the revelation of a private heart, and she felt the sheath of ice she had allowed to form around her own heart begin to melt. "I have to admit," Tibby says, "that Homer reminded me very much of my father as he sat and fished, calmly and quietly." They spent the day on the water, and later he took her to Bamberg to meet Betty. Tibby was surprised that Homer's mother and her own had the same first name. The two women hit it off, delighted with each other.

Sometime soon after, as she sat with Homer and some friends watching a movie in her house, she realized that she had fallen in love. "The room," she says, "seemed to get brighter and the final chunk of ice fell from my heart." She kept the revelation to herself. She had not told him about all her past mistakes, the things she regarded as shameful secrets; she expected that when she did, he would fade out of her life. But she knew she needed to find that out and invited him over, still as a friend, telling him she needed to talk to him. That night, as everything she had locked inside poured out, Homer sat quietly and listened. His own secrets, the dark and bloody things he had kept hidden for so long, had not forgiven himself for, did away with any inclination he may have had to judge her; he listened as the wounded know how to listen to the wounded. She sensed that ability in him, though she did not yet know what it came from, and she was able to open up to him.

A few days later a tornado struck the area near Homer's trailer, and when he went to see if there was any damage, Tibby, confronted with the fragility natural disasters always bring, realized that she needed to tell him how she felt. She invited him to her house, the house she had inherited from her grand-parents, a place of safety for her, and told him she was in love with him.

Homer and Tibby were married on February 14, 1995, in a quiet ceremony in her mother's living room.

# CHAPTER EIGHTEEN

# The Song of a Soldier's Wife

*In a typical story of that time, a young girl would marry a young man in a hasty wedding; they would only spend ten days, or a week or even only three days together, and then the man would go to the war, never to return. His death would be known by the authorities, but since the announcement of casualties would affect morale, it would be decided to conceal the news for one year, then five years and then ten years. The girl would reach her 30s and then more, still waiting for her husband, still nourishing the hope of his return, while still struggling to survive life during time of war: digging underground shelters, enduring evacuations, nursing her parents and her in-laws, her youthful nights spent without the company of a man. This tragedy of women's fate happened everywhere.*[24]

—LE MINH KHUE

Dam's widow, Pham Thi Minh, looks worn by the harsh realities and disappointments of her life. Though she did not seem concerned with the lack of acceptance by the Hoang family, she had her own regrets about not going to meet Dam just before he went to the war. "I wish I could have had a daughter with [Dam]," she said, "I would have never married again. My current husband was also a soldier, wounded in the war, but he is an alcoholic, and I'm miserable. I keep thinking, if only I had a daughter with Dam, then my life would not be this miserable. . . . I know war. . . . It was horrible—all the young people had to go. My biggest memory of that time was when we had ceremonies to see young people off to the front. Families and everybody would come see them off, and we all cried, even the officials. We did not have much hope that they would come back, and so it was as if we were parting, forever parting."[25]

In Vietnamese culture, a childless woman such as Pham Thi Minh is regarded as unfulfilled, in a sense still a child herself, no matter her age. But beyond the social pressure to have a child, there is the simple and profound ache of loneliness that is another legacy of the war, particularly for women. "You had to work in the fields for food and you have to take care of the eldest and youngest in the family and at the same time you have to try to fight against the enemy from the sky and on the ground," said Da Ngan, a woman novelist who was a Viet Cong fighter in the South during the war. "It seems to me I experienced all the bitter tastes of the war. . . . When I began to write, I wrote about the things that I understood best. That I was haunted by the most. So my theme, the theme of my writing is the fate of the women. Many writers like Bao Ninh describe the lives of soldiers, the hardness of the war. But my theme is the fate of women in the war."[26]

Thousands, unlike Minh, did not ever have the chance to remarry. Many of the girls who had gone as teenage volunteers to serve on the Ho Chi Minh Trails spent their womanhood in the war and came back old before their time, often wounded or wracked by illnesses, undesired and outcast. It was a situation Ho Anh Thai described in *The Women on the Island*, a novel about a group of women veterans kept on as a labor brigade long after the war has ended. At a group meeting, one of them expresses her misery: "We have peace now, but the men we were waiting for never returned. . . . But if at least I had a child, I would be consoled in many ways. If I hadn't been so concerned with 'preserving' myself all those years ago, at least I could have had a child with my beloved. And at least I wouldn't have to suffer like I do now. But he's dead, with all the rest, and who did I keep myself for? What do I need with my virginity, when all it does is bring me loneliness? The collective can help me strengthen my will-power, it can console me a bit. But the collective can't bring me private happiness."[27]

The traditional Confucian role of the woman subordinating self in favor of family (or in time of war, in favor of the state or the revolution) is a vein that runs through Vietnamese literature. The most famous woman in Vietnamese literature is the character Thuy Kieu, who, in "The Tale of Kieu," Nguyen Du's famous nineteenth-century epic poem—the national poem of Viet Nam—is virtuous, but allows herself to be sold into prostitution to protect her family. The virtue of female self-sacrifice is so deep that it trumps even sexual virtue. The woman poet Ho Xuan Huong challenged, or at least revealed the price to the soul of, that notion of duty with the subtle, subversive sexuality of her poetry.[28] But second in fame to Thuy Kieu as a female icon is the narrator in "The Song of the Soldier's Wife," the role Pham Thi Minh was expected to fulfill, waiting patiently and sadly at home for her warrior husband:

> Your way leads you to lands of rain and wind—
> mine takes me back to our old room, our bed.
> We turn and look, but all has come between—
> green mountains and blue clouds roll on and on.[29]

"The Song of a Soldier's Wife" is attributed (in the original Chinese version) to an eighteenth-century male poet, Dang Tran Con, and there is still some controversy about whether the version most Vietnamese people know was translated into Vietnamese by a woman poet, Doan Thi Diem, or a male scholar, Phan Huy Ich. Its protagonist models a traditional Confucian feminine ideal of—or, interpreted differently, reveals a different, more subversive feminine yearning for—peace, and an end to a seemingly endless war, passed down from one generation to the other like a curse. It is the subtext of Pham Thi Minh's cry that she wished she had had a daughter, not a son, a seeming contradiction of the Vietnamese desire for male children. A whole vein of ancient proverbs proclaims the value of having sons: "One boy, that's something; ten girls, that's nothing." "A hundred girls aren't worth a single testicle."[30] But sons go to war. They disappear.

Daughters do as well. The Confucian ideal of submissive femininity in Viet Nam had always been contradicted and challenged by the female warriors, who (mainly for that same reason, the death of their men) populate ancient and modern Vietnamese history. Every city and major town has a main boulevard called Hai Ba Trung, named after the two Trung sisters who, after the Chinese killed their husbands, led an insurrection in AD 40 and set up, for a time, an independent state. The Trung sisters, usually depicted mounted on war elephants, are seen on family altars, in temples, and on postage stamps; their four slogans—*"Foremost I will avenge my country, second, I will restore the Hung lineage, thirdly, I will avenge my husband. Lastly, I vow these goals will be accomplished"*— are memorized by schoolchildren.

The modern incarnations of the Trung sisters are the women, such as Da Ngan, who fought as combatants in the National Liberation Front, and those who joined the Youth Volunteer Brigades in the North. There seems a need these days in Viet Nam to turn to the idealized past these women represent, reflected most recently in the great enthusiasm that greeted the publication of the diary of Dr. Dang Thuy Tram, a young army doctor killed in Quang Ngai in 1970. Her diary, like Dam's documents, had been saved from burning by an American soldier, who later returned it to her family.[31] The sincerity and purity of her patriotism, the clarity of her belief, expressed in deeply personal and passionate language, reminded—or informed— Vietnamese readers of something they felt was missing, extracted from themselves and therefore nameless, as the country went through the sea changes and upheavals of globalization, a turn away from the communal to the individual that was economically desirable. Although this was no small matter in a country that had suffered the deprivations Viet Nam had, at times it left many feeling that a certain idealism had been subtracted from their lives. Dr. Dang's voice, from the pages of her rescued diary, reminded people of who they were, or at least of who they had at one time wanted or thought themselves to be. Hundreds of thousands of copies were sold.

Le Minh Khue—the woman who sat across from me at a breakfast table in Boston—would have been condemned to be a legend like Dr. Dang, if she had not survived the war. She had been a member of the Youth Volunteer Brigades—but unlike the manless and childless women Ho Anh Thai described in *The Women on the Island*, their lives forever frozen in the war—Khue was able to marry and have a child when she returned to Hanoi, after four years on the Ho Chi Minh Trails and another five as a war correspondent. Her life during those years could be an exemplar of the idealistic, battered generation of young northerners, at least the educated men and women from the cities who experienced the war and its aftermath. She is the daughter of schoolteachers who were brutally wrenched from the lives of Khue and her sister during the upheavals of the Land Reform movement of the 1950s. Her father was denounced as a class enemy and was murdered by a mob, stoned and then drowned in a village pond, and her mother committed suicide. Both girls were taken in and raised by an aunt and uncle, dedicated communists who, although she came to regard them as too naïve, unwilling to see the flaws in the system, imbued her with a revolutionary and patriotic fervor that led her to lie about her age, at fifteen, and enlist in the Youth Volunteers Brigades. She never forgave those responsible for the death of her parents, but by the time she was in her second year of high school, her hatred had been transferred to the Americans invading her country. That same year, in a village south of Hanoi, she had seen women clutching their children protectively to their chests, frozen by fire into a row of melted statues after an American bombing attack.

Sent to the Truong Son Trails through Thanh Hoa—the same route Dam followed—Khue helped explode or defuse unexploded American bombs, the former by digging carefully around the impacted missile until enough space was cleared to delicately pack in gelignite charges, an activity that took the lives of many of her friends. She served in the volunteers from 1965 to 1969, in the southern part of North Viet Nam and in Quang Tri, working the system of trails that snaked near Khe Sanh, just south of the DMZ. The Youth Volunteers consisted of high school kids, mostly girls; the boys would stay in only until they were old enough to go to the regular army. Small groups of teenagers would be responsible for maintaining a kilometer of trail, disposing bombs, filling in craters, and often constructing coffins and burying dead soldiers. Khue describes one situation in her autobiographical story "The Distant Stars"—her first published fiction, written when she was nineteen and still in the war: "There were three of us. Three girls. We lived in a cavern at the foot of a strategic hill. The trail led past the front of the cave and on up the hillside somewhere, very far. It had been punctured by bombs, mixing the red and white soil together. Neither side of the trail had any sign of vegetation. There were only stripped and burned tree trunks, uprooted trees . . . and twisted parts of cars, rusting in the earth." Yet the girls sustained themselves with the way the trail, and the country, would be rebuilt into something new and wonderful when the war was won.

"All . . . of us understood this. We understood and believed it with a fierce faith."[32]

Khue was discharged from the Youth Volunteers in 1969, the year of Dam's death, but unable to bear what she felt was the indifference and hypocrisy of life in Hanoi while soldiers were still dying in the South, she became a war correspondent, witnessing many more battles until the final victory of her side. In a speech given to a writers' conference in Korea, she recalls feeling not triumph, but a sense of premonitory dread: "In 1975, I was 25, moving with a troop of soldiers from our base in the jungle to the city of Da Nang. After the jubilance of flags and flowers, people who had been on both sides of the war became bewildered by something they found strange and difficult to adapt to. Writers normally have a strong sense of premonition, and looking at that city where the Americans had chopped down all the trees to eliminate the Viet Cong's hiding places, exposing the bare fronts of the buildings, the heated tin sheets of the roofs, the stores filled with a plethora of imported goods in a city with no large manufacturing industry, I had the premonition that eventually the conflict would continue between the two sides despite the fact that the guns had fallen silent. The winners were too full of confidence and haughtiness to remember that the losers were also Vietnamese."[33]

The fear that the war that had split the country would remain an open and suppurating wound between the two Vietnamese sides became one of the connecting themes of her writing, a theme she has sometimes been in trouble with the authorities for pursuing. In a story called "As Fragile as a Ray of Sunlight," her character is a PAVN woman doctor who falls in love with one of her patients, a wounded South Vietnamese POW, whom she never sees again, but with whom she always hopes to be reunited. "Now twenty years have passed and many barriers have been torn down. And yet her hope has never been fulfilled."[34]

All of Khue's fiction is about loss, separations from other people, from one's conception of oneself. About the loss of love. Love was easy in the life-and-death clarity of war. She remembers walking over a plank bridge in the middle of a stream, holding a box of ammunition, when she was spotted and attacked by a single American plane, its rocket splashing and exploding into the water near her, freezing her in fear, an image of herself, the slight teenager and the multi-million-dollar aircraft freezing in her mind also, an encapsulation of the war. A young soldier finally ran out onto the bridge and pulled her back to shore. She immediately fell in love with him. Close to death, and with many young heroes around her, she fell in love often. "Men," she wrote, "were purer then. The war reaffirmed their worth, living as they did always on the cusp of destruction. . . . During such times, any Vietnamese man could be a hero, and Vietnamese women lived through their inspiration. . . . This love, springing from admiration, sustained Vietnamese women from battle to battle. Vietnamese men also were bound by a purity of intent during the war, and this attitude affected the way they regarded and respected women—and were respected by women."[35]

But the war that created such men also rendered them empty husks, as unfit for peace as Homer. "Those same men became completely different people when they came back from the war and were separated from their rifles. They felt impotent to deal with a life that needed reconstruction; they had lost the idea or value of beauty and sustainability. . . . In the time of peace, women eventually no longer faced grave material deprivation but instead became spiritually exhausted, starved of affection. They could not enjoy a cultured form of love, or even of sex—Vietnamese men being exceptionally ignorant of this highly rated activity. Incompetent in management and construction, the man who was the hero of the past became the loser of the present. The young generation, growing up and seeing the bad example of their elders, had to struggle hard to create and confirm their own values."

"The war years were both the worst time and the best time for me," Khue had told me before. They were a time during which the depth of sacrifice could still be tied to a purity of hope. The sorrow of war for her was her fear that its sacrifices were not worthy of its results. In all her stories of material and spiritual corruption after the war, the three girls in "The Distant Stars"—like Dr. Dang—are always there, an invisible, disappointed audience peering out of the mouth of their cave at the wasteland still around them. Seeing how distant the stars still are, the dream from the reality. The three girls become an invisible but prescient—and disapproving—presence, the wandering souls, in Khue's postwar fiction. The world they envisioned being built out of their sacrifices does not appear. Their elders, deformed by war, could not create a beautiful peace. "I want to speak about the tragedy of our country thirty years after the war ended," Le Minh Khue said. "What I mean by this is that the culture of Viet Nam was heavily devastated . . . and that devastation has had a bad effect on every aspect of our lives."[36] One of Khue's translators, Dana Sachs, wrote that Khue's "change in outlook [after her first story, "The Distant Stars"] parallels a pervasive sense of disappointment both among Vietnamese writers from the North and within post-war Vietnamese society as a whole. Le Minh Khue's language of lost ideals uses stylistic qualities such as narrative detachment, complex characterizations, contrasts between past and present, and precise, telling details to convey that sense of disillusionment."[37]

A language of lost ideals. In her stories, families murder each other over American dollars, pimp themselves to foreigners, and have extramarital affairs to give some purpose to lives and relationships that have become meaningless and loveless. Towns will sell off their own cemeteries, memorializing the war dead, to land speculators. Sons will kill fathers for possession of some American bones they can sell: "Dao and I dug them up," Tham said. "There was a chain around the neck with a name printed on it. The end of the name had peeled off, but the words 'Tony D' were still clear, and you could just read the serial number on it. Dao took the tag to try to find a buyer for the bones. Dao knows what he's doing—these are 100 percent American bones. He even took the measurements."[38]

In the end, the prevailing sense of loss and waste, of disillusionment, in Le Minh Khue's stories, reflected also in the work of the other postwar Vietnamese writers—Bao Ninh, Ho Anh Thai, Da Ngan, the exiled Duong Thu Huong, and many more—is the rebuttal to the contention that a sense of meaning and of national purpose, which the American combatants lacked, prevented trauma. Their "Good War" no more lacked an aftermath of psychological wounding than World War II had for American veterans.

And here is where the loss of the capacity to love and trust that Khue and Bao Ninh described in their generation of veterans mirrors the sense of displacement and the shell of emotional numbness that marked Homer and his generation of veterans. For many of Khue's peers, particularly writers—by avocation and profession seers—the perceived rupture of the social contract, the loss of faith in the ability of authority to create a society worthy of the great sacrifices of the war, was a wound from which they could not recover, even while they struggled through their art to communicate the wisdom that could be gained from that wound. The same "destruction of the capacity for social trust" that Homer felt, and that is so embedded in American writing about the war, is also prevalent in the black humor and depictions of corruption, bleak situations, and hopeless relationships in the work of the *doi moi* Vietnamese writers. For the American veterans, that loss of trust was ultimately caused by loss of faith in an authority that led us into a war whose circumstances, Michael Norman writes in *These Good Men*—its "maddening politics, its sad history, its mismanagement and bungled prosecution—exposed more dramatically than in any other war the lunatic motives that lead to organized butchery and the awful waste that results from it. In our era, it was easy to see that the sacrifice had been for nothing and that perhaps nothing was worth the sacrifice."[39] The Vietnamese on the other side of that war for the most part do not question its justice or necessity, but rather the failure of vested authority—those given the mandate of heaven—to create a postwar society worthy of the sacrifices of their generation. Kien, the protagonist of *The Sorrow of War,* asks another veteran, "Isn't peace better than war?" The other replies: "This kind of peace? In this kind of peace it seems people have unmasked themselves and revealed their true, horrible selves. So much blood, so many lives were sacrificed—for what?"[40]

The disappointment isn't merely a sense of ideological failure; there is anger and disillusionment both with the abuses and incompetence of the communist system and the inequalities and cultural erosion of the free market system that replaced it— or even, in the case of Le Minh Khue, simply with "men," the traditional holders of power in a Confucian hierarchy. What elevates disappointment into trauma is the price that the veterans had seen paid for the flawed postwar world they received: the piles of corpses, the young girls Khue stood next to robbed of their lives—the ashes of victory.

"I remember," she says, "many of my friends who were killed during the war and I think that perhaps they were luckier than me, because I am alive and I had to witness all of the suffering of thirty years of war and the post-war life and they don't have to suffer all these things. . . . Over the last thirty years, each day is a different war. Of course, I feel badly about losing my friends. They died young, they died bravely, and they never had the chance to experience happiness. But I believe if they had lived, they would suffer like I have. Most of my writing is not directly about the war. I prefer to describe the indirect aspects of war, and generally, I prefer to write about the spiritual legacy of our country. I think that war, the aftermath of war is like dioxin; it will take a very long time to get out that dioxin, that poison out of our system."[41]

"The war ended more than 30 years ago, but I don't know when its consequences will end," Pham Thi Minh had said. "The war still lingers, like blood trickling in our hearts."

# CHAPTER NINETEEN

# The
# Attic

He had not spoken much to her about his experiences in the war, but Tibby was certain that Homer's intensity and the way he threw himself so deeply into his work hid some deep, unexpressed pain. It was probably part of her attraction to him. After their marriage, the inner stress he was under became more apparent to her. It was never something she feared as a threat to herself; it was never manifested in that way. She could see that instead he turned it all in on himself. It was something she recognized. "Homer confessed that he had had deep suicidal thoughts many times. I began to understand why he had isolated himself on ten acres of land so far from his job where he lived alone with only the woods and his garden for company. He told me about his addiction to adrenalin sports after Vietnam and also about having a drinking problem when he first returned from the war. Very gradually, I began to see how Homer's experiences in Vietnam had shaped and damaged him. He was strengthened by his command experiences and devastated by the loss of some of his men and the killing of others in combat. . . . My family understood this. Uncle Wally's experiences and my father's combat experiences (of which he rarely spoke) gave them an empathy that possibly other families would not have had. Within the safety of our relationship, Homer began to open up to me. On our first New Year's Eve together, Homer lit a candle for one of his close friends who died in Vietnam with him. He cried as he lit the candle and I hugged him tight."[42]

As long as he was working, Homer was able to keep his focus from swinging back to the memories. In 2004, however, he retired from his job, and he and Tibby bought a house in the mountains of the Pisgah National Forest in western North Carolina. "[Once he retired] I made it my goal," Tibby said, "to break down these barriers. And things have changed so much in the last three years. . . . I think having the time to go ahead and confront some of these memories helped."[43]

Homer confronted some of them through the movies. He and Tibby had gone away on a trip. When they stopped at the video rental in town on their way back, Homer saw the cover of the film *We Were Soldiers,* Mel Gibson's adaptation of the story of the Ia Drang battle. As one of the survivors of that battle told me, the film is "85% real, 15% Hollywood." The Hollywood part is Gibson leading a *Braveheart*-style charge to break the back of the North Vietnamese resistance. But both in terms of the terrain and the fighting, the film is startlingly real, and the scenes of North Vietnamese soldiers swarming the perimeter at Ia Drang had to remind Homer of Hill 467.

"I went to bed and took a nap," Tibby says, "and started hearing what I thought was an animal wailing." She got up and went in the other room, to find Homer in front of the screen, hugging his knees. "I didn't realize I was making enough noise for her to hear," Homer says.[44]

When I spoke with Tim O'Brien, at a conference about the thirtieth anniversary of the end of the war, I asked him the question probably hundreds of people had already asked him, the question I was asking myself: Why do you continue to write about it?

"Because it validates my memory," he'd answered.

Why would anyone need to validate memory?

For him it had been like this, Tim said: "You go through a day of bewilderment and lost-ness, and I mean lost in all kinds of ways, geographically and spiritually. And at the end of the day when the other guys would horse around, after we dug our fox-holes for the night, I'd spend the last half-hour of twilight writing these little anecdotes about an event of that day, or a thought I may have had. Or I'd just simply describe a moment of astonishing beauty. A lagoon at sunset or the color of a mountain ridge. Putting it on paper. It's the same impulse that makes us want to take pictures at birthday parties or at weddings. You know you're getting married, or you know there's a birthday, but it fixes it in a way that you have to validate memory. My childhood was real, there is the sandbox and there is the photograph."[45]

That had been the impulse, at the beginning. We needed to confirm that it happened the way we remembered it, because the country was busy either not wanting to hear or turning it all into more acceptable myths, killing the dead all over again. They clamored in Homer's head to have their stories told before they were again lost. Everything had been real. What happened existed as Dam's journal existed and as Dam's soul existed in that journal, the soul his family knew was there and wanted returned. It existed as its own obligation.

⁓

In Joseph Campbell's description of the "Journey of the Hero" monomyth, the journeyer is self-driven into exile by a sense that something essential is lacking in the community that nourished him. He goes down into a dark place peopled by demons, accompanied by a guide of doubtful nature, and there receives a wound. But the traveler survives that wound, and not only learns from the wounding but brings that received wisdom back to the community.[46] The hero uses what he has learned—the wisdom of the wound—to change or fill what was missing in that community. The heroism is not so much in the journey as in the return; the journeyer makes the choice of moving back into his world again and attempting to fix it. That contemplation and universalizing of the hard-won wisdom of wounds is the difference between memory as therapy and memory as art, the difference between the therapeutic and the heroic. Philip Caputo describes the process in his postscript to *A Rumor of War:* "The job of the battle-singer is to wring order and meaning out of the chaotic clash of arms, to keep the tribe human by providing it with models of virtuous behavior—heroes who reflected the tribe's loftiest aspirations—and with examples of impious behavior that reflected its worst failings."[47]

Art, myth, and psychology mix, each an incarnation of the other. The need of some writers to wound the place they come from so that it can learn what they have learned, what it is responsible for, and so be worthy of homecoming, is echoed in Dr. Judith Herman's description of trauma and recovery. Trauma occurs, she writes, when a horrible event or events cause a break in one's own life narrative. On the other side of that break, you can no longer see yourself in the same way. Recovery from trauma starts to occur when you are able to tell your story, in sensory detail, to people willing to listen without judgment and willing to be changed by what they hear—in other words, when you can be taken back into a community that is willing to be wounded itself, willing to break through a comforting shell of protective myths and learn what you have learned.[48] "Healing from trauma depends upon communalization of the trauma,"[49] writes Jonathan Shay. The damaged past must be brought back up into the light and contemplated for meaning before it can be mourned; it is what the individual must do for himself or herself, what the artist can create for the community, as O'Brien creates, in art, the face he could not bear to look into before. If this communalization does not happen, you remain forever alienated, forever exiled, forever outside your community—you are what Hoang Ngoc Dam came to be for his family, what the Vietnamese call a wandering soul.[50]

Homer had reached a point, with Tibby's urging, where he needed and wanted to confront his war memories by sharing them in a way that would make people listen and be changed: changed enough that he could rejoin them. Time, Tibby, and the movies—seeing his experience, all he had learned to keep shut inside, made into story—began to liberate him to tell his own story

He did so through his own medium, creating a Web site that contained a detailed account of his time in the war, complete with journals, commentaries, lexicons, cross-referenced photographs, letters, and stories.[51] It was his way of taking on the mantle and duty of his given name. But when he tried to remember, incidents would flee from him, his mind refuse to seize them. While he was getting the site together, he called his mother and asked if she still had any of the letters he had sent her during the war. A few days later she called back. "She had kept all the letters I'd sent her from Vietnam, and she said 'I've got some stuff here that looks like medical drawings and it looks like it's written in Vietnamese. I think you sent it to me while you were over there.'"[52]

At the time he had written a letter to his parents telling about the young North Vietnamese soldier he had killed, flatly, without emotion, as if writing an After Action Report for himself, filing the incident someplace deep in his mind and heart, to be opened up, whether he chose to or not, at a time when murder was not the normal and desired goal of each day. He had turned over to S-2 the documents he'd taken from Dam's body, but later he asked the intelligence officer, a friend, if he could have the documents back. When he had received them, he had packaged them neatly and sent them back to his mother in Bamberg, asking her to keep them for him. Now the details of the incident came flooding back to him in a rush.

Homer's memories had remained locked in the darkness of the box his mother had kept for him, in the greater darkness of the attic. He drew them out now, into the light. At first he went through his letters. Although he had deliberately left out of them any graphic details, he was able to read what he had not written between the lines, spurring his memory. Finally he turned to the two small notebooks and documents scrawled in alien letters. He picked up one book, opened it. As he stared at Dam's elegant writing and delicate anatomical drawings, the memories of that moment of his first kill came flooding back.

Later he would show the captured documents to Tibby. "I remember looking at the beautiful artwork of human anatomy that Dam had drawn," she says, "and feeling anger at the waste of such an incredible life."[53]

"I realized that I wanted to try and get those back to whoever they belonged to, just simply because it belonged to them and it would probably be the last thing they had from that individual," Homer says. "So I was really interested in giving them back, but I had no idea how I was going to do it."[54]

He asked his friends, anyone else who had been in Pleiku, including Tom Lacombe, who by now had written his own book, *Light Ruck*. Tom and his wife, Jean, operated a small country store up in the Blue Ridge Mountains, near Skyline Drive and the Shenandoah Valley. He was from my part of Maryland, the flatlands of the Western Shore of the Chesapeake, but like Homer, he had chosen after the war to live in mountains. He also had an ancestor who fought in the Civil War (though on the Union side), and he had as well a need, and a way, to deal with his ghosts. "When I came home," he says, "many Americans didn't want to know about Ziggy, didn't care about Beaver, or Bill, or Morris, or Lew, or Hill 947 or LZ Swift. A couple of years after the war, I started writing about my experiences, as a way of remembering, a form of memorial."[55]

We met at a book festival where Tim had been invited to read from *Light Ruck*. A few weeks later, he asked me if I could help Homer find the family of the man he had killed.

Hoang Ngoc Dam

Homer R. Steedly, Jr.

Homer R. Steedly today

Homer and Tibby Steedly

Homer R. Steedly, Sr.

Mom's Passport Photo
for trip to America

Betty Steedly ne
Babette Gumbmann,
passport photo

Left to right:
Homer, Nancy, Anthony, Linda

Hoang family altar.
Photos of Dam and brother Chi, both KIA on left,
parents Hoang Dinh Can (father) and Pham Thi Lanh
(mother) on the right.

Front row, left to right: Hoang Minh Dieu, Hoang Thi Tham,
Hoang Huy Luong, Phan Thanh Hao, Hoang Thi Tuoi, Hoang Thi Dam,
and Dam's widow Pham Thi Minh.
*Photos by George Evans.*

Lt. Homer R. Steedly, Jr.

Captain James W. DeRoos.
*Photo by Homer Steedly.*

Homer and his platoon sergeant

B Company soldiers bathing at Polei Keng
moments before a mortar attack.
*Photo by Homer R. Steedly, Jr.*

B Company Weapons Platoon survivors of Hill 467.
*Photo courtesy of Robert M. Granger.*

E Company GIs on Fire Support Base 20. At the far
left is PFC Frederick Herrera, one of the three MIAs
just before the battle for Hill 467.
*Photo by James W. DeRoos.*

George Evans' friend William Edward Dick, Jr.

The cover of
Hoang Ngoc Dam's notebook.

Pages 1 and 2 of the notebook.
*Photos by Homer Steedly.*

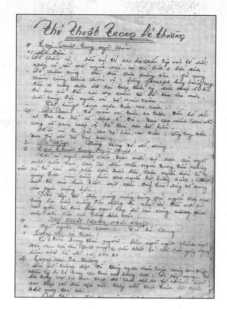

Dam's medic's notes:
midwivery skills

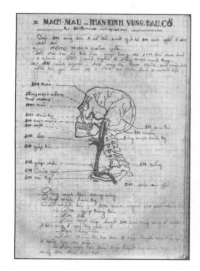

Dam's drawing and notes of
brain and neck injuries

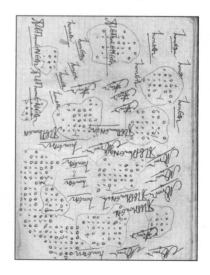

Last page of notebook,
with tic tac toe game.

*Photos by Homer Steedly.*

2005: Author handing Dam's
documents to brother Hoang Dang
Cat as Dam's army mentor Pham
Quang Huy looks on.
*Photo by George Evans.*

After the document return: Daisy Zamora, George Evans, and
author (far left, front two rows) with the extended Hoang family.
To the author's left is Hoang Minh Dieu, Phan Thanh Hao,
Hoang Huy Luong, Hoang Thi Tuoi,
unknown, and writer Y Ban. Dam's widow Pham Thi Minh is
directly behind Phan Thanh Hao, two rows up.

Homer returns, 2008:
bringing offering to the family altar

Homer placing incense sticks
in front of Dam's photograph.
*Photos by Jessica Phillips.*

Army driver's license of Nguyen Van Hai,
taken off Dam's body.

In Vinh, left to right, front row: Lt. Col. Nguyen Thi Tien, Nguyen
Van Hai, Homer; back row:
Doug Reese, author, Bill Deeter.
*Photo by Jessica Phillips.*

The ceremony at Mang Yang Pass;
left to right, Tuoi, Dieu Cat, Homer, and Luong

Hoang Minh Dieu.
*Photos by Jessica Phillips.*

Mang Yang Pass:
the concrete retaining wall at the
base of the hill where Dam was
killed.

Mang Yang Pass:
The tree the patrol used as a spotting point.
*Photos by Homer Steedly.*

Homer hands Dam's remains to sister Tuoi at
Thai Binh station. Translator
Doan Anh Quan on train.
*Photo by Jessica Phillips.*

The funeral:
Homer at Dam's altar

The funeral:
Homer and PAVN pallbearers.
*Photos by Doug Reese.*

The funeral procession from Thai Giang to the cemetery

Homer throws the first dirt into Dam's grave.
*Photos by Jessica Phillips.*

# PART THREE

# WANDERING
# SOULS

# CHAPTER TWENTY

# The Missing

We want the bones. We want all the bones. You will hear this. Good people will say it. They are all good people. They say it. They say: We want the bones. And they mean it, they mean what they say. They carry it into sleep, into their children, into the voting booth. We want the bones. That's what we want. We don't want the ghosts. You keep the ghosts. We don't want them. Just the bones.

Your ghosts are driving us out of our minds.

—GEORGE EVANS, FROM "A WALK IN THE GARDEN OF HEAVEN"[1]

No, I told them, there are no American bones here.

The Americans left years ago and took their bones with them.

These skeletons, scattered all over our land,
Belong only to Vietnamese.

—VAN LE, FROM "QUANG TRI"[2]

In the Vietnamese belief, the spirits of those killed away from home, through violence or accident or war, wander the earth aimlessly, far from the family altar. One hundred and forty-two from Dam's home village of Thai Giang, including both Dam and his younger brother Hoang Dang Chi died in the war.[3] In 1972 Dam's father, Hoang Dinh Can, and his mother, Pham Thi Lanh, were given official notification of Dam's and Chi's deaths, one after the other. Dam's younger brother Hoang Dang Cat recalls: "My mother died when she was 58. . . . After she received the news of Dam's death she began to have heart problems. Then with the news of my second brother's death, Mr. Hoang Van Chi, she became worse. She had gotten wind of my second brother's death from people who wrote back from the front, and became very ill, so the family had to ask the authorities to not notify her in order to prolong her life, but she still passed away."[4] Their father passed away a short time later.

Dam had "cavorted with happiness" when he found he was being sent to the front; Pham Thi Lanh had wept, and sniffed his clothes after he left. She understood the enormity of what she would lose and the likelihood of it happening, as it had generation after generation in Thai Giang, in Viet Nam.

Before Pham Thi Lanh passed away, she consulted several fortune-tellers—perhaps the right term is mediums—to try to locate her sons' remains, or to see if perhaps the notifications of their deaths were incorrect. One told her that Chi was gone, his body in the ocean; something that turned out to be true. Cat says: "My brother Chi—some people told us they heard the news on the BBC announcing that my brother Hoang Dang Chi had been captured. But I heard from a person named Hoang Mai Nam, who is my uncle's son, and was the political officer at the island Con Dao prison. My brother was on a ship or a motor-boat without numbers going out to the island, on a commando raid, and my cousin was the one who was supposed to rendezvous with him. But the boat was bombed by American aircraft and sank."[5]

The same medium then told her that Dam was still alive, but had gone abroad, and that he would return one day "in glory." The revelation puzzled and disturbed Dam's family, and they tried to keep what the woman said to themselves. If the other villagers heard it, they might assume that Dam had deserted, gone over to the enemy. But the rumor leaked out anyway and continued to circulate, even though Dam's family would receive more information about the circumstances and place of Dam's death through his friend Pham Quang Huy, who had finally returned from the war.

The last time Huy had seen Dam was when he was treated for his second wound, at the H67 dispensary unit; the last he had heard of him was when the nurse, Sinh, told him how Dam had died and where he might be buried. The family was grateful for the news, which held out the possibility that Dam's remains might actually be found and brought back to rest in the village. Is this what the medium had meant by "return in glory"?

By 2002, the Hoang family was doing well. Cat, still a farmer, became the head of the local Party organization, Tham passed her medical exams, Luong had become an engineer, and Tuoi owned a restaurant. It was time, the family decided, to see if they could find Dam's grave and bring him home. They had talked about it for years, and with Huy's retirement, and hence his ability to help them search, and their own growing prosperity, it seemed time to meet what they felt was an unfulfilled duty. "In the spiritual life of Vietnamese people," Cat explains, "we believe in *song gui thac ve*, which means that people who live in this life need to rest in their home soil after their death, so their descendants will remember and light incense for them, and we the living will be at peace. If we can't find his body, then we will forever have to think about an unfulfilled task, because according to our tradition everybody has to go back to his place of origin to be buried."[6]

The two brothers, Luong and Cat, and brother-in-law Dieu traveled south with Huy to Dam's old battlefield. Luong says:

"In the provincial office they still have a lot of documents about my brother. The province provided us with a Russian jeep to go look for his remains. We found a lot of guerillas of that time because Mr. Huy can speak the local, ethnic dialogues. We went to the mountain near the spring where they think my brother had died. Mr. Vang, a guerilla, took us there."

Huy explains: "I found a unit head who was a member of the ethnic minority group, the Banhar, who had buried Dam. Four people died there, two Vietnamese and two ethnic minorities. In 1978 there was a unit that was tasked with getting the remains and bringing them back and to bury them in the military cemetery. We came out there to get the remains of the four into the cemetery, but regretfully they made a mistake and now we don't know which one of the four was Dam. The [Banhar], one, they are not very educated; two, they are not concerned very much with remains; three, they have a custom that after three years, they just destroy their cemeteries, they don't keep the remains. So when they were unearthing the remains of the four, they placed each one in a bag, they put them in a woven basket, like a woven knapsack and they carried that over to the soldiers who were tasked with this, but they didn't clearly mark who was what. So we know [they buried them] in the cemetery of Ayunpa with thirty other soldiers. . . . [B]ut of the thirty-four we cannot be sure [which was Dam]."

Before the trip, the family had once again consulted a medium, a woman from their village. Luong recounts: "She told us the general area, told us the cemetery, told us the order of the graves. And it matched what we found when we went."

I ask if she had known anything about the site beforehand. "She drew a map. When we followed it we were happy to find [the graves], but the problem was that the medium said you may find a grave that had the wrong middle name or the wrong accent marks. But when we found the one grave in that spot on the map, it was a grave without any name at all. When we got there we had the one grave that they had been pointed to had some dried flowers on it, and that gave us the sense it may have been the one, but we were not sure. So we called the medium, and she asked us if there were any special objects around. But we did not tell her, because we wanted information from her, rather than give her information from us. So then she said, then get a betel nut and chop it up and tell me if it is empty or if it has some things inside. But we said we were not going to tell her that either, we were not getting information from her. So then she said to go get an egg, because it is a custom to do an egg and a chopstick."

"An egg and a chopstick?" I ask.

Luong, caught up in the story, ignores me. "But even if it worked," he says, "it would not tell us anything. We did not trust her anymore. So now we do not know where my brother is."[7]

The brothers had hoped to find Dam's bones and bring them home to be placed among the family tombs. But all they could do was grieve for all the anonymous dead in that place. There were no remains, and no objects to be put on the family altar, to draw his soul back to the family hearth.

Dam had become one of the 300,000 wandering souls—the missing in action from the war—that still haunt Viet Nam. In our conversation, Huy had reflected the widespread denial that the war lingers in any significant way in the form of psychological trauma. It is as if the arc of trauma and recovery has been given corporality in the form of the dead who still need to be discovered, disinterred, and brought home again, wrapped into the lives of their families.

Without their remains, or at least some object or objects that belonged to them, being brought home and the proper ceremonies followed—without, that is, commemoration and contemplation, a physical knitting back into the community—neither they, nor their families, could find peace, in the simplest and most profound meaning of that word. As long as they remained lost, the war would never be over.[8]

It is hard to imagine 300,000 missing in action, the emotional toll of knowing not only that the sons and daughters, husbands and wives who went to the war would never return, but also that one would also never know how they died, nor get back their remains. Yet there is a parallel in our own history. In spite of its essential difference—our involvement—the Viet Nam War has, rightfully, been compared to the American Civil War, a war in which families often had combatants on both sides, which resolved the different self-definitions of the country through massive murder and set its future direction, and which killed off a sizeable portion of its population. Some 620,000 Americans died in our Civil War—the equivalent of six million Americans out of today's population. Half of those casualties— the same number as in Viet Nam—were never identified. In an interview with *Washington Post* reporter Bob Thompson, Harvard President Drew Gilpin Faust, author of *The Republic of Suffering: Death and the American Civil War,* described how the families of dead soldiers tried desperately to find the remains of their loved ones and their inability to work through their grief when they couldn't.[9]

That same desperation, filtered and magnified through Vietnamese culture, is still a driving force in many Vietnamese households, and perhaps for similar reasons, which go beyond custom, or which custom had been created to address and soothe.[10] "We believe that people who live in this life need to rest in their home soil after their death, so their descendants will remember and light incense for them, and we the living will be at peace," Cat had said. But if a body could not be recovered, then at least objects that belonged to that person could be placed on the family altar and allow the family the peace of which Cat spoke. The Hoangs had failed to locate Dam's body. They did not yet know that his notebook and other papers had been sitting in an attic in Bamberg, South Carolina, and were now back in Homer's hands.

Although the face-to-face encounter that had cost Dam's life was rare in that war, Homer's impulse to hang onto the documents was not. Nearly all North Vietnamese soldiers and Southern National Liberation Front fighters kept journals or diaries, in which they wrote and copied poetry, their thoughts, and the events of their days, and it was common practice for American GIs to take and keep these or to give them to intelligence. So many personal documents were captured that eventually thousands were put on microfiche and are now stored in the National Archives. No one knows how many thousands more were taken by individual GIs, to be brought home, stored away, locked up. The lag between locking the documents away and bringing them into the light again, the need, decades later, to not only confront and tell the unfinished past, but also to redeem it through concrete acts, was also a common reaction. Over the last ten years, many veterans have made the effort Homer vowed to make back in 1969: to find the families of the men or women whose documents and diaries they kept and return them. To date more than 9,000 have been returned to veterans' organizations in Viet Nam through the Vietnam Veterans of America Initiative Program.[11]

No one has epitomized the need to name and return the dead more than a former lieutenant colonel in the People's Army of Viet Nam named Nguyen Thi Tien. She had engaged in a one-woman, decades-long search to find and bring such artifacts—and even remains—back to the families of the missing.

She did not look like any colonel I had ever seen. Waiting for her in a café in Hanoi where we had arranged to meet, scanning the faces of the people entering, Phan Thanh Hao and I looked right past her when she walked in. Both of us expected someone more severe and humorless, not this grinning woman wearing a mauve silk scarf with a Ralph Lauren logo on it, a tastefully subdued gray blouse and dress, and a string of pearls.

As soon as we sat, she looked at me, her face stamped with concern, and asked something Hao did not catch.

"She is asking about a Wick?"

I nodded. "Wick. Sedgwick Tourison."

"Yes," Tien said. "I worry so much about his health. Is he taking care of himself?"

Wick, a former army intelligence analyst, fluent in Vietnamese, was the man who had put me in contact with Tien. He and Tien had developed an e-mail friendship. They shared an interest in the missing. After Wick had retired as a highly decorated chief warrant officer—working in Cambodia and Laos as well as Viet Nam—in 1978, he went to work for the Defense Intelligence Agency's Special Office for POW/MIA Affairs as acting branch chief of the Analysis Branch from 1983 to 1988, when he resigned in protest against the way the MIA issue was being handled.[12] In 1991 Wick had published a book, *Talking with Victor Charlie,* that described his experiences in military intelligence from 1965 to 1967—"Not including," he wrote to me, "many issues too painful to put into print." What he couldn't describe led, on July 1, 1998, to a nervous breakdown, during which he almost killed himself. "Just too many Viet Nam memories I kept bottled up for three decades appeared out of nowhere," he explained. Retired, he works part-time as an interpreter for cases with Vietnamese complainants or defendants. The job is often emotionally wearing. "Each time I approach the court," he said, "I am back in Viet Nam getting ready for another interrogation session which, when I was with my Vietnamese counterparts, was quite brutal. I can say that now, I could not say that in 1998." What had helped him the most was his relationship with Vietnamese friends—particularly those who had been on the other side of the war. He met Tien through a mutual friend, Tham, who worked for the Vietnam News Agency. Mrs. Tham's father was a PAVN captain whose remains were somewhere in Laos. "If you want to understand how deeply the issue of recovering remains affects families," she told Wick, "you need to meet Tien."

Wick did, and the two began to e-mail each other frequently. His fluent Vietnamese, Tien's military background, and the intimate distancing of the Internet allowed him to open up in ways he could not previously have done. "My relationship with Colonel Tien is a very special relationship that has done more than the VA to begin the process of healing," he says. "She knows everything about me, my previous work during the war, and the daymare ghosts that haunt me each time I go into a court to interpret. . . . I have described many of the ghosts to Tien, the worst of which was watching a prisoner being beaten to the point that he died. His body was dumped down a well. There is nothing I could have done at the time to stop the two ARVN interrogators, for reasons too long to go into here. But, I've seen it all and kept it inside."

He had seemed fine when I'd seen him, I told Tien, and she smiled and nodded. I was touched by her concern. "It is strange how those who used to hate us so much have now turned into being our healers," Wick had said to me.[13]

Bringing ghosts to rest was a role Tien had been performing for years, though she had not started out her life with the idea of becoming a professional army officer, let alone the legendary angel of the missing she would become. In the university she studied literature and then museum design management. But she had grown up in Nghe An province during the war, in a farming village outside the provincial capital, Vinh. The province, located just north of the 17th parallel, is famous as the birthplace of Ho Chi Minh and for the tough nationalism of its inhabitants. As a child, and as a teenager, too young to go to the war herself, Tien had experienced the intense bombing of that province; she had witnessed the deaths of many of her friends and had watched the endless stream of soldiers moving to the South, to disappear into the war. "There were so many of my friends who left and did not return to school," she said. "The day we parted and they went to battle, we young women fled behind the school house to cry our hearts out, not knowing if our boyfriends who were leaving would return to continue their schooling or not. They left forever and never returned."[14]

When she graduated from university, she taught folklore at Da Lat College in the South for a few years before having what she called "an inexplicable urge" to join the army. In 1994, then a major, she became deputy director of the Military Region 4 museum in her hometown of Vinh. One of her duties was to categorize and store recovered artifacts from battlefields and burial sites, the pathetic remnants of lives. She was not directly involved with efforts to locate and recover bodies, though she knew that by that time army teams had recovered 15,000 remains, of which only 600 had been positively identified.

What would become the driving mission of her life was solidified for her one day when she went to Thanh Hoa to meet an army recovery team bringing actual human remains back from Laos. "It was January 13, 2000," she recalls. "The team had found a group of thirty markers, out in the jungle. Just a clearing in the jungle." Sixty bodies were disinterred from that place, but only two had anything with their names on them. She had stood in the rain trembling during the Buddhist ceremony marking their return, staring at the markers on which only the words "war martyr" had been written; seeing the endless stream of friends and relatives who had disappeared from her life into the war; and wondering if any of them might be among the dead she had just helped bury. And thinking of those they had left behind, the families and lovers who would never know what had happened to them. "I made a silent vow to the souls there," she says, "that I would do all I could to find all their names."

There is a passage in Philip Caputo's memoir *A Rumor of War*, in which Caputo comes across a packet of letters and photos from some Viet Cong he and his men had killed. They made

him wonder "if the other side had a system, as we did, for noti-
fying the families of casualties. I hoped so. I did not like to
think of those women, dreaming of returns that could never be,
waiting for letters that would never come."[15]

This same vision had seized and motivated Tien. And yet in
that similarity was also a telling difference. Caputo wanted to
bring peace to the living, Tien to assuage the living and the
dead, wrapped inextricably as they are in Vietnamese families.
"Each day I light incense in the room where the artifacts of the
war dead are kept. The atmosphere is filled with silence and
the scent of incense. I sense, next to each artifact, the soul of the
nameless departed who is not yet able to return to his family. . . .
It is my constant fear that time will move on too quickly and
the items in this room will continue to lie here silently just like the
other artifacts that remain cold and lonely in the wilderness."[16]

She started going out with the army teams looking for
gravesites in the jungles of Laos or in distant provinces. The
teams were usually all-male, and the terrain they searched was
often very rough. At first they were reluctant to take her, a
middle-aged woman. But the soldiers came to respect her dedication. She would sleep under their trucks, just as they did,
and would slow-crawl with them through streams, mud, and
heavy bush, the ground still scattered with unexploded ordnance, to get to the remains of dead soldiers.

Over the following years, alone or with the army teams, she
investigated the locations of battles, finding hastily dug single
or mass graves. Rotting in the earth would be wallets, water-
damaged photos, carvings, and combs made from the fragments
of airplanes—a fact that reminded me of a famous short story
by Ho Anh Thai called "A Fragment of a Man," in which a war
widow who has never recovered from her grief tries frantically
to reconstruct her life with her husband from the fragments, the
scraps, she hunts for in their backyard, including such a comb,
carved with her husband's initials.[17] It was the first story of
Thai's I had ever read, and Tien's descriptions of what she found

was another moment for me in which Vietnamese fiction was suddenly illuminated and given context by the reality that had created it.

Trained in restoration and reconstruction through her museum work, Tien was horrified to learn that most of the time the soldiers on the recovery teams were immediately burying the objects they found with bodies next to those remains. She had to convince them that the spirits of the dead wanted her to use those materials to find their families.

For the most part, she relied on DNA and other scientific methods to detect or confirm her finds. The clues to their identities were often minuscule: two banknotes sandwiching an employment certificate, on which she found, with a magnifying glass, the fragment of a seal from an army engineering unit; the faded, blood-stained picture of a soldier's mother whose style of dress was from a particular region that Tien's own mother helped identify. I asked her about the "egg and chopstick" that Luong had mentioned. She grinned skeptically and explained the custom to me: "A chopstick is stuck in the earth of a gravesite, an egg placed on the point. If the egg doesn't drop, that's the correct grave." She laughed. "If they do it enough times, they'll eventually manage to balance the egg."

In spite of her belief in the efficacy of science, she still prayed to the spirit of the dead she was trying to name to help her return them to their families. At times she would rely on what she called the invisible bonds among family members: a mother, sick at heart because her eighteen-year-old son went to war without ever having a proper meal because the family was poor and he was always hungry. Her son's body was in a mass grave. Tien was able to identify a scrap of aluminum with the words *Cung An*, eat together, inscribed on it in the rotted uniform pocket on one of the skeletons; it was his mother's nickname for him, and DNA testing confirmed that this was her son. Tien had dozens of similar stories. "The war has moved further away, further into the past," she wrote to me later, trying to articulate her passion. "Only those people who are tied to their nation and to her people forever still remain, even though it is only through half a shirt, a button, a razor blade, a pen, a comb or the picture of a mother. They all glisten with the soul and sadness that sustained the life of the person who carried it."[18]

Something in Tien's obsessiveness, her very need to bring the missing home, had allowed her to develop an affinity with them, whether it was in the way her mind processed and connected the bits and pieces of evidence to their sources, or the way her eyes learned to see the ground. It was an affinity proven by her success. She had done more as one individual than teams of searchers, sometimes traveling thousands of kilometers in a week, rushing to get to a recovery site whenever she was notified—as her reputation grew, soldiers on the MIA teams agreed to call her whenever their team located remains—before the objects could be buried. She used any transportation she could to get to the sites, at times even hopping freight trains. Her fame also grew as a result of her method of locating families. She would publish photos of found objects in the newspapers and appear with them on public affairs television programs, consciously building up her own legend in order to get people to watch and listen. She began to get hundreds of phone calls and letters, begging for her help; by the time I met her, she had received over 5,000 letters. Soon she noticed that her fame also had a different effect. It is considered unlucky to touch the dead in Viet Nam, except during certain ceremonies, and when she traveled in buses or on trains, people would edge away from her, leave her plenty of space, afraid she was bringing the belongings or even the actual remains of the deceased with her. Sometimes they were right. She carried bones in her rucksack, and could feel them jutting into the skin of her back, pressing toward her heart.

"Were you ever scared of the dead?" I ask.

"At first. I was touching the dead with my bare hands. It is not something we are used to. I'd have to stop and take a deep

breath. But not any more. I burn an incense stick at the site, and
I tell them: I'm trying to bring you back to your family." She
smiles. "These days I'm only afraid of time. But I am tired."

"Why did you take all this onto yourself?" I asked.

"Have you ever seen our military cemeteries?"

"Some of them."

"Then you've seen those same rows and rows of headstones
without names. They were like blank pages to me, but each one
was a life that needed to be recalled. I felt an urgent need to fill
in the names on those empty headstones."[19]

CHAPTER TWENTY-ONE

# The
# Altar

Homer's tabula rasa was his Web site. He had spent hours scanning Dam's documents into it, and I spent more hours staring at them, taken by the delicacy of the drawings, the careful penmanship of the writing, its neatness made poignant by the fact and manner of the writer's death. Homer had contacted Lacombe; Tom had contacted me. But the idea of finding the family, in the wake of the national upheaval that the war had been, in the sea of 300,000 missing, seemed far-fetched. I had tried, ten years after the war, to get in touch with the family of a friend of mine who had been killed flying a mission I was supposed to be on, only to find that his relatives had died or moved away. How much more difficult would it be in Viet Nam?

Tom had also e-mailed Doug Reese, a veteran who was married to a Vietnamese woman and now lived in Viet Nam, arranging and leading tours for American vets. Reese saw a reflection of his own experience in Homer's. He had been an army advisor to an ARVN unit in the Mekong Delta when he was sent as liaison

to the Navy Swiftboats working his area, assigned with a contingent of ARVN troops to one captained by a Lieutenant
John Kerry. He had been on Kerry's boat when the future senator came ashore and shot a Viet Cong; at that same time, Reese
had shot and killed another VC who'd been waiting in ambush.
During one of his initial returns to Viet Nam, Reese met the
brother of the man he'd killed the day that he had stepped
ashore with Kerry. When he heard about Homer, he became fascinated with the similarities—if not of their stories, of their
need to attempt to close those circles, confront the killings of
their youth.[20]

Now Lacombe thought Reese's on-the-ground knowledge
might help. I asked him for advice on how to proceed; he rec-
ommended turning over the documents to the Vietnam Veterans'
Association in Hanoi, which had its own methods of finding
families.

That sounded right. But meanwhile I e-mailed two of my
closest friends in Viet Nam: Phan Thanh Hao, the translator of
*The Sorrow of War* and my collaborator on the series of books by
Vietnamese writers my publisher in the United States had put
out, and Ho Anh Thai. I sent along the scans as e-mail attachments. They both told me that the best solution was to take the
documents in May, when I was planning to go to Viet Nam anyway, and to hand them over to the Vietnamese Veterans' Association, as Reese had suggested. I e-mailed back, saying that I
would do that. But meanwhile, could they possibly write some
articles about the situation and see if anyone responded?

Thai agreed, saying he would get something published in
*Lao Dong* (*Labor*), one of the largest newspapers in the country.

But Phan Thanh Hao sighed when she saw my request, a
cold weight filling her chest. The story I had described in my
e-mail, I reminded her, was a real-life version of *Song of the
Stork*, a film directed by her son, Binh, and produced by her
daughter-in-law, Hanh. In 2002 they had asked me to write part
of a script for that film. Both their parents had been deeply af-

fected by the war, and they wanted the story told. But they did not want to do what they claimed the American films about the war did—leave out the story of the other side, dehumanize the Americans. They wanted me, instead, to write a substory into the script about an American soldier who nearly kills a North Vietnamese soldier, a poet. Looking down at his wounded body, the American sees the poet's journal and takes that book instead of the man's life—or maybe because it is the man's life. Twenty-five years later he wants to find that former enemy or his family and give back the journal. I wrote that section of the script for them, but always had my doubts about its likelihood. I didn't buy that the American would leave an enemy alive. And how would he ever find the other soldier again? It all seemed too neat.

Now I had been confronted by the story of a man who, except in one significant particular, had done in real life what the character in the film had done. It was a synchronicity I'd come to expect from Viet Nam. But it was also one I could not ignore, any more than Hao could. The fact that I had written the script called a kind of obligation to itself: like all Viet Nam war fiction, it owed something to the dead, for the stories, for the fact of being alive to write the stories. And I understood how Homer needed an ending, needed to confront the grief hidden away in an attic for over thirty years, to confront the humanity of the man he had killed. It made his story our story.[21]

Hao knew that my mention of the film was a not very subtle way of implying her own responsibility to help; she knew that I would sense her reluctance, but she also felt that obligation was a real one. When she opened the attachments containing the scanned documents, she felt a chill go through her. During the war she had worked in a volunteer search and rescue squad; after bombings she and the other volunteers would dig the survivors and the dead from the debris, an experience that had left her still unable to stand the smell of barbequed meat. She had also worked for the ministry of information after the war, and as part of her job had recorded or synopsized the stories of veterans, spoken and written: "I had been involved with interviewing hundreds and hundreds of veterans, listening to hundreds and hundreds of poems. When I moved out of my job as a press officer, I feel I could totally forget the war and forget everything. When I had to read Homer's website and saw all the documents, all the diaries; it was my nightmare."[22]

Hao approached her editor at *Giao Duc & Thoi Dai (Education & Times)*, Y Ban, who is also a well-known novelist; many fiction writers in Viet Nam make their livings as journalists. Hao knew Y Ban had recently been caught again in the lingering nightmare of the war: her father, after suffering for years, had died of the effects of Agent Orange. Y Ban looked at the photos of Dam's documents and told Hao to go ahead and write the story.

Hao's and Thai's articles came out in both papers on April 30, 2005, when all over the country there were ceremonies and special issues marking the thirtieth anniversary of the end of the war.

In Thai Giang, the Hoang family had recently observed the ceremonies for another anniversary—the day of their mother's death. The sadness of the day was always exacerbated for the family because they knew their mother had not been at peace when she died, the circumstances of her sons' deaths still unknown to her or to them. Pham Thi Lanh had died in 1974, a fragile woman. The information the medium had given her, that Dam was abroad and "would return in glory," was a source of both agony and comfort. "So we encouraged her to believe it," Dam's sister Tham says. She was not a skeptic herself. "We even attended séances," she says, "during which Dam would appear and always say he was very sad and cry. We thought he was sad because his wife had re-married. But he never said that, only 'I'm very sad.'"[23] They were still not ready to forgive the life they believed Dam's widow had taken from them.

But Pham Thi Minh had also, for many years, refused to give up hope that Dam would return, even after getting the official notification of his death in 1972. "I lay in bed and thought, if there was only some news. I hoped that I would hear that he was some place, that he had lost his arms and legs and could not tell the family. . . . I hoped for that, just that he would come back. But it did not come true."[24]

The morning the newspaper articles came out, Dam's sister Tham was on her way to work when a neighbor, excited, ran up to her, rustling the special edition of *Education & Times* in front of her. Her eyes fell on Homer's photo—a thin, young, blond foreigner—and then on the photos of Dam's documents. She saw his name, "Hoang Ngoc Dam, 1966," written in looping letters, surrounded by his drawings, and felt a wave of weakness pass through her. "Suddenly, I couldn't stand. I ran right to my husband, and I told him: 'Dam has returned.'"[25]

Within minutes the entire family heard what had happened and gathered in Cat's house, passing the article back and forth, crying, repeating Tham's words. They read the article over and over, particularly Homer's description of Dam's demeanor during their confrontation, his refusal to lower his weapon and surrender. The sudden, sharp sensation of grief he felt was surprising to Cat, perhaps because he had been very young when news of Dam's death had been given to the family, years after it actually occurred. The article, the photos of the documents, and his brother's drawing and writing suddenly made Dam real to him, a legend of his youth given flesh and weight and now wrenched out of his life again. But the sadness was mixed with a great swell of pride, an emotion that grew partly out of the vindication this event would now allow the family, after the whispers that had spread through the village after the medium's pronouncement that Dam was still alive and abroad. His feelings were just as mixed looking at the face—the faces—of the American who had killed Dam. The newspaper had printed the face

of the young Homer next to a present-day photograph. In the
first picture, Homer sat in the front seat of a jeep, covered with
dust, hatless, his blond hair matted down in a kind of soup-
bowl haircut that emphasized his youth, only the eyes old in
that boy's face. If the photos hadn't been next to each other, Cat
would not have connected the young soldier to the older man,
who was bearded, his hair below his collar, his face gaunt and
lined. The man who had killed his brother. Yet he felt the hatred
die in him. It had been war; this man had done what soldiers do
in war. "Our family and the people of this village feel very
proud," he said later, "because the American, our one-time enemy, the man who had killed my brother, now praised him."[26]

The others, passing the paper back and forth, murmured
their agreement. They were grateful to the American. They were
grateful to his mother, who had clearly understood the importance of what her son had given her, keeping it so carefully after
all those years. A brother they had thought lost to them forever
could come home.

Someone found the telephone number of the newspaper.
Cat called, asking for Phan Thanh Hao. She wasn't there, but he
was connected to the editor, who gave him Hao's cell phone
number.

Hao e-mailed me that afternoon with the news. It was three in
the morning in the States, but I had been sleepless and had
turned on the computer. The house was completely dark except
for my desk lamp, the little circle of light it created on my desk.
When I read the message, I turned away from the screen. I
looked at the wall in front of my desk, where I had a poster
from the old *Streetfare Journal*, the series of poetry on posters for
buses that the poet George Evans had edited. This one had his
poem "Meeting the Enemy." "There was a time," the poem read,
"we would have killed each other." Everything suddenly seemed
heavy with portent. My hands, I saw, were shaking slightly. I

had not really expected the newspaper articles to succeed, had resigned myself to taking the documents to the Vietnamese Veterans' Association, where they would at least be preserved and commemorated. The existence of the family had been unreal to me, as outside my imagination as the actual life of Dam had been to Homer. To any of us, I thought. He had been a ghost for us long before he became a ghost, a force as much a part of the jungle, the land, as the tiger who had seized Homer's soldier. I realized that I had assumed the family was dead or impossible to find because I had given up the hope for redress and completion that their existence implied; it seemed not too easy, but rather too neat to be possible. I closed my eyes, and suddenly sobs were shaking my shoulders. I turned off the lamp and tried to stifle them, to not wake up the house.

The family, Hao had written, were very excited. They wanted to get the documents back, and they wanted Homer to come himself, "to place them on the family altar."

# Chapter Twenty-Two

# The
# Letter

On April 22, 2005, Homer e-mailed the following letter, through Hao, to the youngest brother of the man he had killed:

*Dear Mr. Hoang Dang Cat,*

*I would love to have given the documents back personally, but I can't possibly afford a trip to Vietnam. I am retired, on a fixed income and with recent health problems, just don't have the money. Even if I did, I am afraid I am far too shy to meet with strangers, whose language I do not even speak. I was raised on a small farm and have always been very shy. I still do not know how I managed to be a Platoon Leader and Company Commander in the Army.*

*I am very touched that you have an altar that keeps Dam's memory alive. It makes me feel good to know that his brave soul is still honored in such a wonderful manner. It hurts to think of the hundreds of thousands on both sides of that tragic war, who still mourn the loss of their loved ones.*

*Sometimes the guilt of surviving can be overwhelming. What will I say, when I enter into eternity? Is there a little known footnote to the* commandment *"Thou Shalt Not Kill,"* that forgives killing in combat? Look what I did in the ignorance and folly of my youth. I thought I was a true patriot. So why doesn't that give me comfort at age 59?

Dam and I met by chance on a trail. He and I saw each other and both of us attempted to shoot the other. I lived. He died instantly. For over a quarter century I have carried the image of his young body lying there lifeless. It was my first kill. I wish I could say it was my last. Why did a medic die and I live? I don't know.

Maybe someday humanity will gain the wisdom to settle conflicts without sending its youth to kill strangers. . . . People should know what our leaders are doing when they resort to armed conflict to solve political problems.

In my dying moment, Dam and many of his comrades will surely call to me. I am not afraid . . . only saddened. Perhaps we will meet again as friends.

Respectfully yours,
Homer

"I just can't do it," Homer told me. He asked if I would take them instead. A day later, the documents arrived by Express Mail at my house. He had let them go.

# CHAPTER TWENTY-THREE

# The Documents

I hesitated a long time before I opened the padded envelope. I knew that for the Hoang family what I had now was literally a piece of Dam's soul. For a moment I felt a kind of resentment, fueled by an atavistic fear. What was I releasing into my home? I had not killed this man. As soon as the thought came to me, I tried to struggle against it. One of my Vietnamese friends had written me, when I told her that Homer might come over, that she would not want to meet the man, was not sure she could look into his face. Homer could have been me, I replied to her. He could have been any of us.

I opened the envelope and drew out the notebooks and papers, the smell of very old, very dry paper wafting to my nostrils. Everything had been kept in pristine condition. I looked through the documents, as carefully as if I were an archaeologist examining an ancient and precious text. On one of the title pages, Dam had drawn an elaborate red-and-green orchid, and his name, Hoang Ngoc Dam, under the date 1-1-1966, in the kind of ornate lettering teenagers use to inscribe their school notebooks;

another, previous page was decorated with a hand-drawn pair of surgical scissors. The book was divided into sections about treatments for different types of wounds, though surprisingly the first section was Midwifery. Page after page was illustrated with beautifully done medical drawings: head and neck arteries, bones of the leg, the hip, and so on, as if he had copied an entire medical textbook. The work was beautiful in itself, and it was astonishing to think of Dam painstakingly creating those images in jungles, tunnels, and caves, under bombardment and artillery fire. On the last page was the only drawing that did not seem neat: scrawled grids, five squares per line. I wondered if they were tactical positions, battle plans, but when I showed them to a friend, Ho Nguyen, who taught at a nearby college, he grinned and told me they were Vietnamese tic-tac-toe; he had played the same game when he was a kid.

Seeing and touching Dam's neat, precise handwriting, the letters tiny, using as little space as possible, and the exquisitely done anatomical drawings, I thought of Homer's anguished cry in his letter to Cat: *Why did a medic die and I live?* The book raised the question war always raised, that war should always raise: Who is this that has been lost to us? But what stabbed me was the hope that these meticulous drawings and notes revealed. The book was an amulet bound and filled by a young man trying his hardest to give himself the illusion of a future.

Ho Nguyen was also very moved by the documents, and the two of us sat together as Ho went through them, translating, sometimes with tears in his eyes. The notebook was not the only document. Inside it were four separate "Certificates of Commendation" that Dam had received. All of the other documents belonged to another man, apparently an army truck driver named Nguyen Van Hai. The first was his license, affixed with his photo. Hai was a very handsome young man, and one of the other papers seems to have been a love letter and a poem to him from a girl he left behind:

When you left I was speechless; I couldn't find the words to say.
In every step you take away from here, I carry with me the feeling that I have. . . . Our feelings for each other are as wide as the
ocean. What is in your heart is also in my heart. Your image has
faded away beyond the bamboo hedge, but you brought me to
life. I was so moved when you told me to wait and do my duty,
so touched that I didn't know how to reply to your words. . . .
Now you have left to fight the Americans and I must stay here to
build the country. But I will see you again one day.

> *As long as there is still Heaven*
> *As long as there is still earth*
> *As long as there are still clouds*
> *You and I will meet again.*

When you left I didn't know who to talk to, to be with. You left
behind your spirit, which inspires me to keep strong. Now that
you are on your way, I wish you good health and success in the
fight against the Americans to save the country, so that we can be
reunited one day. I promise to fulfill my duties as a younger sister
should while you are away, and when you sit to your meals, remember that there is still a younger sister who waits for you.

Was Nguyen Van Hai one of Dam's patients who had died?
We hadn't found out anything else about him, though now I
would take his documents also to Dam's family. There were
other letters in the packet, and a black notebook, filled with
high school math problems that Homer may have recognized
from his own high school books and copies of poems by Ho Chi
Minh, in tiny handwriting.

Someone wrote:

I miss you like a son misses his father. I bought some cloth, and
will buy some for your family if they need it. On August 26–28

the hamlet was bombed and children and old people had to be evacuated. Remember to write to me.

On the bottom of that letter was a note from a mother—Hai's or Dam's; it was not clear whose:

Your departure had made me miss you so much; I will never forget you, son. I feel sick with missing you so much.[27]

"I don't know where to put these," I said to my wife, Ohnmar. It didn't seem right to just lay them in my in-basket. For one thing, I didn't want to look at them all day, to be reminded constantly of the burden of them. For another, what if something happened to them? Ohnmar touched the packet.

She is from Burma and maintains a small altar in our son's room, where she burns incense or candles and meditates. There are no family photos on Burmese Buddhist altars. But when I told her of my unease at having these objects from Dam in our home, where they would stay until I took them to the Hoang family to be placed on the altar of their ancestors, she smiled and shook her head.

"Put them next to the altar," she said. "Dam will be our guest."

# CHAPTER TWENTY-FOUR

# Transit

During the flight I kept Dam's notebooks and papers in a plastic baggie, in my carry-on bag. Every once in a while I took it out of the overhead compartment and checked, as if I was afraid Dam's soul, drawing closer to Asia, would take off ahead of us, leaving behind a bag full of fragrant smoke.

At Incheon airport in Korea, where we had a stopover and transfer, we sat in a restaurant, eating Korean soup. The poets George Evans and Daisy Zamora, coming from San Francisco, were to meet us at the gate for our Viet Nam connection, but when I looked up—there was no wall on the concourse side— I experienced the sudden lag and shock of seeing their faces emerging from the multinational procession of transient souls. I called out to them.

A few moments later, George looked up from the table and repeated the double take I'd done when I'd seen him. He rose and called to an Asian man passing outside. The man's eyes widened in surprise; he and George shook hands, laughing at the serendipity. George brought him to the table and intro-duced him. Nguyen Do was a friend of his from San Francisco, a Vietnamese American poet and translator on his way to Hong Kong. In my jet lag, everything seemed weighted with significance, as if fate or Dam had created this nexus. In any case, it did not seem something that should be ignored. I cleared the table and took out the documents. As Do looked at them, translating and reading some of Dam's words to us, his face softened. "You are doing a good thing," he whispered, closing his eyes, and then he rose and drifted back into the passing crowd, a momentary emissary nominated and pulled from the stream of the world as if to keep us mindful of what we were doing.

Later, Phan Thanh Hao would call Dam a "sacred soul," who drew together those who needed to come together.

We were an odd little squad he had brought together in that airport restaurant. That year, before Tom Lacombe had contacted me about Homer's documents, I had made plans to interview some of the American and Vietnamese writers I knew who had been in the war. A friend, Marc Steiner, who hosted a daily NPR show in Baltimore, and his partner, Valerie Williams, had started an independent production company, the Center for Emerging Media, and they wanted to create a series of hour-long programs based on the thirtieth anniversary of the end of the war.[28] Besides the interviews with the writers, the programs would focus on how our group of Americans responded to a country so intricately tied into our own histories. We were to represent a cross section of the Viet Nam War generation, the war protestor/soldier dichotomy that had become a kind of fuzzy shorthand for the cultural split the war had fissured in America; we were to see what that mix might stimulate, in terms of good radio, as we ambled through Viet Nam.

I don't know how good we were at being a representative cross section. Marc and the two technicians, Steve Elliott and Neelon Crawford, had marched against the war, and George and I and the other vet with us, Woody Curry, had marched to it, but all of us had ended with the same sense of obscene wastage. The only difference—not a small one—was that to three of us the wastage had faces and flesh. Valerie was too young for the war; its hold on her now was mythological, through its ripples into her own progressive politics and her partner's life. Marc had been a red diaper baby who grew up in the poor sections of Baltimore, a street fighter, the only white kid in his neighborhood and school; later he had been a full-time civil rights and peace activist. He carried scars from razors, knives, and clubs, from both times of his life. Many of his friends had gone to the war he had avoided out of moral sanity; he felt a good man's mix of righteousness at that decision and guilt about the bodies and souls that may have taken blows in his place. Now the earmark of the anniversary had made him decide, against the objections of his management, that he needed to examine again the war's stamp on his life, on the lives of his generation.

George and Daisy were there at my request. They had met (and married a few years later) while teaching at the same program in Boston where I had encountered Le Minh Khue and other Vietnamese writers, former enemies—an experience I had shared with George. He and Daisy were also veterans of opposing sides, although in their case, of different wars: George had been a medic in Viet Nam and Daisy a Sandinista guerrilla. For Daisy the Vietnamese struggle had always been a model and an inspiration since her own days in the jungle, dreaming of Nicaragua as a country run by poets. But dreams rarely survive the victory of a revolution, and she was going to a country where her equivalents, the artists born of that revolution, had learned that worn lesson. No matter. "To go to Viet Nam is for me like going to the promised land," she told me, laughing.

That worried me. But then again, I thought, we all came to Viet Nam looking for something lost—a notion less dangerous, more hopeful than it had been when it had helped fuel a war.

Daisy would be searching for the untainted purity and ideals of her youth; Marc and Valerie perhaps for that same reason, a chance to once again wrap the personal in the historical.

And I was looking forward to doing the interviews with the writers. In recent years the blind arrogance that had produced the Viet Nam War in the first place had been leaving members of another generation dead or broken among the stones and sand of Iraq, and I felt that the foundation of belief in the efficacy of words that had sustained me as a teacher and a writer had crumbled under my feet. I wanted, basically, to see my Vietnamese friends, assure myself of their existence, as if the new war had somehow threatened the very idea of them, of our connections to each other, the capacity of our witness to touch any weight on the direction of the world.

But my real faith had shifted to Dam's documents, to the weight and feel of them, their faint pulse under my palm. I was going to see if grace could be pulled from pain.

I wanted also to witness the way my two fellow veterans would react to being back in Viet Nam for the first time since the war. I had returned several times; the country had shifted out of the war for me, although I knew it only took a peripheral glimpse of a shadow moving over the flank of a jungled mountain, a finger curled around the handle of a cup as if it were a trigger, to reveal itself once more, everything layered on top a dissolving pentimento. How would they see the country; what were they looking for?

Woody (Woodrow) Curry came from the same Baltimore neighborhoods as Marc. He directed a center for addicts in that city now. He had been an infantryman in Viet Nam and had come back addicted himself, to drugs and alcohol and isolation. He'd pulled himself out of it, earned a master's degree in psychology, and developed a kind of Buddhist-oriented counseling. Later his ring-encrusted fingers, scorpion pendant, and the scorpion tattoo on his arm would give him an instant nickname and make him an instant legend to the Hanoi street kids, who gravitated in flocks to the tall black man with the infectious laugh walking down Le Thong Kiet Street; he drew them around himself as they were drawn to him, like found luck.

He wanted now to see the country that had pulled him off his own streets, only to become a nebulous dream when he found himself back on them, a needle in his arm, oblivion in his veins. The memory of a girl he had killed, shooting her from a helicopter when she revealed a weapon, contended with the memory of a girl in An Khe whom he had loved, as if she were a hope for redemption. There was something he needed to confront in Viet Nam: himself, of course, but he wasn't sure how he would do it, until we went to Cu Chi, where he would meet a Vietnamese guide of his own age. The two would show each other the puckered flesh of their wounds, raising trouser cuffs and shirts. He had vowed not to go into the famous tunnels there, now widened for tourists. "You were here," the guide said Woody nodded. "25th Infantry," he said. The man nodded back and said, "Yes, that's right," as if a test had been passed. Woody turned from him then and stared at the dark opening of the tunnel, then got down on his hands and knees and crawled into it. He wrote about it in his journal: *I must know this thing intimately. It knows me, it owns me, I must move with it, I must taste it, I must smell it. . . . That's what draws me back into the tunnel. I don't know where else to find it. That's the only place in the universe where I can meet it. There's only one place where I no longer exist. It's both the grave and the birth canal, a trip through the unknown to the unknown. I emerge not me. Someone emerges. I need to become again. I didn't exist moments ago. My whole world ceased to exist moments, hours, days when they all became eternity.*

"There are parts of me, that like most people, I tend to avoid," he explained afterward to Marc. "And that's what makes them so frightening."

"Which is why you had to take that leap into the hole?"

"I had to make it my ally rather than something that immo-
bilizes me. . . . I have to accept it and get friendly with it, so I
can use it rather than be destroyed by it. . . . It didn't necessarily
feel good, but it saved me."[29]

George Evans would be looking for his friend Billy, another
medic, another wandering soul.

Like Marc and Woody, George had been a street kid, the
blue collar North Side Pittsburgh neighborhood of Manchester
standing in for Baltimore. He was the son of an ice man who,
like Woody's father, had come back damaged from World War II,
bringing it home to his family in the form of a constant, derisive
hostility that would unpredictably riff into petty humiliations or
physical violence. At the same time he held the war up to his
son not as damage but as initiation. George had had enough of
it by the time he was twelve and began living on the streets,
plugging into poor families in other neighborhoods to survive,
running with the gangs. His sanctuaries were the public library
and the Carnegie Museum. He discovered in himself love for
the art and reading his father and the street had tried to squeeze
out of him. But he couldn't reveal any of that vulnerability,
could only relax when he was with his best friend, Billy Dick,
also a fighter (what crap he must have been handed for that
name) but like George secretly starting to read, to question the
parameters of his life and the assumptions of his world. Billy's
home became an occasional safe haven from the streets, a place
to sleep and eat, and Billy's friendship a permanent safe place to
let loose the hard hunch and crouch and shift of his life. Billy
encouraged him to finish high school, and then, knowing the
draft would take them both, to preemptively enlist in the Air
Force. George agreed; he thought it would be cool to fly planes.
Billy, more grounded in reality, figured it would keep them out
of the infantry and give them more geographic choices than
Southeast Asia. But Billy had a bad knee from a sports injury,
and when they went to the recruiter, he was rejected. George

wasn't. He went into the Air Force, but not, he found, into the air. Instead he was trained as a medic and sent to Africa. (Later, in Viet Nam, he would be crew chief in charge of the Cam Ranh Bay hospital ER.) Billy was eventually drafted anyway; apparently the army wasn't concerned about the condition of his knee. For a time he seriously considered refusing to go or running away; he did not believe in the war. It was not a matter of fear. He had begun to seriously study the percepts of nonviolence, to move his own perceptions out of the mind-sets of the street. But the neighborhood would not stand for draft dodgers any more than it would abide artists or poets, and when the pressure got too great, he decided to take conscientious objector status. He would fulfill his military obligation as a medic, as would George, as would Dam.

Soon Billy was sending George letters from Viet Nam, warning him it was a bad scene, not to come, to avoid it at all costs. But it was too late. Around the same time that Billy had gone overseas, George was transferred to a small dispensary at McGuire Air Force Base in New Jersey, a dream job, and as far from the war as one could get in the air force. But two of his other close friends from childhood had been killed by then, and he was restless. "I was bound and determined not to stay put in New Jersey," he says. "I wanted to go to the war. I wanted to see what was happening to my generation, so I volunteered." It was a decision he would, as was not unusual, come to regret.

On September 19, 1968, SP4 William Edward Dick Jr. of Team 11, 41st Civil Affairs Company, First Field Force, eight months into his tour, was killed in Binh Dinh Province, Republic of Vietnam, when the jeep in which he was driving back to base camp, after doing a MEDCAP—a medical aid mission in a Vietnamese village—hit a land mine.[30] His mission that day was similar to the winning-hearts-and-minds duties Hoang Ngoc Dam performed in the villages of Gia Lai.

Six months after that, George left for Viet Nam. Two decades later he wrote a poem called "Revelation in the Mother

Lode," a vision of walking into a northern California vineyard at night and seeing it transformed, its stakes marking the graves of his lost generation, Billy among them:

> *a one time soldier with a trick knee, flagging humor*
> *monsoon debt—and find you enfolded by fog as if by spirits,*
> *and become the visage of all that's been*
> *thrown from the world.*[31]

I have read that poem many times, and that line would become a kind of refrain for me in Viet Nam, a silent mantra for the journey we were on now, each of us looking for what was lost or what we hoped to find, going to meet the family and village for whom Dam, his face framed on the altar, had become all that had been thrown from the world.

# CHAPTER TWENTY-FIVE

# The Return

We left for Thai Giang at six in the morning on Saturday, May 28, 2005. With me were George and Daisy, Phan Thanh Hao, and the novelist Y Ban, who was also the editor in chief of Hao's newspaper. We were carrying the documents Homer Steedly had taken off the body of Hoang Ngoc Dam.

The village is located deep in the rice-growing countryside of Thai Binh Province, southeast of Hanoi. We rode out in a small van, past roadside shops selling large earthen jars of *nuoc mam*, fish sauce, and the new textile and clothing factories lining the Hanoi-Haiphong highway, their products destined for Wal-Marts and Targets all over the territory of the old enemy. They are the form reconciliation takes when it occurs between nations, and they were raising the standard of living here, we were told; but to me they somehow mocked the dead of both sides. The reconciliation we were engaged in now was smaller, more personal, and perhaps, because of that, more possible.

It took us more than three hours to get to the village, even though it is only, as the crow flies, about sixty kilometers from

215

Hanoi. There were no direct roads, and on the way we made another stop back into the war. Y Ban's father had died the month
before, and we visited her family to pay our respects and light
incense at the family altar. When I asked Y Ban how he had
died, she hesitated, as if out of a strange politeness, and then
said he had suffered from the effects of Agent Orange all of his
life since the war; now it had finally taken him.

The Hoang family arranged to meet us at a bridge near the
main road; from there they would lead us to the village. We stopped the van at the top of the bridge and waited. After a few moments another car drove slowly past us, then pulled in front of us
and stopped. Dam's brothers and sisters were wearing the white
headbands that signify mourning. They were all weeping. They
clutched my hand, the depth of their grief surprising me—it
was as if Dam had died yesterday instead of so many years ago.
They asked us to follow them, but for me to keep the documents for now. As we drove through the lush green countryside,
surrounded by rice fields, from time to time they threw pieces of
green and orange paper from their windows—Buddhist symbolic currency. They were leading Dam's soul back to his village.

As we came into Thai Giang, I was stunned to see that the
street was lined with people, hundreds of them, the entire village, most of whom were wearing white headbands, and many
of whom were weeping and keening. I got out of the car, clutching the notebooks, and walked toward the crowd, glancing back
and hoping George would get out and join me. But the rest of
the party was hanging back, hesitant, and I walked ahead, alone
for a time, into the gauntlet. I was here for Homer, as his surrogate, as his brother, and I was walking into the village of the
man he had killed, holding the documents in front of me like an
offering, feeling the naked vulnerability of a man walking point,
as if I were offering my body to something, as if I were a surrogate for more than Homer.

The others in our party had come out of the van now and
caught up to me. George looked dazed. He had only been back

in Viet Nam for a few days and couldn't quite believe where he was. Walking behind me, he thought he saw Dieu, Dam's brother-in-law, staring at him. George is bearded, and Dieu, we found out later, for an instant believed that he could be Homer. "He stood at the door and looked at me," George said. "Not a trace of emotion on his face, a stone, stone cold look. The anger came from him believing that we were deceiving him, perhaps out of fear, out of shame, but once he finally understood it, he was OK."[32]

Meanwhile, Dam's other relatives gathered around us—an entire extended family of aunts, uncles, nephews, nieces, and cousins. His sisters, Thi Dam, Tuoi, and Tham, and his brothers, Cat and Luong, were all weeping, touching the books—as was a woman I found out later was his wife, Pham Thi Minh. The sound of their crying surrounded us, a continuous wail; the sobbing wracked into me.

Later I would think of something Tim O'Brien said to me in Hawaii: "I worry that [the war] is not remembered in suffering, is not remembered in the detail, in the graphic moment by moment by moment by moment unfolding of a tragedy: the sound of a woman crying over the death of a child. That one woman's wail, alone, not multiplied by 300,000 or 3 million, alone, is a horrid cost for any political objective. Being a brand new father myself . . . if my son were to perish in any war over any cause, it's hard to imagine what it might be where I would say, 'Yeah I'll take that wail. And I'll cry for eternity, for that.' The wail of one Gold-star mother or one Vietnamese villager whose daughter lies burned and dead at her feet. And that's just one. And, man, I think a lot of us forget that wail."[33]

Not that day. Luong would say: "It was just like we were receiving my brother's body. Hundreds of people came out, all wearing white mourning headbands."[34] I held Dam's documents in front of me, in my cupped hands. If I was a surrogate for Homer, Dam was the surrogate for the 142 young men from the American war who had never returned to this village.

Yet I didn't see, or even sense, any hostility in that crowd. George did. "Walking into the central square of the village down that crowd-lined street was like running a grief gauntlet—faces twisted in pain, moans and keening sounds. As I've told you, in addition to all the grief, I felt pure anger from the villagers, and hatred, their eyes like spears and arrows drilling through me, pinning me against the air."

Why did we perceive it so differently, even though we were both sharing, apparently, the same sense of surrogacy? When I spoke to Hao later, she agreed with me; she had not seen any hostility. But it was George's second day back in Viet Nam. He saw what he needed to see. Maybe we both did. Maybe he was seeing Billy Dick's accusing eyes, or the eyes of the dozens of corpses he'd shut by running his hands down their faces as if he were closing books. Or the brain-damaged men in his ward, their eyes open, staring blankly. Maybe he was remembering the children he told me he had seen early in his tour, when he went into the emergency room and saw two dead Vietnamese children—run over by an American truck engaged in a game the drivers called "gook hockey," betting on whether or not they could run down kids on the roads—lying on gurneys, "like little dolls." Their mother came in screaming, running back and forth between them, beating at George's chest, her spittle wetting his face, hysterical, lost, her face burned into his mind. They were not the last dead children he saw. "That day I reached and swept the flies from the face of a Vietnamese/girl on the bed of a pickup truck until I realized she was dead and stopped, is the day I will never forget. . . . They crowded her eyes, until her eyes were as black and swirling and/indecipherable as the eyes of Edvard Munch's *Madonna.*/When I backed off, the whirlpool revealed such beauty my spine/melted. Such beauty I thought I couldn't live another moment. Such/ beauty my soul dissolved. My heart died and/ revived, died and/ revived, died and revived."[35]

Maybe, I thought, he was seeing those kids.

"I clearly remember thinking," he said later, after leaving the village, "'Now they have me, finally, and now I pay,' and kept thinking that. . . . Staggered by the power of it, tipped off balance, I caught myself and braced to face it, like a medieval sin eater, tempered by another thought: 'Take it, be strong, they deserve to give it and you deserve to get it, it's your responsibility, their pain belongs to you.'

"The refrain, 'Now you pay,' came to mind, then kept repeating with variations. 'Now you *really* pay,' for the war, for being part of it, being involved in the horror brought to Viet Nam, and for not being able to do anything effective to stop it, on any level, or make up for it, the two things about that time that have haunted me most the past decades."[36]

Surrounded by that small sea of grieving people, we walked first to the People's Committee office, where the family and town officials greeted us. Hao and I sat down at a long wooden table, across from the local party leaders. Then Cat—I didn't know any of their names yet—walked up next to me and I stood up. Pham Quang Huy sidled over next to Cat. I unsealed the plastic bag in which I had kept the documents, drew out the two notebooks and the papers, and handed everything to him, feeling both a sense of relief and loss.

He touched the covers and then began going through the small stack, still crying. At first he picked up and thumbed through the other notebook, containing Nguyen Van Hai's papers, and I saw his face squeeze in a momentary twinge of uncertainty. I imagined him thinking: they have brought papers from the wrong man, it is all a terrible mistake. But then he came across Dam's notebook, his brother's signature drawn beautifully on the cover page, the sketch of surgical scissors. Cat broke, his wailing eerily echoed and then magnified by the other people in the room, the crowd pressing in at the door and windows. It was O'Brien's wail, a grief so naked I thought it would enter my heart like the permanent scream in Homer's ears.

The mourning for Dam began to affect George in a different way: "My friends dead in the war came to mind at one point, and I concentrated on them briefly, thinking that moment in Thai Giang I survived long enough to experience was for them as well as for Dam, a sort of cleansing of war filth. It's difficult to sort that out clearly, but I felt it, felt a renewed, powerful sense of how much life was wasted on both sides, and how that was a moment of truth for me, the one who lived, for proving that I could take the pain on everyone's behalf, the pain I deserved, an apex of pain for the internalized suffering I've lived with—that we've all lived with, those of us who participated and survived."[37]

We walked in procession to the community center. Its veranda was ten deep with people. They crowded around us, needing to touch us. Inside, on a stage, an altar had been set up; on it were incense and flowers and a large photo of Dam. It was flanked by two Vietnamese veterans, both old and frail, standing at rigid attention in dress white uniforms. The small, hot hall was packed with men, women, and children.

A series of village and district notables mounted the podium and made speeches. Finally, Cat rose. His voice breaking, he thanked Homer for allowing the family this release. He bowed toward me as he spoke, and when he was finished I climbed onto the stage and presented the documents, wrapped in the national flag, to him again. He placed them on the altar. Looking at the flag, brother Luong felt a swell of pride and completion watching these Americans, his former enemies, who had come all this distance to honor Dam. The grief he felt now, he realized, was mainly because his parents could not be alive to see this day. He had read a translation of Homer's account of shooting Dam, and what had given him solace, all these years after the war, was Dam's refusal to surrender to Homer. It again gave the lie to the rumors people had spread since the fortune-teller had told the family he had gone abroad. Now the prophecy, and its second half, that one day Dam would return in glory, had come true. "Homer said that my brother had the proud stature of a superior person," Cat recalled later.

"He can rest peacefully," Tham added. "When that American shot him, he looked directly into that man's eyes, and maybe he thought that this man also has a good heart, so he let him keep his notebooks and papers for thirty-six years. I think Dam must be happy now, in another world, satisfied with what the American has done."[38]

Perhaps not completely. As Tham spoke, one of the television cameramen trained his camera on me and Hao. Almost immediately, one of the camera lights exploded in a shower of hot glass shards. A small piece landed on my shirt and burned a small, cigarette burn-sized hole. Another, larger piece struck Hao, who was talking to the monk, landing on her chest and burning her skin.

"He is still a bad shot," she said to me, grinning.

At the moment the ceremonies finished, a soft rain began to fall. We walked through it to the Hoang family's compound. Thi Dam, the second-youngest sister, had been weeping throughout the morning, continuously, her face so suffused with pain that I couldn't look at her. Finally Daisy, unable to bear it, put her arm around her shoulder, and the two collapsed against each other. She had been drawn back, Daisy told me, into the grief of her own war.

At the house, dozens of people had crowded inside, and more milled around in a patio area under some fruit trees outside, where tables and chairs had been set up for a huge feast. The family altar was against the wall. It contained photos of Dam; his brother Chi, killed in the prisoner of war camp raid; and their parents. People kept filing in to see and touch the documents, and children stared at us, softly pulling the hair on my arms and George's, the way I remembered Vietnamese kids in the war doing, amazed at our monkey hairiness.

I sat next to Cat and Pham Quang Huy, the veteran, Dam's friend, who later would tell me some details of Dam's death and burial. I had brought the papers of Nguyen Van Hai, the driver, along with Dam's, and I asked Huy if it was possible to locate his family as well. He looked at me in surprise, blinking. But hadn't anyone told me? Hai was alive; he would come to the village soon and collect his things.

We ate with the family for about an hour, the conversation falling into a jokey easiness, markedly different from the grief and tension of the morning. Something held tight and hot in our chests since that morning, and perhaps for over thirty years, had suddenly been released, leaving us light and a little dizzy with its absence. I was told many times that they wished Homer could have come. They would always welcome him, they said— the village had even offered money to purchase a plane ticket for him. He was now a part of them. Cat said, "If after he killed my brother, he did not pick up the documents, then we would never have seen my brother's documents again. But after killing my brother, Homer's human feelings arose, and I remember reading the article in which he said that my brother was too young, and in just the blink of an eye, he'd shot. You know that, in wars, everything happens within a few seconds, and afterwards, even if he had regrets, there was nothing he could do. I read Homer's diary about that many times; how he had given the documents to his mother and how they haunted him, so that now that he can't come here. We all sympathize: And we want him to come here, and not worry about anything; it is just that now he and our family have some connection."

Phan Thanh Hao said, "In Viet Nam, you know, we have a certain spiritual relation that we call karma. . . . We think that Dam was a sacred soul. He was so sacred that he could gather us together: the ones who have fought, and the ones who were thirsty for peace. He was so sacred to gather all of us here, to do this thing, to meet today. So that is what we believe."[39]

After I returned from the village, it was a few days before I could bring myself to sit down and write to Homer and describe what had happened. A day later I received two e-mails in return. The first was from him: "I have a huge lump in my throat. I am sure I would have been a basket case, if I had been there. I am still trying to comprehend the totality of your e-mail. . . . I know it must have been difficult. Knowing that the family has the documents give me great peace of mind . . . will get back in touch later, after I stop sobbing."

The other was from Tibby: "When I asked Homer how he felt after reading your e-mail tonight, he said, 'Complete.'"

# PART FOUR

# INTERLUDE

CHAPTER TWENTY-SIX

# The Pisgah
# National Forest

The original Cherokee name for Pisgah Mountain, rising almost 6,000 feet above sea level, is the sibilant Elseetoss; the ridgeline over which it towers was called Warwasseeta. The name Pisgah is Hebrew, from the fourth chapter of Deuteronomy. It is the mountain where Moses stood and was allowed to glimpse the Promised Land. Not far from the American Pisgah, in the same range, is Cold Mountain, the inspiration for another story of a soldier who needed to leave his war and find peace in his love of a woman and of a place.

Tibby first came to the Blue Ridge Mountains and western North Carolina in 1970, to attend Brevard College for a year. She had been enchanted by the beauty of the place: the winds soughing through mountain laurel, balsam, and pine forests that clung to steep granite slopes and thickly blanketed the more gentle swells of the lower hills; hushed, bowered glens and coves jeweled with wildflowers; waterfalls, blurred by rainbow mists, arcing from granite cliffs or sliding over moss-furred boulders; shadow-dappled creeks swelling clear and clean over black-and-gray rocks smooth-worn or patched with lichen, the creek banks thick with ferns and wildflowers with wonderful names—hairy beardtongue, fly-poison, Turk's cap lilies, turtle-heads, mountain Saint-John's-wort, skunk goldenrod, and white heart-leaved aster. The same deer herds and bear packs that wander elsewhere through the Appalachians ranged there, but the Pisgah forest was famous for peregrine falcons and for a strange breed of white squirrel, said to be the descendants of two animals that escaped from an overturned carnival truck.

Soon after her marriage she brought Homer, to introduce this place to him and him to this place. The mountains mantled with forest, tendrils of mist and cloud drifting and curling over their flanks, evoked the Central Highlands, but transmuted here to Homer's home ground, sieved through that mist, through the way he could see it, pristine from the debris of war, in his wife's eyes, made into a kind of peace. He and Tibby had stared at the green hills and mountains and promised one another that they would live there if they ever had the chance.[1]

That chance came after Homer retired, when on a vacation trip back to the area, they discovered a house for sale in Transylvania County, in the foothills of the Pisgahs. By then Homer had found that the connection he had envisioned was a geographical fact: the Pisgahs, their topography, flora, and fauna, existed in a connected geological belt with the Truong Son range in the Central Highlands of Viet Nam, formed after the last Ice Age.

Two months after I returned from Viet Nam, my wife and I, and Marc and Valerie, sat in the Steedlys' living room. Bits of the natural world brought the forest into the house: a willow branch fastened on the wall, vases of wildflowers, and wood carvings of bears. Sometimes the intrusion was more than symbolically. A few times a local black bear had come to visit; it had sat on the glider on the front porch. Homer was awakened by the barking of his two dogs. He told them to be quiet, that there was nothing, and then had to apologize to them when he looked outside and saw the bear looking calmly back at him.

The Steedlys' house sat on the heavily wooded slope of a foothill, off a narrow country road with the lovely name Pisgah Shadows. The area behind the screened porch at its rear opened into a forest-encircled garden. Homer, constructing to another vision Tibby had wanted to solidify in this place, had put down a white graveled pathway, its edges marked by clusters of ferns and hostas. It wound its way to raised plant beds, filled with yellow-fringed orchids, foam flowers, and jack-in-the pulpits, and then meandered to a brick-rimmed pond, its dark surface crowded with swaying flag irises, dragon flies skimming above them.

The flowers are often the subject of Tibby's and Homer's photographs; they are both serious nature photographers. I looked through a stack of Homer's close-ups of flowers and plants: beads of sparkling dew on deep green leaves, a bee settling on the bristle heart of a sunflower. In this country of sweeping landscapes, they showed a focus on the minutiae, the fine details of its consistency. In the middle of the stack, the war intruded: a photograph of a convoy of soldiers, armored vehicles, and trucks fording a river at Ploei Kleng. I had seen it before on his Web site. Some of the soldiers were bathing in the river, their nudity fragile in contrast to the war machinery, the reddish dust raised by the machines tingeing the air. It is a photo that reminds one of a Renaissance painting. Seconds after it was taken, Homer told me, the ford was hit by enemy mortars, the shrapnel exploding among the men in the water.

In the living room, after watching the film Marc and I had brought back from Thai Giang, we sat in stunned silence for a while. I told Homer how eager the Hoang family was to have him visit them. One of the Steedlys' two dogs, Dottie, pushed her forehead against my side, and I scratched her ears. Tibby looked at us and smiled. "She usually doesn't take to strangers," she said, and then told me how the small, white-faced dog had come to them. When she and Homer were out for a walk, Homer had noticed the dog cowering under a low bridge, looking starved and, from her cowering reaction to his advances, obviously abused. He had sat with her for over an hour, talking softly, and had finally stuck his hand out. When she sank her teeth into his thumb, he had not reacted, just let her grip him until she understood he would not harm her, and then she had come out and become their dog. It was something, said Tibby, who had just watched a village mourning her husband's kill, that she wanted me to know about Homer.

I'll go there, Homer said. He was ready now.

# CHAPTER TWENTY-SEVEN

# The Cuc Phuong National Park

But I didn't know if I was. A year and a half later, back in Viet Nam to, among other things, make the arrangements for Homer's visit, I struggled uphill over the sharp, slippery rocks of a jungle trail, sweat running into my eyes.

To my generation, at least that part of it that fought in the Viet Nam War, a certain giddy madness is evoked by the idea of national parks in Viet Nam. Seeing the signs for the park at Cuc Phuong, in Ninh Binh Province, took me back to those times in the war when we would fantasize coming to Viet Nam one day as tourists, the deadly jungles we were patrolling or flying over turned into commercialized attractions, Jungle Worlds, the lovely beaches into umbrella-dotted resorts where ex-VC waiters would bring mai tais and cold beer out to our beach chairs. We never believed those daydreams, though they all came true. On this day, trudging with Le Minh Khue and Ho Anh Thai up a mountain trail (our goal was to hike the eight kilometers to a famous 1,000-year-old tree) that runs through the riotous undergrowth of pre-historic-looking ferns, orchids, climbing and hanging vines, and thorn and flower bushes, all

tangled under the tree canopy of the jungle; helping support a
panting former NVA Youth Volunteer who had once moved
more lightly up other trails that would look exactly like this—
and being supported by her when my own heart started beating
like a mad drummer in my chest—I had that sense I sometimes
have that I was moving through a dream that I was actually having in the war. It was a way of seeing Viet Nam I could not shake,
no matter how many trips I made here, no matter that I knew
the country better now than I ever did in the war. It all edged
and overlapped in my mind again now, and I tried to make a different comparison, to see it the way Homer might when he came
to Viet Nam, a blending into a series of tugging dichotomies
between this place, so like both the deadly jungle in which he'd
fought, and the safe envelopments of the Pisgah Forest: mountain paths that might wind under dark tunnels of mountain
laurel and rhododendrons to segue into the path we were on
now winding uphill under the gloomy canopies of huge, vine-
strangled trees. It was the way I wanted Homer to see Viet Nam,
tied to some present peace, instead of seeing it as I did, in layers, thinly shelled over both memory and a perception couched
by memory and films and books.

But I didn't know if it were possible for any member of my
generation to see the country other than through the prism of
the war. A few days before we decided to explore the Cuc
Phuong, we had stopped at the famous cathedral at Phat Diem.
The complex consists of a series of buildings and shrines spread
over a huge, paved square, watched over by a statue of the founding priest, Father Six, the limestone boulders he had piled to test
whether the boggy ground would hold the weight of the buildings still there. Other such slabs lie heaped up at the base of the
bell tower, placed there so the local mandarins could sit throned
atop them and monitor the Catholic rites. The cathedral is quite
beautiful, and like many Catholic churches in Nam Dinh and
Thai Binh—as I had noticed when I first went to Thai Giang to
see the Hoangs—it is a strange mix of French cathedral design

and Chinese architecture: European-style bell towers next to dragon-scale-tiled roofs topped by pagoda towers, their tiered levels marked by tile awnings with upturned tips; stained glass windows and friezes decorated with lotus flowers and dragons and Christian saints. Outside the church grounds we had seen an odder representation of foreign symbols that have either conquered or been conquered by Viet Nam. In the center of an artificial pond rimmed with green scum was a large stone turtle, the sacred symbol of Hanoi and resistance to foreign invasion; atop its shell sat a large, red-and-white plastic Santa Claus, one hand raised in greeting. It inadvertently brought back to me—and, I suppose, commented on—the old antiwar chant: Ho Ho Ho Chi Minh/NLF is going to win.

But even more resonant of the war—or its representations—was the canal that runs along the road going into Phat Diem, clusters of empty plastic bottles and trash clumped in its dark, greasy water. Looking at it, I recalled the scene in Graham Greene's *The Quiet American* when Fowler, who had come to Phat Diem to report on the war, comes across perhaps this same canal, with so many human bodies floating in the water that it looks like a kind of stew.

And thinking of Greene, I remembered walking Nguyen Qui Duc's dog a few days earlier. I had stayed in his house this time; Duc is a repatriated Vietnamese American who returned to live in Viet Nam both because he had always wanted to come back, and to take care of his mother, who suffers from Alzheimers. The cost of the needed caregivers in the San Francisco area, where Duc lived and worked at a local National Public Radio station, was prohibitive.

He and his mother—and two full-time helpers—live in a big, ancient Hanoi house. A steel gate shields its inner courtyard from a busy street, and three stories of high-ceilinged rooms and balconies look over parts of the city. His dog, Moto, also lives there. Moto is a bulldog, small and close-furred, with a barrel chest and a flattened face and huge, strangely beautiful eyes. Early each morning he came to my bed and stared at me, and I got up and got his leash. We walked over a small bridge and along the Ho Tay Lake into which John McCain had parachuted during the war. More than once, as people in the neighborhood stared, it struck me how I would look to them, though the connection I imagined wasn't to McCain, but rather to an American walking his ugly dog over a bridge, the ghost of Alden Pyle, the Quiet American, transmuted here from Saigon. I couldn't shake that way of seeing the war, and its interpretations shelled inside everything, or coexisting with it, as the Buddhist and Catholic styles and art and mythologies edged into each other at Phat Diem, no matter how many new friendships and experiences in Viet Nam layered themselves between the present and the war.

How would Homer take being here, and how would the Hoangs react to him, each of them faced with the physical presence instead of the idea of the other? Now that his trip was becoming a reality I'd helped create, I was full of trepidation. Homer had felt completed, he said, when he heard the story of how the documents had been returned. How would he feel if the family found his presence too painful or grating—what would that do to the wound in his heart—and theirs— that had begun to knit together?

"I don't know what I would feel if I were them," Khue said. We had finally reached what Khue and I—panting, struggling, both of us too out of shape for jungle hiking—had begun to call The Fucking Tree (as in Thai-oi, when will we get to the fucking tree?), and were sitting under a very effective, wordless sign posted above our heads: a picture of an endangered civet, half of a civet couple, with a hunter shooting it and the mathematical formula $2 - 1 = 0$.

I touched the cool, muscular trunk of the tree, looking up at it and then back at her. She held my gaze.

"I think about our friendship, that it's the same thing. If we can forgive each other . . ."

She tapped my chest. "You," she said, "have nothing to forgive me for." And then smiled, though I knew, deeply, she would never truly believe in the symmetry I was suggesting. Nor should.

"The Hoang family is very insistent that they wanted him to come."

"They are strong people," she admitted. "And they seem sincere. But you don't know how the rest of the village may react."

"What you may need to think about, grandpa," Thai said, "is the way his coming may affect the family, in the village. It's true; they are good people. But others may talk about them, get jealous, think they are getting rich from this American."

"I don't know what to do about that."

He smiled. "Just be careful. You may be met by stones."

"*Chieu oi,*" Khue said. "To be frank," she said. "If you had killed Phuoc I would not want to meet you. How would you feel if someone came who had killed Adam?" Phuoc is her daughter; Adam, my son.

She looked away, into the forest, and I wondered if she were glimpsing, between the leaves of this place, the forms of the girls her own daughter's age who had died next to her on the Trails.

"Just think about it carefully," Thai said again.

But what came into my mind was something Duc had told me about an American veteran who had participated in the My Lai massacre. Wracked—stretched on a mental rack for years—with guilt over what he had done, he wanted to meet the survivors of a family whose other members he had slaughtered, in order to confront his past, heal. What a terrible thing to do, I'd said to Duc. He had met one of the family members, who had agreed—"with teeth clenched in hatred," Duc said—to smile and meet the man; it was national policy now to be friendly to the Americans, and he would obey. The American would find his healing by opening wounds in them, as if they existed on earth only to heal or define him. Was I looking at the Hoangs in the same way, needing Homer to go to them, to receive their forgiveness and grace, almost as much as he did?

Before coming back, I had e-mailed a message to Duc: "Tell me, my friend, do you think I'm doing the right thing? I've pushed for this, mainly because the Hoangs have said they wanted it to happen and—for that reason—I thought it will be a good thing for both them and Homer, about whom I've grown more protective, as I find out what a truly good man he is . . . hard-worn but the core of innocence never destroyed. I was very against the event you told me about—the My Lai killer going back to meet the family; outraged that he would try to find his peace at the expense of theirs. Of course I know Homer's situation is not like that, and, again, the family has been very clear that they understand the circumstances and are grateful for his keeping the documents and the information he was able to give them—and really want him to come. So now that it is actually happening, I hope I'm right. I've been working on the book about him and Dam for about six months now, deeply taken by it, and in the course of doing it I've gotten to know Homer well. As I said, he's a good man, the best of us, and I want a happy ending, or at least a resolved one for them and him, yet as a writer, or just as a man moving through his times, I sometimes have doubts, a lack of faith in both."

"I think you and Homer are doing what is proper," he had replied. "As for the My Lai guy, I can only hope that was his first step toward some act of decency toward the remaining members of the family he killed, and to all the others who suffered needlessly."

But I was still not sure.

After our time at the 1,000-year-old tree, we hiked to another of the park's attractions: a cave used by prehistoric forest dwellers some 7,500 years before. Scrambling up the path, using creepers to help us pull ourselves up, I could see why they had picked this spot: the cave mouth was near the top of a vertical limestone face, easy to defend; from there it would be easy to spot any movement in the terrain below, in spite of the thick jungle. Looking out of the cave's entrance, above the tree line, I could see the jagged teeth of the limestone karsts and the lushly jungled mountains rolling on for miles, a sensation of the country suddenly opening up after the claustrophobic closeness of the forest. Inside was a large chamber; to its right a narrow gap led into another series of antechambers, pitch black, their ceilings rising twenty feet or more above my head, suggestive shadows from the clusters of stalactites and stalagmites flowing across them when I shone a flashlight around. Khue and Thai declined any exploration beyond the entrance cave, and coming back I saw they had lit joss sticks in a small pit near the cave mouth and were praying to the spirits of whatever ancient ancestors had dwelled there.

I looked at Khue's face, her eyes closed, her lips moving silently. I did not know for what, or to whom, she was praying. She was kneeling at the mouth of the cave. Like me, but more than I ever would, Khue still saw the terrain, the shape of the landscape, from the mouth of that cave in her memory. It framed everything.

When she and her friends had emerged from the caves on the Ho Chi Minh Trails that sheltered them, we killed them if we could. Often she had buried others we had killed. They had come to symbolize a kind of perfected human being in her eyes, as the dead tend to do, if their death is seen as a kind of sacrifice. She survived years during which those companions in her cave had died next to her, shredded with shrapnel from American bombs or blown up trying to defuse them. Her first contact with Americans had been Hemingway, London, and Steinbeck. In her second contact, she had seen the head of one of her favorite teachers blown off in a bombing attack.

*If you had killed Phuoc*, she had said. The founding legend of our friendship was based on the need and the ability to forgive all of it. We had all taken enough from each other, even if it wasn't proportionate. But suppose when we met she had known I had killed one of her friends in the cave?

Khue rose now, and caught me looking at her. She shook her head, a wordless acknowledgment of what she could see I was struggling with.

"Bring him. It's not up to you," she said, reading my mind, and Thai nodded, repeating her words in English.

If she meets Homer, I thought, I know she will like him. If she looks into his face, as she had once looked into mine.

What I was afraid of, I knew, was that it really could never be over.

Before coming here, I had gone out to Thai Giang again with Duc and Doug Reese to talk about Homer's pending visit. We had stopped in Thai Binh and picked up Huy and Dam's brother-in-law, Dieu, and had taken them to lunch. The conversation had drifted into war stories. Dieu told us that he had been in an infantry unit that had also gone down the Ho Chi Minh Trail, but he had fought in Quang Ngai, where I knew he had ambushed the American LRRP unit, and in Quang Nam provinces. He had been wounded in the fighting around Hoi An, an area near where I had once been for a time. I hope I didn't shoot you, I said, to relieve some of my own tension, and he laughed and said, no, it was a South Vietnamese soldier.

Actually, the word he had used was puppet soldier, and I could see Duc stiffen a little next to me, though he was used to the term by now. Duc had left Viet Nam in 1975, when he was seventeen, and had had a successful career as a journalist in the United States. When he was ten he had been in the city of Hue and had witnessed not only the destruction of the old gracious Imperial capital during the 1968 Tet Offensive, but also the capture of his father, Nguyen Van Dai, a South Vietnamese government official. Duc's father spent twelve years imprisoned in the North, eight of them in solitary confinement, in a hole often filled to the level of his bamboo rack with water, while his mother kept the family alive after the defeat of South Viet Nam by selling noodles on the street.[2] But Duc said nothing then, did not comment on Dieu's use of the derogatory term, and when Huy inquired where he came from, perhaps hearing something in his accent, Duc only answered, "Hanoi."

Later, in the car, Huy spoke of the military cemeteries and the Hoangs' desire to identify Dam and bring him home. He spoke about the government's efforts to help find and repatriate such remains. Duc peered at him. Did he think the government should also help find the remains of South Vietnamese soldiers?

Of course not, Huy said. They were the enemies of the nation. It was up to the Americans to help find them, if they wished. Dieu listened, nodding.

As Huy spoke, I thought of the Confederate cemetery and monument at Point Lookout, Maryland, near my home. More than 3,000 Southern prisoners died there; their graves are not marked, not even by blank stones. There are two monuments. The smaller was erected by the state; it is inscribed with the Old Lie, *Dulce et decorum Est pro patria Mori*. The larger was not erected by the federal government until the 1930s; before then there was no question of building memorials to the enemies of the country. I've heard that analogy before, Duc said later, when I mentioned it to him, trying to comfort him with the idea that civil wars lasted for centuries after the fighting stopped. "It doesn't matter," he said, anguished. "Can't Huy see that my father loved this country also?"

I thought of the pain Huy's words had unknowingly caused my friend as I stared out at the Cuc Phuong forest—staring out of the mouth of a cave as Khue and her friends had done—trying to peer into the near future. The complex agonies I had stirred into here.

When Doug, Duc, and I had arrived in Thai Giang, we found that the Hoangs had decided they wanted to do more than simply meet Homer. "We want to take a trip to [Dam's grave]. That is our wish," Dieu had said to me. Dam's bones were still among the thirty-four sets of remains, the blank tombstones of the Ayunpa cemetery in Gia Lai Province. If Homer would come there with them, they were sure Dam would draw them to the right grave. "We feel that my brother's spirit is connected to Homer in some way, and so with his presence here, we would hope that will help us bring the remains back," Luong said. Whatever had passed between Dam and Homer at the instant of death had not ended then, they felt; it had stirred Homer to keep the documents and to find someone who had allowed him to return them.

Their plans had deepened my concerns. I didn't share the Hoangs' confidence that bringing him to the cemetery would achieve what they wanted. What would their reaction be if they didn't find Dam?

Yet our visit to the Hoangs in Thai Giang had otherwise been comfortable and pleasant. It had been quieter than the time I'd brought the documents: no crowds, just the family sitting in Luong's living room. Cat had lit incense, as Khue had, at the altar of their ancestors, in front of the photographs of the two war martyrs, brother Chi and brother Dam, and the notebook Homer had taken and I had brought back, which was now permanently placed in front of the second photo.

"We hope you will welcome these guests into our home," Cat had said, speaking to the photograph as if he were speaking to Dam himself, as we sat in Luong's house: Duc, a Vietnamese man who had to leave his homeland when he was seventeen, while his father was still confined in a northern prison; and Doug Reese and I, two Americans who had fought against them.[3] "Dam is a sacred soul; he has drawn all of us together," Phan Thanh Hao had said, and I knew the Hoangs truly believed that Homer's visit would allow them to finally bring Dam, and more than Dam, to rest. "As a veteran I know you cannot bring back the dead," Dieu had said. "But we wish to acknowledge that the war has gone on too long."

The Hoangs were as desperate as Homer was, as the three of us here in the Cuc Phuong were, for an ending. They wanted a body so that they could unearth it and then finally bury it for good.

# PART FIVE

# HOMECOMING

# CHAPTER TWENTY-EIGHT

# Thai
# Giang

H omer Steedly Jr. returned to Viet Nam on May 20, 2008. Through the plane window as we circled in to land at Tan Son Nhat, he could see the green grids of rice fields, the wide river snaking below, and then the tangled sprawl of houses, buildings, and gleaming towers solidifying out of the brown haze that hung over Ho Chi Minh City. He hadn't had a chance to visit this place in its former incarnation as Saigon during the war, and so its octopus growth since then didn't register now. His first landing in country had been at the American base at Cam Ranh Bay, and his two tours had all been in the jungles of the Central Highlands; he had never taken an in-country R&R or gone to Saigon or Vung Tau, or the other Vietnamese cities presented to GIs as prizes for surviving portions of their tours.

The airport terminal he walked into from the umbilical transit corridor was clean and modern, lined with floor to ceiling windows that were slightly beaded with condensation from the air-conditioning. Except for the sudden memory of the heat he felt, conjured by its breath on the outside of that glass; except for the line of old American revetments and rusting Quonset huts he could still see edging part of the runway; except for the people pressing against the barriers beyond the customs area, some of them in familiar cone-shaped hats, their shouted words vaguely familiar, a dim memory under the ringing in his ears; except for the customs officials, wearing the uniforms of the old enemy, the red star on their garrison hats, peering up at him from the photo on his new passport as if looking for the young lieutenant hidden under the mask of his years, he could have been anywhere.

It had been nearly two years since Homer had told me he wanted to meet the Hoang family. The reason that it had taken so long, and the reason he was able to come now, was due to another family tragedy. After a long, debilitating illness, Tibby's mother, Betty Dozier, had passed away. Homer had not wanted to travel while Betty was ill; he and Tibby had been able to spend much of her last days with his mother-in-law. Betty Dozier had been married to a soldier and had been the main caretaker of another, her brother, his mind frozen to the battlefields of World War II. "She understood Homer more than any of us," Tibby says. "She knew how important it was for him to go to Viet Nam, and she knew we couldn't afford it. If her health had been good, she would have paid for the trip. As it was, she made sure in her will that there would be money for both of us to go." [1]

But Tibby's own health at the time precluded her accompanying us. There were four in our group now: Homer and I, Doug Reese—whom I'd asked to make arrangements in Viet Nam for the trip—and Jessica Phillips, a young radio producer. When Homer had told me he was able to make the trip, I'd contacted Marc Steiner to see if he wanted to come along again and do a sequel to our original program. Marc had just been fired from WYPR in Baltimore, the end move in a long-standing feud with the station director and board of trustees. He was eager to go to Viet Nam and record the end of Homer's story, but was burdened with the complications of his situation. Jessica had left the station to work with Marc in his new production company. "I'm going to let her go with you instead," he told me. "She's very good, bro."

If the three men with whom she would travel represented our country's old relationship with that country, Jessica was part of its new connections, or at least her family was. The Phillips owned a famous Maryland seafood restaurant chain. Over the past few decades, as Chesapeake Bay became depleted of the crabs and oysters that were the mainstay of its fishing industry, the family had begun importing more and more from Asia, rousing the anger of local watermen. The bulk of the shrimp they now brought into the country was processed and shipped from Nha Trang. Viet Nam was not a war. It was a business opportunity.

Our plan was to spend a day in Ho Chi Minh City and then go north to Hanoi, where I would visit my writer friends and let Homer acclimate a little to modern Viet Nam before meeting the family of the man he had killed. I thought of it as a kind of reverse of the army's homecoming policy for the Viet Nam War: men pulled out of the jungle one day, on American streets the next, a shock to the system Homer had experienced twice. On his final trip home, after his second tour, he had looked out the aircraft window and seen fuel spilling out of a leak in the engine. Is that supposed to do that? he had asked the flight attendant, who turned pale when she saw what he was looking at. Soon afterward the plane had made an emergency landing in Alaska, and the men, in their tropical uniforms, were ordered to sprint across a runway where the temperature was fifty below zero. The air burned on Homer's skin like fire as he ran, as if he no longer belonged in the same atmosphere as the country to which he was returning, the shock of that run a precursor of all the other shocks and displacements of a homecoming for which he had not in any way been prepared.

We would do it differently now, I thought. Let Homer see the country at peace first; let him experience the throngs of people in the cities and the countryside who had either been born

after or had militantly forgotten the war, the people who would
not see it stamped on his face. I had brought George Evans out
to the village and its grief right after he landed; it had shocked
him, made him see enemies where there were none. I would not
repeat that mistake with Homer.

After Thai Giang, on the original schedule, we were to travel
south with the family; stop at Vinh, which is located in a province
just north of the old division between the northern and southern
parts of the country, and visit Tien; and then go to the Ayunpa
cemetery at Azaban, in Gia Lai Province, where Dam's remains
were buried. Doug Reese and I had not believed the family would
have any more luck than they had had in the past in identifying
which grave, among the thirty-four, was Dam's. But we would
pay our respects in the cemetery, we thought, and then leave
them, go back to the Mekong Delta, and visit Camau, the southernmost town in the country, where Doug had been stationed
and where he had met the brother of the man he had killed.

Earlier that month, Colonel Tien had told me she would
go south with us to Gia Lai when we went with the Hoangs.
That same day I had received a message from Phan Thanh Hao:
the Hoang family had consulted a famous medium, who had
told them exactly where Dam's grave was located among the
thirty-four unidentified bodies in the cemetery. Based on her vision, they would be able to get permission from the authorities
to disinter his remains and bring them back to Thai Giang. They
still wanted Homer and me to accompany them. In fact, the
medium had told them it was essential that we go along. When
Tien found out, she was not happy with their decision to rely on
magic. I shared her skepticism, and I hoped their decision to use
the medium would not preclude her coming with us. But the
family's faith, Hao told me, was in the medium; she had located
many remains for many families. Through her they had spoken
to Dam; she had told them things that only he could know.

The Hoangs' certainty convinced Doug and me to have a
backup plan. If they actually found Dam, we would need to go

back north with them, to the village, to participate in the funeral. How did Homer feel about that?

Whatever they need, he said. That was what he was here for.

*Here* was Saigon, insisting on its original name, whatever the name of its latest victor. Homer was buoyed up by the friendliness of the people, by the energy of the commerce that seemed almost to pulse in the heat. But the noise assailed him. His hearing still contained the scream of the shell that had exploded near him on Hill 467, these days a silence growing over it as well, cushioning it, but slowly muffling out the rest of the world also. The hearing aid he wore tried to diffuse and order noise, but Saigon overwhelmed it, as would all the cities of Viet Nam: the constant blare of horns, un-muffled engines, loudspeakers blaring the commercials that had replaced party slogans and admonitions, the shouting and screaming and shoving for space. The country had four times as many people as it had had when he was last here.

Sleepless, up at dawn, he called my room and we walked around the green oasis of the park across the street from the hotel, watching the grace of the elders doing morning tai chi exercises, the exuberance of the young people jogging or hitting shuttlecocks back and forth. He found flowers and plants he would see at home, searching out connections the way Daisy Zamora had, though not for the same reasons. There was no tenseness in him when he was among the people. They did not look like enemies to him; they never had, and now they smiled and laughed, and he ate their food and found it to be wonderful.

On the second day, on our way to the airport, the hotel staff loaded our bags into the back of a taxi van. We decided to stop first at a restaurant and let the taxi go, but when we helped the driver unload, we found two large backpacks that did not belong to any of us. They must have been in the hotel lobby, Doug said. I felt sick, thinking of whomever these belonged to, their trip ruined. We paid the driver 100,000 dong to take the packs back to the hotel—surely, we reasoned, he knew we had his number, would simply do what he had to. Besides, we were here to learn to trust our fellow man. Who never showed up at the hotel. Who taught us once again not to romanticize that which you wanted to save you. Someone else would pay the price of our desired delusion. An old story.

In Hanoi, our hotel was near Nguyen Qui Duc's house, and we had coffee and *pho* with him in a small café and then walked with him around Ho Tay Lake, where McCain had once parachuted after bombing this city. Duc needed to get out of the noise, he told me. He had finished his house in Tam Dao, in the mountains north of the city, and if we could, we should come up; it was a sanctuary for him. Bring Homer, he said, after whatever happens. After, or if, Dam's remains are returned.

"How's your mother doing?" I asked him.

"Some good days, but more bad ones. Some days now she thinks I'm her husband, thinks I'm my father. She berates me for abandoning her."

His words reminded me of his plans to bring his sister's and his father's ashes back here. His father, Nguyen Van Dai, was finally freed in 1980, after twelve years in prison, and reunited with his wife, who also went through searing hardships and tragedies during that time. One of the worst was the death of Duc's sister, Dieu-Quynh, who suffered from mental illness for many years. When Duc returned to Viet Nam the first time, he had done what the Hoang family wanted to do with Dam's bones—brought back her ashes, in his case to the United States. Now he had brought both hers and his father's back here.

"What have you done with your father's ashes?"

"They're on a shelf in the house, along with my sister's. I was going to put them in my mother's family mausoleum in Hue. But they've been giving me a hard time. We're of royal descent, and so on. The reality is that they are afraid to have a funeral for someone who had been a political prisoner associated with the old regime. I'm sick of it, sick of royal blood and all such crap. He's the man who supported your sister, I say to them. I don't care. I'll dispose of him myself."

We both looked at the lake. The reflections of the trees and flowers and buildings wavered on its surface, the light bright and lovely and vivifying the colors. But a rim of impacted trash lay just beneath the surface, visible under the oily sheen in the water. Duc laughed.

"No, don't worry; not here. I'll scatter them in Tam Dao. In the mountains."

Tam Dao is a mountain village north of Hanoi. The house he built there is made of the naked native stone of the place and overlooks hundreds of miles of mountains and forest, much of it thick with the same tall pine trees one sees at Da Lat, the town where he grew up. He had re-created Da Lat there, as he had re-created a San Francisco arts and café scene in Hanoi.

We walked to the John McCain statue. The John McCain memorial, some Americans called it, but what was memorialized was not him but his capture. His name is misspelled, McCann, and the sculpted representation of one wing of his airplane has USAF on it rather than the correct initials, USN. Otherwise, the representation of McCain imprisoned in stone, held forever captive in the past, seemed accurate. And not just for McCain.

"Let's get out of here," Homer said softly.

"I couldn't have come here ten years ago," Homer said that night. He meant of course Viet Nam, though where we actually were was with Duc and his girlfriend, Lien Dung, in the Café Cong. "Cong" means communist: the small, sidewalk café was, in name and décor, an ironic homage to a recent past apparently, or wishfully, distant enough to be subsumed into nostalgic parody. The collage of posters and photos on the wall included Party figures, slogans, and, I noticed now, several images of GIs, from war movies or famous shots by David Duncan or Nicholas Ut. An American expat sat with us, an artist named Bradford

whose father was a Viet Nam vet, and who had done a book of
photographs of zippo lighters used by troops in Viet Nam, inscribed with epigraphs of the "I'm the meanest mother-fucker
in the valley" variety. The ironical quality of the café and his
book was somehow negated or contradicted by the presence of
Homer and the reason he was in Viet Nam. Irony needs distance.

"I don't dream. Or rather I don't see images when I dream,"
Homer told me as we looked at the pictures in the collage. We
were talking in low voices, the others around us, Duc and his
friends, engaged in their own conversations. "What I remember
experiencing is a kind of waking dream. A waking nightmare."
On his second tour, he told me, he had taken over a unit that
had become slack and rebellious. He had ordered a patrol to set
up a listening post outside the perimeter. But the patrol leader,
he had been warned by the man he replaced, had a reputation
for sandbagging—only going out a few yards in the darkness and
settling in comfortably for the night. In the command bunker, on
the radio, Homer had ordered the man to cross a stream a few
hundred yards past the wire and set up along a possible avenue
of approach on its other side. Look, Captain, the patrol leader
had replied, the stream is swollen with floodwater and running
fast; I could lose people going over. Homer didn't believe the
man and angrily ordered him to take his men and go across.

"But he wasn't lying," Homer said, his voice strained. One
of the men, weighed down by his equipment and weapons, was
swept away by the current and drowned. "I sent him out. He
had to cross a little intermittent stream, you know the little dot-
ted blue line on the map that means it's a couple of inches deep,
or a foot deep or something, something you could walk across—
well, he said it was a raging white-water rapids and I just
thought he was lying because he didn't want to go out. So I
browbeat him into trying to cross the rapids. Well, he lost a guy.
The guy trying to go across drowned. We never found his body.
That has haunted me all my life." His voice rose and almost
broke and then he stopped and looked into his beer. "You know

I forced that guy to make a decision and try something, and of course I didn't know, you know? But still, I used my intellect to browbeat this poor guy into doing that, and it probably messed his mind up the rest of his life, too, and that bothered me." He stopped speaking again and stared at the beer. Around us the conversations continued, people talking about Bradford's installation piece, a new poet from Saigon, the food at Bobby Chin's, whether Nguyen Huy Thiep would ever write again. Viet Nam was not a war. Homer's hand had gripped the beer glass hard. "That's what I dream about. But there are no images. It is a waking dream. I wake up in the middle of the night and I don't know where I am and it's dark because we didn't have any lights on in the bunker while I was doing all this—just the ambient light from the moon—and I wake up confused, because I think I'm there. I think I've just passed out and I'm back on my feet again, I'm trying to find the radio and then I touch some furniture or something and I realize I'm not there, I'm back in the world."

We had been talking and e-mailing, on and off, for a year about his experiences in the war. But this memory, which he called his worst, had only come out now, sitting over beers in Hanoi. This Viet Nam, the modern country prosperous and peaceful enough for its young people to afford a sense of irony, the cities where he had never been, especially this, the enemy capital, were bringing the past back to him in a rush of the images he denied he could see. Welcome to the funhouse, I thought, and ordered two more beers.

The dream, he said, melted into the day.[2]

In the morning we went to Thai Giang. It was a gray day but oppressively hot and humid by six in the morning. In the back of the van we carried a large memorial wreath, a circle of yellow and red flowers set on a bamboo tripod. I had ordered it the night before, but when it arrived the hotel staff had refused to let it sit in the lobby—its commemoration of the dead would bring bad luck, might make other guests reluctant to enter. We had set it next to a row of motor scooters parked outside the front entrance. No one disturbed it.

Jessica, Doug, Homer, and I sat quietly, too aware of what we were doing to relax. We had picked up another person, Bill Deeter, a former air force officer, and now a civilian consultant to the U.S. remains recovery team. Bill, a stocky, bald man with a generous beer belly and belly laugh, spoke, wrote, and read perfect Vietnamese. He had interviewed the brother-in-law, Hoang Minh Dieu, and was particularly interested in meeting Lieutenant Colonel Tien and seeing her museum if we went to Vinh. As we headed out of Hanoi, Quan, our Vietnamese translator and arranger, received a telephone call from the family. They needed to know if we had left. The medium had to make arrangements for a zombie to follow us and protect us. I glanced in the side view mirror, and Quan saw me and laughed. "Is he there yet?" he asked.

"I'm not sure. What kind of motor scooter would a zombie ride?"

"*Dream*," he said, grinning.

Bill laughed. "Bich Hang [the medium] is famous. She was on the Discovery Channel."[3]

It was the first time Jessica and Homer had been out of the city, and as the green fields began to surround us, stretching to the horizon, Jessica asked what was being grown in them. "Rice," everyone else in the van said simultaneously, but softly as a prayer. A breeze blew swathes through the stalks. At the edges of the field, boys sat on mud-caked water buffalos, and white egrets waded, lifting their legs carefully, one by one, out of the muddy water. I watched Homer watching the countryside. He saw it, he said, through a farmer's eyes. He wanted to connect to it, not hold it at the safe distance he had the last time he was here. He saw the concrete telephone poles that marched through the paddies and thought, good idea, wooden telephone poles in farmland never lasted. He saw two stores selling rice seed and thought, of course. Stores selling seed. He saw a boy

plowing behind a water buffalo and saw himself behind a mule.
The road went from highway to a two-lane road, to a one-lane
country road, along a berm lined with areca trees. Among them
was a row of shanty restaurants offering "Thit Meo," cat meat.
As the roads grew narrower, more filled with pot holes, we
seemed to be funneling down into what a guidebook would call
a different time. It was, though perhaps not in the way that
cliché was meant to be taken. We were moving into a world
where zombies were called to us on cell phones and dead souls
demanded attention, a universe ordered by different and more
ancient rules. We were nearly to Thai Giang.

And then we saw the dead man.

A truck and a bus had stopped in front of us, blocking the
road. The man was being pulled out of the water-filled ditch at
the side of the rice field. As he was lifted, a small crowd around
him, his head fell back, mouth open and streaming water, and
his long hair hung down, fallen back from his forehead, his
chest bare and splotched with mud. Jessica drew in a sharp
breath. "Not a good sign," she said somewhat desperately, echo-
ing my thoughts. I had been, I realized now, psychologically
holding my breath since we left Hanoi, hoping everything
would go smoothly. In my journal that morning I had written,
"It's 3:40 AM on the morning of the 24th. I can't sleep. Too much
anticipation, all the possibilities running through my head.
What if Khue and Thai are right, and they attack him? What if
he just can't take the confrontation?" I looked at Homer looking
at the dead man. He had seen many dead men, but to have it
happen here and now, on his way to meet Dam's family, to see a
corpse pulled out of a paddy. A drowned man. The man's bare
chest began to heave. Water spewed out of his nose and mouth.
Resurrection. One of the women near him tilted back her cone
hat and laughed. Several men helped to somehow drape the revived man over the front seat of a motor scooter, and the driver
took off, wobbling. The little knot of vehicles unraveled, and we
continued to the village.

At the People's Committee House—the place where I had first given Hoang Dang Cat the documents—Homer and I sat across from the village chairman, drinking the inevitable cups of green tea. We passed all of the groups' passports over the table to him, and then listed our names, ages, and what the Vietnamese literally translated as "homelands," meaning hometowns or states, in a notebook he gave us. The chairman, wearing a pressed white shirt, was a slim, middle-aged man with a full head of black hair. Unsmiling, he closed the notebook and then pointed to a map of Thai Giang on the wall, an amoebic shape, its edge bisected by the Song Diem Ho, the Diem Ho River, Hoang Ngoc Dam's true homeland, and began to list statistics. The village area was 4,500 hectares, and 605 families lived here. How many people, I asked. He looked at me blankly for a second, and I realized my mistake. It was never a matter of individuals. About 6,500, he said finally. Some 70 percent of the village area was planted in rice fields. They had two crops a year. He looked at Homer. There were 200 people from the village killed in the war, he said.

"I thought there were 142," I said.

He nodded. "Those are the war martyrs from both the French and American wars. Most from the American war." "War martyrs" meant soldiers. "Every family in this village had at least one person who fought. There are fifteen heroic mothers, women who gave and lost their only child, or at least three children, to the war."

Homer remained silent.

"How does it feel to meet American veterans?" I asked the chairman.

He looked into my eyes and didn't smile. "I have met many of you before," he said, and closed his notebook.

The obelisks flanking the war memorial did indeed list 200 names from all the wars. Now I noticed how many of them were

Hoangs. I asked Luong, who had met us there, if they were all related. No, he said. Some were, but there were three large Hoang clans in the village.

After we had laid the wreath, he led us down the alley, between stone walls, to his house. Homer bore a tray of fruit—spiky, red-shelled lychees—to lay on the family altar. Ducks scurried out of our way, and curious children stared at us. The gate to Luong's courtyard was twined with fragrant bougainvillea flowers. A small, long-haired man in cutoffs and a sleeveless T-shirt suddenly rushed out from it and put a large TV camera in our faces. We had been forewarned that a crew from Vietnamese television would be here, but their presence still surprised me, seemed intrusive. He began to gesture wildly, motioning us to keep walking. I kept at Homer's flank, ashamed of the sense of relief I felt that the stares, this time, were on him and not on me, as they had been the first time we'd come to the village. As we entered the courtyard, the cameraman, a sound man, and someone I presumed was a director or producer, were, respectively, thrusting the camera and microphone in our faces or directing the others to do so. The director, I found out later, was a writer named Minh Chuyen, a veteran himself, he confided to me later, over beers. But it felt wrong that they were there, in the middle of this culminating meeting; they were taking the moment out from itself, as if its importance or significance would only occur later, in their film.

From inside the house I heard a woman screaming. Jessica edged between Homer and the sound. Through the open door I could see Dieu, the brother-in-law, dressed in an olive PAVN uniform, a red and gold veterans' badge on his lapel. He looked grim also. The women of the family were lined up against one wall. What I had feared was happening; the fact of Homer's coming had overwhelmed the intention of forgiveness. The screaming—it was not the wailings of grief I had heard on my first visit, but a shriek of rage—was now forming into a string of words or a chant. The woman began stamping her feet. Everything was edging out of control.

"What is she saying?" I asked Bill.

His listened for a moment, his forehead creasing. "I can't understand her." He shook his head. "She's babbling. Talking in tongues."

I looked in the door. The woman screaming was Thi Dam, the next-to-youngest sister. She had, I remembered, a normally dark complexion, but now her skin was beet red, almost purplish, as if starved of oxygen. She was standing in profile to me, her face tilted up. Her throat bulged, the swell of it moving up and puffing out her cheeks; her mouth gaped like a drowning person gasping for air, a high-pitched howl coming from between drawn lips. Tuoi, the youngest sister, knelt down in front of her and placed a small recorder in front of her mouth. The other women gathered around, hugging her, stroking her.

She's possessed by Dam's soul, Dieu explained matter-of-factly to Bill and Quan. It's OK; he knows you're here.

The woman suddenly fell silent as Homer entered, bearing the tray. There was only the hum of the electric fans. The air inside was stifling and heavy, and the fan blades only moved it around tepidly. As Homer placed the tray on the altar, Tuoi handed each of us a small bundle of lit incense sticks. Homer was staring at Dam's photo, sitting at the edge of the offering tray, in a tandem frame with his brother Chi. Luong cleared his throat. As the eldest brother, he wanted to welcome us. To welcome Homer and to express their gratitude that he would come. Luong, Cat, and Dieu smiled at Homer. He was still staring at Dam. It was the first time I had ever seen Homer with tears in his eyes. When he spoke, he started out evenly. "I'm Homer Steedly. I'm a farmer's son that got sent halfway around the world and wound up killing people that I didn't mean to." Homer's voice broke then, the way it had when he'd talked about the drowned boy. He struggled to go on. "And I've come here today to try to bring a little peace and resolution to the tragedy that all of us have suffered. And to honor all, all the soldiers who died on both sides of that war. And to pray that we never have to do anything like that again. Accept my deepest apologies. I'm so sorry."

As he spoke in his soft accent, Thi Dam began to scream and wail again as if in response to his words.

To see the emotion, the raw grief, seizing and shaking this man who rarely revealed emotion was too much for me. I tried to think of what was happening as a kind of science-fiction story. The soldiers of future wars each required to confront the family of their victims, help them find the remains, exhume them, carry them back, and rebury them. Each soldier required to do what Homer was doing here.

Something else seemed to relax in the room. We each walked up to the altar and placed our bundles of lit incense into a small ceramic bowl of sand set in front of the photos. Dieu, suddenly businesslike, his body jerking with energy, motioned us to sit down at the table. He preened a little, in his olive drab uniform, smoothing its front with his hands, and then took out a calendar. Would he ever go to confront the families of the Americans he killed? Like Homer, he could know their names. Was the question a fair one? I remembered our conversation with Pham Quang Huy. He was not a man with regrets, or who admitted to regrets. He had done the right thing, the only thing. Would the families of those families receive him the way the Hoangs were receiving Homer now? I felt a swell of admiration again for the courage or compassion or need this family and Homer were demonstrating.

Each group must have a leader, Dieu proclaimed, and he would be the leader of this group. Food was brought out, and we ate as we began to talk about the schedule for the next days: a train to Vinh and then Qui Nhon, two vans to Pleiku and then to the Ayunpa cemetery at the vaguely Middle Eastern-sounding town of Azaban. As we spoke in one part of the room, Thi Dam began moaning and babbling again, the deep yet shrill sound rising at times to screams. She was squatting near the altar at the far wall. The other women were caressing her shoulders and legs as she crouched. She raised her face, and the stream of words spilled out. Her voice was high-pitched and unnatural and made the hairs on the back of my neck rise. Dieu, Luong, and Cat went on calmly discussing the plans; we were disagreeing about the time needed, Doug insisting on sticking to the schedule we had already agreed upon. As they argued, the women lined up against the opposite wall kept kneeling and stroking Thi Dam, who twitched and wailed, as Tuoi held the small recorder to her face. Next to her, I saw, was Dam's wife, Pham Thi Minh. She had not looked at Homer. She seemed much older than the last time I saw her, her face intent, listening to the spirit of her first husband (her second, I found out later, had died earlier that year).

"It will be alright," Dieu said, looking at me looking at the women, at his possessed sister-in-law. "Dam has told us to go with you to bring him home. And then everything will be alright."

Finally, we all shook hands. Tuoi glanced at us and clicked off her recorder. She was to come with us on the journey.

I went outside. Behind the house, clumps of green bamboo and breadfruit trees bordered a small, beautiful pond. Homer came out and stood next to me.

"You doing OK?" I asked.

A small flock of white ducks spilled over the bank and into the pond.

"I couldn't stop looking at his photograph," he said softly. "His eyes kept following me, the whole time we were there."

# CHAPTER TWENTY-NINE

# Vinh

Any tension we had felt during Homer's initial meeting with the Hoangs was gone that evening, as we sat at a long table in a hotel restaurant in Nam Dinh, waiting to catch the 8:00 P.M. train to Vinh. It would arrive there at 1:00 A.M., and we would check into a hotel before going to meet Lieutenant Colonel Tien in the morning. When the family—Cat, Luong, Tuoi, and brother-in-law Dieu—had gotten into the van with us, the atmosphere had changed to that of a family outing. Now at dinner they laughed, joked, slapped Homer on the back, and teased Doug about keeping up with his young wife. It could have been an excursion to the beach, if one were going to the beach to disinter one's dead brother. Part of the hilarity came from the relief that this was finally happening.

At the dinner table, many of their questions to Homer were about his mother. How old was she? Was she in good health? Did he have a photograph? Her careful preservation of Dam's documents, of, in their view, Dam's soul, and perhaps the absence of their own mother, had brought her into their family. Downing Hanoi beer, I felt again a sense of apprehension. They were smiling at Homer, and he was more animated than I had ever seen him, smiling back, laughing at their teasing. I thought again about what would happen if they could not find, or could not bring back, the remains. Would they turn on him, take out their bitterness on the man who killed Dam?

Tuoi looked at me and put on an exaggerated expression of exasperation. She reached over and yanked the corners of my mouth up into a smile, then laughed hysterically. "Waynekarlin, waynekarlin," she repeated, shaking her head, running my names together as the Vietnamese always did.

Some time later, on the train ride to Vinh, Jessica and I asked Homer how he had felt, going to the village and the Hoangs' home, whether seeing Thi Dam's possession by the soul of her dead brother had bothered him. He just smiled. "It wasn't the first time I've seen someone speaking in tongues. I'm from the South, and my close friends and our family when I was young were all black people. From time to time when they were grieving, one of their family members would do the same thing. I've seen that several times, that's not surprising to me." He smiled. "It's a little scary every time that happens because you know it's going to come out. But I thought what came out through her was a very positive thing. I felt sorrow, not so much for her, as for the other family members watching her. You could see it in their faces, just watching her." His smile faded. "That's when I broke down, the first time. When I looked at their faces, my voice cracked and tears flowed, which is unusual for me. The other time that I really got emotional was when I was presenting the incense to the altar. As I'm putting the incense up, I look up and there's Dam looking right at me. And then I look to the right and there's his brother's picture—he also died in the war. And I tell you the rest of it—we were there for an hour or two and every time I'd break my concentration and relax a little bit, I'd turn and look around the room and there would be Dam's eyes looking at me again. It was weird. It was like we made eye contact the whole time I was there. It was a little scary sometimes. I would be talking to someone else and I'd turn my head and there was eye contact—not looking in my direction, but direct eye contact. Like, you know when someone looks at you from exactly across the room? That's exactly what it felt like. I don't know what was going on there. I think the lady was channeling direct thoughts to me or something."[4]

The next morning, in Vinh, Homer, Jessica, Bill, interpreter Quan, and I took a taxi to Tien's house early. She was waiting outside her front courtyard gate. Next to her was a short, slim, elderly looking man dressed as Dieu had been, in an olive-green PAVN uniform. He had two red and gold badges on his lapel, and a wispy Ho Chi Minh beard. When he smiled at us, I could see that his teeth, like those of many of the veterans, were discolored. He shook hands with us, his grip hard and calloused, a farmer's hands, Homer would say later.

Tien's living room or salon was a high-ceilinged, narrow room, furnished with dark, heavy, Chinese-style furniture, but with natural light illuminating the room from the front door. Her husband greeted us and invited us to sit around the long table in the front of the room. At the head of the table Tien had placed a large antimony Statue of Liberty—a souvenir of her trip to the United States. I remembered how, on the book tour I'd done with Khue and Thai, such statues had been their gift of choice to bring back to friends and relatives. We had emptied the Joyce Kilmer rest stop on the New Jersey Turnpike of all its Lady Liberties when we stopped there.

The old man sat across from us and kept smiling, his eyes wide, as if he were afraid that if he blinked we would disappear. It was a feeling I shared.

"This is Nguyen Van Hai," Tien said, grinning. She had said the name outside, but the meaning hadn't surfaced in my mind until now. I stared at his face, seeing in it now the handsome face on the driver's license that had been in Dam's possession. Homer got it at the same time I did.

"Well, I'll be damned," he said, and rose, extending his hand. "It's a pleasure to meet you, sir."

Tien's grin got wider, the hostess who had pulled off a surprise party. "He lives in the countryside," she said happily. "He drove forty kilometers in, on his motor scooter, to see you. I want the Hoangs to give back his license and papers."

"I thought they had," I said.

"Not yet."

Homer, meanwhile, had moved over next to Hai. He had grasped his hand again, the idea become flesh.

"He's a farmer?" he asked Tien.

"Yes."

"Tell him I am too."

Hai nodded, patted Homer's arm.

"We all wondered," I said, "how Dam came to have his documents."

He had been a driver on the Ho Chi Minh Trail, Hai said, pointing at one of the badges on his chest. He had driven for four years.

Homer nodded and saluted him.

That day, they had heard an American helicopter, and they—he and his codriver—were out in the open; they knew they would be hit. As the helicopter dove down, shooting its rockets, he had run away, leaving his rucksack. Later, he supposed, Dam must have come across the wreckage, or some other soldier had taken his papers from it and had given them to Dam.

"Why would he do that—did you know Dam?"

Yes, of course. Everyone did. Dam treated him once, for malaria. But he was known for being very good at surgery.

"What did his dispensary—the place he treated you—look like?"

It was a bomb shelter. Perhaps three meters by four meters, with a log roof covered by camouflage.

"I thought he was dead," Homer said later. "And then to find out that he actually knew Dam and that that was why he had the documents. . . . [H]e and I hit it off immediately. You look at his hands—those are farmer's hands; strong hands, you know? Yeah, he and I just connected immediately. We could have sat around a pot-bellied stove and talked for hours. In fact, we did. I like him. I like him a lot. You know it's strange, he's got a bad right knee and I've got a bad right knee, too. There were a bunch of strange coincidences that happened as I was going over here. I left North Carolina as the cicadas were singing. I get over here—and what do I hear? You can hardly hear, the cicadas are singing so loud."[5]

After tea, Tien called the hotel and asked the Hoangs to come over. I knew she was still troubled about their decision to rely on the medium, but apparently she had decided to accept the inevitable, or at least to respect their determination She would meet them at her museum. We can walk there, she said cheerfully to us. She was still triumphant about producing Nguyen Van Hai.

Tien's museum was a separate building, part of the Military Region 4 military museum. She had designed the facility solely to hold the hundreds of artifacts she had excavated from burial sites, as yet unclaimed. In the center of the large, high-ceilinged hall was a statue of a Heroic Mother. Around her, lining the walls, were display cases filled with neatly arranged and labeled relics: combs fashioned from aircraft metal; canteens; ponchos; cartridge belts; photographs of mothers or sisters or friends; and always diaries, letters, journals, snatches of poems. In places, there were series of peep holes in the walls. Looking into them, face pressed against the wall, you saw that the shallow, cylindrical tubes contained the same kind of artifacts as lined the walls. The effect was like peering into the grave. What would we find in Dam's grave, if we got that far? The medium had told the

Hoangs, apparently, but had also told them not to share the information. The walls were covered with photographic murals of the living, posing in groups, arms around each other's necks, gathered casually in jungle clearings; in all the pictures that Tien had chosen, the groups and clusters of young men and women soldiers were smiling.

I remembered the display room dedicated to Heroic Mothers in the Army Museum in Hanoi. It contains photographs of the women as they stand stiffly, hung with medals representing dead children, or having the same draped around their withered necks by equally bemedaled officials. There are other museums, in Ho Chi Minh City and at My Lai, dedicated to displaying American war crimes. But this was the only museum I had seen in Viet Nam that commemorated the fallen of their side of the war, not twisted into the heroic poses of massive, socialist realism-style statuary, but through the pathetic individuality of the small, personal objects they held precious or necessary. It made them individual and real, and it was the closest in spirit that I had seen in Viet Nam to the Vietnam Veterans' Memorial, with its simple listing of names, which focused also on the human cost of the war rather than on the abstracts of heroic national sacrifice. I wondered if it had been as controversial here as the Wall had been at first in the United States.

Homer was looking at a case holding some canteens, remembering, he told me, a firefight after which the North Vietnamese, as usual, had dragged off the bodies, leaving only the same canteens and web belts he was staring at now. How many people had he killed, he wondered, whose faces, unlike Dam's, he had never seen? All the artillery and mortar rounds he had sent off, all the times he had just fired at muzzle flashes from the jungle.

I suddenly felt a hot light on my face and turned to see the TV camera on me. The cameraman turned to Homer, motioning for him to stand and gaze up at the Heroic Mother. Homer complied for a second, but then shook his head. "I'd like to help you out," he said softly. "But it's not me." He walked away.

I went up next to him. He was looking at a series of metal markers, shaped like spades or shovel heads. Each was only inscribed with a painted number: 267, 498, etc. I asked Tien what they were.

"Each marked the number of dead we found at different sites," she said.

"I was afraid that's what they were," Homer said.

As we left, Homer helped Nguyen Van Hai, who had a bad knee, down the steps of the museum, Hai clutching Homer's arm. At the bottom, the two grinned at each other. Homer rubbed his own knee and displayed his own hand to Hai, a farmer's hand, then picked up Hai's and placed it next to his own, as if to demonstrate their connection. Hai nodded at Homer and smiled.

Later, as we sat with the Hoangs, back at Tien's house, the smile became puzzled and somewhat sad. They had not brought back Hai's documents, though they had a photocopy they could give him. Their failure to bring the license troubled Homer, though he was determined to like the Hoangs and withheld his judgment. "I can make him an exact copy," he offered, trying to salvage the mood. "Same kind of paper and all. I'll send it to him." But I could see that Tien was annoyed, and Doug Reese was furious. "It's not theirs to keep," he said. "Look at that poor old man."

"Look," I said to Luong, "Dam must have been bringing those papers to return to Hai. Isn't it what he would have liked?" I was puzzled and more than a little saddened at the family's actions. Their grace with Homer had moved me deeply and, like Homer, I wanted them to be flawless. I didn't understand why they did not simply give Hai his belongings—I could see no profit for them in keeping those few pieces of paper.

Luong looked pained. "There is a reason for not giving them back right now. Please be patient and I will explain everything to you later."

It was the medium, he said to me that evening. She had told them that for now Dam said to keep all of the things he had together. They were afraid not to do exactly what Dam said. Everything depended on that now.

I was sitting with Luong in the hotel dining room when he told me what the medium had said. I had spotted the Hoangs by themselves at one table, having an early supper before we caught the train to Qui Nhon. The tandem-framed photographs they were carrying everywhere, of Dam and his brother Chi had been carefully set up at one end. They motioned to me to join them, and I sat down at the opposite side of the table from the photographs. I didn't know if I bought what Luong had said, but I was the guest at this table and it hadn't been my brother who'd been killed. Most of the food was gone, but two full bowls of rice still stood near me. I reached for one. Tuoi tapped my hand sharply and shook her head. I looked up. Luong was shaking his head also. I noticed, for the first time, the family resemblance between the brothers, Luong and Cat, the large, square foreheads and delicately featured faces. Cat was the more emotional, always ready to laugh or weep. Luong was reserved and looked perpetually worried. He tapped the photos of his two dead brothers now, then pointed at one of the bowls of rice and then the bowl I had touched. "Dam," he said. I nodded and withdrew my hand. I had almost eaten Dam's rice.

# CHAPTER THIRTY

# Pleiku

Before we left for the station that evening, we gathered in the hotel lobby. Bill Deeter, who was only coming with us as far as Qui Nhon—he would meet us there as well on the way back—looked pale, his forehead beaded with sweat. He sat down with a groan in a large chair, holding his stomach.

"Are you OK?"

"You know the problem with being the only white guy here who speaks fluent Vietnamese?"

I was squatting next to my suitcase, rearranging some things.

"What's that?"

"You have to go out and drink beer and eat dog meat all night with the television guys."

As I zipped up my suitcase and straightened up, I felt a sharp blow on my right shoulder. I spun around to see Tien grinning at me. She had socked me in the arm. She spoke rapidly to Bill, who smiled and shook his head.

"She said, she can't come with us now—her cold is too bad. But when we come back through Vinh, we should look out the train window. We will see a short woman in a colonel's uniform standing on the platform, holding up a case of beer for us."

I understood why she did not want to come. She waved at the window as the train pulled out.

At Qui Nhon, in the morning, we split up into two vehicles at the train station: the Americans and the Vietnamese TV crew in one, the Hoangs driving ahead to the Ya Yun Pa cemetery at Azaban to arrange our visit and the exhumation. I had thought it was all taken care of before, but apparently there were more bureaucratic hoops through which they had to jump. Meanwhile, we would wait at Pleiku for word from them. We drove there through the heart of the country where Homer had spent his war. Both An Khe and, later, Pleiku, were unrecognizable to him. The winding concrete road that connected the two towns, snaking between the crests of mountains and through the pass, had been a mine-crater-pocked and rutted dirt road in 1969 on which he'd raced, breakneck, covered with a second skin of red dust, dodging B-40 rockets and snipers when he was too impatient to wait for convoys. But the mountains and the grids of the paddies and the lovely rolling countryside between them, the jungle-canopied peaks falling off on all sides, were all the same, the red soil revealed like the wounded earth through rents in the jade green.

The Hoangs were to have ridden ahead of us to straighten out the situation and call us when we could continue to the cemetery. The exhumation, as we understood it, had to take place after dark. But soon we overtook and passed them on the road; they had stopped at a small restaurant to eat. "How are they going to get everything done in time?" Doug asked. He was leaving for the States a day ahead of us and worried about making his connections. His worry was catching. I didn't care about the connections, but I felt a great urge to do this, to get it done. Get it out of the earth. The trip had all been geared to that moment, and I felt it receding in front of me, always just out of reach.

At Pleiku, as planned, we stopped and waited for the Hoangs' call. The small, sleepy ville Homer remembered had been transformed into a sprawling, heavily commercialized post-*doi moi* Vietnamese city, marred by blocks of ugly Soviet-style buildings; the Russians had helped rebuild and develop the city after the war. It was hard to see any of the past, neither its murders nor its charms. I watched Homer looking around. From where we were, he could still see the configurations of the topography—Dragon Mountain and the ridgeline that protected the old American air base.

The American war had started here as much as in the Gulf of Tonkin: eight Americans had died when the Viet Cong shelled the American advisors' compound in this city in February 1965. President Johnson had also used that attack to justify the bombing of North Viet Nam and the deployment of ground troops a month later.[6] Ten years and millions of lives later, when the South Vietnamese had fled from Pleiku in 1975, most of the civilian population—over 100,000 people—abandoned the city along with the ARVN soldiers. On their way out, they had burned down the town, rather than abandon it to the North Vietnamese and Viet Cong.

When the Hoangs still hadn't straightened out the situation by dark, we checked into a hotel, a resort consisting of a row of tile-roofed "villas" set on the crest of some landscaped hills, along the edge of a gulley that plunged down to a creek. The villas were only $20 a night. Pleiku was still not a large tourist destination.

I lay under the white mosquito netting and tried to sleep. There were small recessed lights in the corners of the ceiling, and I couldn't find the switch to turn them off, but I was too weary to call the front desk. A gecko scampered across the top of the opposite wall. I like geckos. They eat insects. But this wasn't one of the quiet ones. It began croaking at me. Probably telling me to turn out the lights. At least it wasn't a fuck-you lizard, I thought. Fuck you, the gecko said to me. There's no way they are going to pull this off. They have to, I thought.

Fuck you, too. We were all doing what we had to do, I told the gecko. O'Brien's character had to see the face of the man he'd killed before he could mourn him. Ah, you literary bastard, the gecko said. Stop seeing everything as stories. This is a real man you may be fucking up, dragging him to stare into the grave. Fuck you. I got up, went to the small desk, turned on my laptop, and began playing some music. A thin green centipede was making its way slowly around the circumference of the room. I watched its patient, futile progress for a while. I wrote in my journal: *After the long train ride—inevitable disappointment. The Hoangs called said they didn't get permission to exhume, got to Azaban late, found no one they had spoken to. Frantic cell phone calls to the fortune teller, who lets them speak to Dam. Hang on a second, he's right here. Pick up, Dam. We wait in Pleiku. The circus is in town today, Dylan just sang from my computer's music files. Desolation Row. You bet. The cameraman hitting on Jessica; I had to tell him to cool it. Tell him I've killed people, Homer said, deadpan. The TV crew tell Homer they want to take him onto a hill, shoot him pretending to be where he shot Dam. No way, Jessica, furious, said. No way. I wonder if we're going into to the kind of situation my cynical friends Khue and Thai would find predictable, if not inevitable. The desire for a good ending turned instead to tragedy and, worse, farce.*

I watched the centipede make three more complete circuits of the room. As if he were acting out some ceremony whose significance only he knew. Maybe he was holding the world together. What would it be like to dig up Dam's bones? It was not a macabre act in Viet Nam. The Vietnamese did it routinely, three years or more after a burial. Took up and washed the bones clean and reentombed them. But this had been almost forty years. The bones would be brown and black, crumbling, Dam's impeccable uniform in rotted shreds.

The centipede made one more circuit. There was light outside the window. I looked at the clock on the computer: Five. I dressed and went outside. At the end of the gulley, the eight tiers of a new, garishly painted pagoda rose into the sky. As I trudged up a path, I saw Homer walking down toward me. I wasn't surprised.

"When you were in the jungles around here, did you have those little fuck-you lizards?"

"Sure," he said. "Fuckyou, fuckyou. It seemed appropriate."

"How are you doing?"

"Actually, fine."

"You don't seem worried about what's happening with the Hoangs."

"You're worrying enough for both of us," he said.

"To tell you the truth, I've been concerned about whether or not we should be doing this at all. Whether it was right of me to bring you here, put you through all this."

He smiled. "What it's doing or nor doing to me is not the point. I want them to find Dam."

"You're a brave man."

He closed his eyes and shook his head, as if I'd missed the point. We fell silent. I nodded at the dining hall, where some of the staff were laying out a buffet.

"Just like your last time here," I said.

"Let's get some breakfast."

We walked over to the buffet, poured coffee for ourselves, dripping in condensed milk, in the Vietnamese style. I buttered a baguette.

"My father was a brave man," he said suddenly. "Much braver than I am. Morally, he was the strongest man I ever knew."

So are you, I wanted to say again. But I knew it would shut him down. I wondered, though, looking at the hills through the window, why he had chosen to speak about, to remember at this moment, his father, instead of the other memories that must crowd this ground.

"He had a big, generous heart. I remember once, he and I had worked all day, some hard, dirty job, earned $20, and then he turned around and gave it to a black man we'd worked with

who needed it more, some kind of family crisis—all to the dis-
gust of my mother."

He looked away. "He knew right from wrong, too. You get
raised in South Carolina, those days, you just accepted the racial
situation. It was like the air you breathed. You didn't question it
because there was never an alternative presented. But he knew
it was wrong. He hated it. I don't know what made him different. Maybe it was the war. Maybe his parents—I don't know. I
remember, all that Ku Klux Klan stuff. . . . I was looking out of
my bedroom window, and I saw a fire next door. They were
burning a cross, though I didn't know what that was at the time.
I called daddy, told him he better go look. He went out the
door, and then he came back in and got his shotgun, loaded it
with rock salt, and told us to stay put. Next thing, I heard two
blasts. Nobody ever tried to get back at him for that, either.
Everyone respected him, knew not to cross him. He was the
kind of man, you knew if you got in a barroom fight with him,
you got in a fight with him for any reason, you'd have to kill
him to win. He wouldn't care if he died, but he wouldn't give
up. People see that in you; they back off."

Earlier, he had told Jessica that for years, until he met Tibby,
he would not look people in the eye. "Not unless I was going to
get in a fistfight with them," he'd said. Looking at him when he
said that—he is not a big man—I had thought the same thing
he now said about his father. If you got into a fight with him,
you'd have to kill him before he'd quit.

He had related the story of his father and the Klan before,
but something had changed in his telling of it. In a moment I realized what that was. "I don't remember images," he had also
told me once. "It's why I have a hard time answering your questions, and Jessica's sometimes. When you ask me, how did I feel
about something, I can't answer. I don't remember, have no images to tie it to, and so the question is meaningless to me." But
now he had described the light of the burning cross as seen

through his window, awakening him, the sound of his father's shotgun blasts. He had described how he felt.

Outside the window, a bird shrieked at us, bringing me back to Pleiku.

"He was uneducated, but he understood everything," Homer went on. "He could see somebody do something—sink a well, fix an engine—and then he could do it. When we did the well-digging business, he saw someone work a dowsing stick, you know, holding a forked stick to find water? And then he could do it. Always found water, too, except one time. He could see what was beneath."

"Is that right?"

"I came home from the war, he looked in my eyes and said, 'I can see you've changed. But don't let it control you in a negative way. Grow from it. Make it into something good.'"

"That's what you're doing."

"I loved him. But you know what? I went to his funeral and I felt nothing. I knew I loved him and I knew what I was supposed to feel. But I felt nothing."

I didn't know what to say.

"What I mean is, I'm feeling it now. I miss him. If I was at that funeral now, I could cry for him. Maybe I will."

I looked at him. Everything he had told me about his father had been an answer to my own doubts about whether or not this trip was a good thing.

# CHAPTER THIRTY-ONE

# Camp
# Enari

*5/27 Tuesday*

*The situation seems straightened out this AM. They found the right people to speak to. The authorities and the medium—or Dam, via the medium, speaking to them, grave to Hanoi to grave, on the cell phone—has given them permission to dig in the daytime, some kind of pass on the curse. We'll meet them at the cemetery—a three hour drive—burn incense at the grave, etc., and they will exhume without Homer. Good!*

I was relieved at their message. They needed, they had told us, Homer's presence, to find and bring back Dam's remains. But if they did not need him to actually be there when they did it, so much the better. "I'm not disturbed about digging up his bones," Homer had said. "I've seen the dead before." So had I, but to see come out of the earth what you had placed, prematurely, in it, seemed too much confrontation. In spite of the way Homer had tried to reassure me that he was doing OK, I was still worried. At the same time, though, I had been looking forward to going to the cemetery, completing what had come to seem the vast, geographic ritual of this journey. There was another aspect to it as well. I'd been writing for months now about Homer's war, Dam's life, and now the places I had read, heard, and written about were becoming real, no matter how changed they were since the war. I remembered the trip I had made in 1993 to the small town in Russian Poland where my mother spent her girlhood. The act of going there allowed me to fill in the details of her stories, move them out of mythology, and see the living childhood of the woman my mother had become. The local people had taken Dam's body with the others and buried him in that military cemetery, erasing him into anonymity of mass martyrdom, and a part of me still wanted to see the place, see the story I was telling move from legend into a place on earth, as if to reassure myself it could truly be finished.

We had driven about fifty kilometers south of Pleiku, following Route 14, a leg of the old Ho Chi Minh Trail now made into a two-lane concrete road, when we received a call from the family. Stop. You can't come. The authorities at the cemetery had not known about the presence of foreigners. We would have to get permission from both Hanoi and the provincial government. Even if we could, it would put us too far over schedule to make our flights back to the States. Had they gotten the remains? No, not yet. There was a delay. My doubts about the whole venture began to surface again. Maybe some myths needed to stay myths.

The repetitive pattern we seemed to be experiencing bothered me the most. We would make a plan, and then we would discover that the plan did not work. We would not get Dam's remains. The authorities would change their minds, decide not to allow a grave to be dug up at the word of a medium. The wishful thinking of the Hoang family would butt up against the reality of being here. Homer would be blamed, or he would feel he had failed to accomplish what he'd wanted to accomplish here, bringing some measure of peace to the family and himself; he, like Dam, would slip back into an encased silence.

We turned around and started to drive back to Pleiku, to await word from the Hoangs. Along the way we made a pit stop near a small hill. Homer and I scrambled up to the top and looked across fields, more rolling hills, and then the rim of jungle-covered mountains. The shadows of clouds moved across their flanks. Look, I've already done what I needed to do, he had told me. If this was as close as we were going to get to Dam's grave, I told myself, it would have to do.

Near Pleiku, just outside the town, we turned right off the highway, onto a smooth, wide concrete road, the red dust and dirt so packed into its surface by decades of traffic that it had been stained that color. "Look at the shape this road is in," Doug said to Quan, grinning. "See—the Americans built this over forty years ago. This is how a road should be built."

It was in good shape, something symmetrical left by us that wasn't contained in cemeteries and rows of unmarked graves. The traffic was mostly farm vehicles: small trucks, tiller-tractors, carts. We drove for about three kilometers.

"There," Doug said.

The location of what had been the Camp Enari guard post was marked in the center of the road by a concrete slab and a pattern of bolts marking where posts had been. Homer nodded. We stopped and got out. There was nothing to look at now, but being here, in the place itself, allowed the images he thought he no longer had to surface. When he had come for the first time, the plane had landed at the army airfield on the other side of Pleiku, and he and the others had been driven down the road we'd just traveled in buses with wire mesh on their windows, to prevent grenades from being tossed inside. The men were unarmed. He'd been told to get off on the tarmac beyond this gate and pointed toward the sandbagged positions of the company he would join, on the other side of the field. As he'd started to trudge toward them, he heard a whistling scream, an explosion, and then a slap of heat against his skin. More rockets began to

fall around him, and he spotted and rolled into a small depression between the perforated metal tarmac and the uncovered
ground, trying to press himself as low as he could. His first day
in the war. What he remembered now was the dirt in his face,
the red dust puffed up by the breaths from his nose. It was the
red soil that would cover his fatigues, stain his skin, work its
way in so that when he had the chance to bathe or shower, he
would see it worm out of his pores. It was the red dirt that always covered all of them, like a second skin. It was Viet Nam. It
was the same red dirt whose absence astonished him when he
saw Dam coming around the bend on that mountain ridge trail
dressed in spotless, parade-ground khaki, not a trace of the soil
on it. His cleanliness in this unclean place, encompassing a care-
fulness, a stubborn dedication to preserve some standard in
spite of an environment that made it seemingly impossible,
somehow reminded Homer of his father, of the aspect of his father that existed as some core of himself, a mirrored brother, his
secret sharer.

Homer knelt by the side of the road, near the footprint of
the American guard post, scooped up some of the red, red soil,
and packed it carefully into a small plastic baggie.

They had found Dam, the Hoangs told us the next morning,
calling from the cemetery at Azaban. They had finally gotten
permission from both the authorities and, through the medium,
from Dam. He had told them which row, which number. They
had come such a long way to this strange country, he had told
them, through the medium. They could dig him up in the daytime; it didn't matter. He wanted to be pulled into the air by
their hands; he wanted the dirt from this place shaken from his
bones; he wanted to go home.

# CHAPTER THIRTY-TWO

# The Mang Yang Pass

What I liked was that I had no history in the soil of this particular place. I knew, in the abstract, the history of the area we were driving through now, speeding back down Highway 19 from Pleiku to An Khe, retracing our earlier drive. I had Homer's stories of it and the reading I had done to put his stories in context. The rugged, jungle-covered hills and mountains of the Mang Yang Pass, squeezing the road around above us now, had been stage sets for sweeps and raging battles and ambushes and holding actions and meeting engagements, a slaughter that continued until 1975, when the People's Army of Viet Nam had finally been able to complete the surgery it had attempted so many times before, to race down this highway and cut the country in half so that they could finally knit it together, so they could at last liberate Pleiku to become the hub of futile tourism and ugly Soviet-era architecture it is today.

In June and July 1954, the last battle in the war with France had been fought on this road, then called Coloniale Route 19, and on Coloniale 14, the road to Azaban where Dam's bones had recently rested. The remains of the massacred soldiers of Groupe Mobile 100 force were buried somewhere on this ridge-line as well, after that unit was ordered to retreat from Anh Khe to Pleiku and was ambushed and decimated at kilometer marker 15 by two Viet Minh battalions.[7] That slaughter took place just a week before the final cease-fire that marked the end of the French-Vietnamese war, the war that foreshadowed and fore-warned our own, though its After Action Report, had there been one, would have had the word "none" scribbled under the category heading Lessons Learned. The deaths of those Frenchmen, whose ghosts American soldiers would later claim to see, oc-curred fifteen years before Homer and his men would hump these same ridgelines, where he would kill Hoang Ngoc Dam, in his impossibly clean fatigues, in this haunted, alien, perversely beautiful place.

I knew all that, but none of the images of my own war would tangle and segue here into that history. I could look at the country as Jessica was looking at it now. I didn't have to envy her.

"What beautiful scenery," she said.

The minivan the Hoangs had hired pulled into the hotel en-trance at about one o'clock that afternoon. When the door slid open, Cat jumped out. He saw me and laughed, and then came over and flung his arms around me, tried to lift me off the ground. Tuoi came over and patted my back. They had him, they said. They had their brother. I looked into the van. Dieu and Luong were sitting solemnly, their backs straight, in the rear seat. Between them was a cardboard box, perhaps two feet long. Multicolored shower massage heads, the words on the box re-ported, in English. Pictures of the same. Two red ribbons were fastened around the box at each end.

It had been like this, Tuoi told us, excitedly. She had reached into her bag and pulled out one of her shirts. The sleeves were caked with mud. They had called the medium. She had let them speak to Dam. He was happy they were there. She had been the one to dig. Some of the time, she had dug with her hands, inside the sleeves of this shirt, until she felt his bones through the cloth. And then on her skin. She had found many bones. In the grave, as the medium had said, there was a bowl, and a red poncho in which the body had been wrapped. And, she said, looking at Homer, there were three bullets among the bones. But he had said he had shot Dam with one. But perhaps he did not remember, she added hastily. Homer shook his head, looking at the box. He may well have fired a quick three-round burst, he said; it was an automatic reaction, which may have registered in his memory as a single pull of the trigger.

Later, when Jessica and I interviewed the family, Luong stopped Tuoi from repeating what had been found in the grave; the medium had forbidden them, he said, to tell anyone. I distrusted the neatness of it, of all of it. But what shone in Tuoi's eyes, and in Cat's, was the fervor of belief.

What Dam wanted, Luong told us, was very simple. At first he had wanted us to visit a cave and the location of one of the field hospitals where he had been during the war. But now he said that wasn't necessary. He only wanted to go home. He only wanted this: that as we drove back from Pleiku to An Khe, we should stop somewhere on the Mang Yang Pass, take his bones out, and perform a small ceremony, light incense for his soul. Those performing the ceremony, Luong said, should be the family. And you. And Homer. It must include Homer.

Driving through the Mang Yang now, we look at the side of the road for a likely place to pull over. Finally, at the apex of a sharp curve, the road dropping sharply down after it, we see an emergency truck slow-down ramp—a dirt track onto which a truck with brake failure could pull—rising at a thirty degree angle up the side of a small, steep knoll, a tree on its top. There, someone says, or maybe more than one of us says, and we pull over to the side of the road, just before the sandy ramp. There is a small, level area of bushes and wildflowers, which drops off on its edge to a steep valley. Across the road is another small hill, a nub on the side of a large hill or small mountain, about 4,500 feet high, its slopes thickly covered with jungle, some slabs of old concrete retaining wall along its base on the road. It doesn't rise to a peak, but rather to a long, narrow ridgeline. On it a single tree, perhaps 150 feet high, stands above the other trees.

"C'est bon," the cameraman says. "Montons la." He points at the small hill. Homer looks around, up at the mountain, at the road. He is still silent. He walks off a little by himself. He brings his camera down to the faces of the flowers he knows he will see, when he goes home, in the soil of the Pisgah National Forest.

The Hoangs get out of their van, Luong holding the box in front of him. The three television men trudge up the small hill, carrying the heavy tripod and camera. "Shit," Jessica says. She is staring at the Marantz recorder.

"What's the matter?"

"I have twenty-four new batteries. I've been putting them in here, one batch after another, but nothing works. This machine is dead."

"I have some from my camera," Homer says. He gives them to her. One by one, they fail.

"Shit," she says again. "I don't know why it's doing this."

We hear a sudden shout from the hilltop.

"Can you use the camcorder?" I ask.

"I hope so."

We climb up the hill. The cameraman is cursing; the director and the sound man look distraught. They had set the tripod solidly on a level patch of ground, to film the ceremony, when a sudden gust of wind knocked the machine over. It had smashed against some rocks and is now useless. We look at each other and laugh, in that way Americans laugh when they feel a melodramatic situation can be defused with irony. I remember how the camera light had shattered, pieces of glass burning a small hole in my shirt and on Phan Thanh Hao's skin, during the ceremony at the communal center in Thai Giang, when I had returned the documents.

"I'm getting the feeling that Dam doesn't like staged events," Jessica says.

Homer is staring at the hill, his face strained.

"I was here," he says. "We fought here."

I look at him. Are you sure, I was going to ask. But it is not a question you would have to ask this man.

We turn to look at the Hoangs. They have draped the showerhead box with a red national flag and placed it on Dieu's black briefcase. In front of the box they have arranged a bottle of whiskey, a plastic water bottle, a pack of Era cigarettes, and boxes of butter cookies and small chocolate cakes. We sit on the ground around the box, Homer and I and the Hoangs. Luong pushes incense sticks into the ground next to the bottom edge of the briefcase, and Dieu rests the tandem photographs of Dam and his brother Chi on top of it, he and Homer holding the edges of the frame steady, on either side of the contained bones. I cup my hands over Luong's to keep the wind from blowing out the match as he lights the joss sticks. The smoke curls up into the mountain air. Cat begins to weep, the sobs catching in his throat, and then Tuoi, tears streaming down her cheeks, as Luong chants a prayer, his eyes closed, and I begin to pray also, the words of the mourner's kaddish coming to me, strange but not strange in this place, where I have tried to tell myself I have no history. I hear Homer's name and then my own, subsumed in the Vietnamese of Luong's own chanted prayer, the others repeating his words now, over and over. A wave of dizziness lightens me, and I edge out of myself; the result of anticipation and sleeplessness and heat, certainly, but for an instant I am open to something in this earth that grips my heart and then releases me, leaves me husked and without form, and I open my eyes and see Homer, his lips moving in prayer, his eyes raised to the mountain.

Luong opens his eyes and looks at him and says something. Quan holds the words for a moment, and then gives them to Homer, like something he is unwrapping.

"He said that Dam thanks you. He said that Dam forgives you."

# CHAPTER THIRTY-THREE

# The Hai Van Pass

Homer sat next to Dam in the Hoangs' compartment. I sat next to him and Tuoi, on one bottom rack. Luong, Dieu, Cat, and Quan sat on the opposite side, smiling at us. Dam was on the foldout table under the window. They had left the shower-head carton undraped, so that other people on the train could not know what it contained. But the photographs of Chi and Dam in their double frame were still on top of the box, Dam's face near Homer's. He and I and Doug and Jessica had the next compartment, but the Hoangs had called us in to sit with them.

I was somewhat worried about Homer. After the ceremony on the hillside, he had remained silent, distracted. Of course, I thought. How would I expect him to be? The ceremony on the Mang Yang was beautiful and strange, but I wished, fervently, that we had been finished after we had gone to the village, when he had lit incense at the altar, under Dam's photo, and rendered his apology. The weight of literally carrying the bones of the man he had killed with that man's family seemed to be pushing him back into silence. And now we would go back to Thai Giang, and he would endure the funeral and burial. It was too much to

ask of anyone. After the ceremony, he had gone off a little ways
and began taking his close-up shots of flowers again. When I'd
gone to him, he'd said that looking at those mountains, he was
remembering all the men he had lost, as well as Dam, the young
man's eyes in his photograph catching and holding Homer's
whenever he glanced in their direction.

Yet the family was happy now. At the funeral, they would
grieve again, I knew, and for an instant I felt envious of the ritual
patterns of their lives, their ability to place grief and joy on their
appropriate tables, neatly tied with red silk ribbons and framed
in front of the backdrop of eternal rice fields and mountains,
those rushing past the window now. They joked with us now, all
of us pressed together tightly, letting Homer understand that the
words they had reported from Dam's soul came from their own
hearts. Only Dieu was still somewhat glum, or distracted, perhaps thinking of the American bones he had left in the soil of
Quang Ngai, though I had no reason to think so except for my
own need to feel there was some symmetry of grief for our own
lost souls.

A little later, back in our own compartment, I asked Homer to
tell me about the fight he had had on the hill where we'd commemorated Dam. He looked at me for a moment.

"You don't understand," he said. "That was the ridgeline
where I killed Dam."

Something sharp moved against my heart. I stared at him.

"I kept looking at it, thinking I couldn't be right," he said.
"But everything was in place. We had been set down by helicopter a little further up the road from where the van stopped,
and we walked down it to that knoll, past those concrete retaining walls. I remember them. The road was different, but I remember thinking then how odd it was that those retaining walls
were there. I remember that curve in the road, just before it fell
off into the valley. I had it on my map, and I saw it. I remember

the shape of the ridge. I remember the men balking; I hadn't re-membered that until then. I wasn't their regular platoon leader and they thought they could get away with it, and I had to start forward, with the medic, and hope like hell they would follow."

He paused, took a deep breath.

"What I remember most is that tree. It's the same tree. You have all those others on the ridgeline, and then that one, with the oddly shaped canopy, towering above everything else. That tree, standing out like that. I used it to sight on, as we climbed our way to that ridgeline."

I was still staring at him, unable to speak again. If it had been anyone other than Homer, I thought, I would have put it down to wishful thinking.

The PA system began playing some Vietnamese equivalent of muzak, a woman singing a cloying song. The rattle of the train on the rails.

"Are you OK, man?" I asked him finally.

He smiled at me. "What I feel," he said, "is serenity."

Later, he and I and Jessica sat in the compartment and talked about it, the countryside going by the window like a succession of framed photographs. Like memories. We were going over the Hai Van Pass. The name means "Sea-Cloud," and it is one of the most beautiful places in Viet Nam. A finger of the north-south Truong Son Range extends suddenly east to the coast here, just north of the city of Danang, the lush green flanks and folds of the mountains descending thousands of feet to the turquoise water of the South China Sea, the train racing around dizzying curves on the crests of the ridgelines. The Hai Van range had been a natural border between ancient Viet Nam and the king-dom of the Chams, a people who shared the Hindu culture that stretched westward from Viet Nam to the Angkor Wat Kingdom in Cambodia, Bagan in Burma, and then to the Indian subconti-nent itself. A border and a pass, wide enough to finally let the conquering Vietnamese on their inexorable march south pour into Champa, exterminating most of the population and incorporating the kingdom.

As we had driven through the Mang Yang Pass yesterday, Homer said, he had stared out of the window of the van, thinking of the many times he had driven through in a jeep, at breakneck speeds, watching for land mines and the road rather than watching the scenery. "When we pulled over yesterday . . . you could see the valley below, you could see the, the mountains, the ridge lines above and you could see this is a real curvy part of the Mang Yang Pass road, so you get a real feel for what the Mang Yang Pass is like. That's why it was such a perfect ambush area. You had the high ground all around you. And these roads that were so curvy and with such steep drop offs that you had to go a little bit slow and of course that's where they'd ambush you—when you had to make those hundred and eighty degree turns. As I'm standing there and the TV crew's getting everything set up, I'm just standing around waiting and looking and admiring the mountains and remembering that I must have been a lot younger then, because they're a lot steeper than I remember them. They're about as high as I remember them, but they're a lot steeper. And, yet, we definitely climbed those things." He laughed. "Rucksacks and all. And as I was looking around; I'm looking across the valley, and I saw that turn with the truck coming around, I suddenly remembered this is exactly where they put us down. What they wanted us to do was start in the valley, walk up the tail end of that ridge line, all the way to the top and then walk the ridge line to check to see if they were putting any emplacements up there for ambushes. And frankly, there were some very steep sections on the nose of that ridge line that we didn't think we'd cover."

He stopped, closing his eyes for a second. I looked out at the Hai Van. From the window a cliff dropped straight down, the train so close to the edge that from that side it could look as if we were flying, suspended in air. During the war, the heli-

copter base at Marble Mountain had been south of here, south
of Danang, and we would fly up and over the pass on our way
to Hue or Quang Tri, into the war.

"So what we did," Homer continued, "is we kind of took
command of the situation and changed our orders a little bit.
We walked up the road, about maybe two clicks from where
we were stopped to have the ceremony, but further up the
road. Then we turned and went up the ridge line and the only
guide we had to know where we were and what we had and
hadn't covered on the ridge line was, if you look at the top of
the ridge line, it's jungle and there's bush eight to ten feet tall and
then there are trees, sixty to ninety feet tall and then there's this
one tree up there that must be a hundred and ten, hundred and
twenty feet tall, just one little tree by itself—well, not a little
tree, it's a big tree. So we used that as a target to aim at when we
went up. We went up to that tree and then we took a left and
went down the ridge line that way and we were coming back
when we encountered—we were coming back in a hurry because we'd already cleared that part of the trail. We didn't expect to find anyone there. That's when we ran into Dam, and the
encounter took place and I shot him. When I realized that, I
couldn't at first believe it was—it was just impossible, that we
would just arbitrarily stop at the exact place. But I kept looking
around and there's no other place in the valley where the road
and the valley and the ridge line all intersect. I was looking
when we were driving in, you know, from the other direction.
At first, I didn't see anything else that looked familiar. Except
that one spot."

"So you don't think it was just a coincidence?"

When I finally convinced myself that I wasn't hallucinating
and this really was what I thought it was, it was very spooky,
as a matter of fact. Because before this, the TV crew who had
this huge tripod, I mean, Godzilla could have shoved that tripod around and not knocked it over, and the wind blew the
tripod and damaged the camera. I still can't believe there was a

strong enough wind to blow that tripod over. That was a monster tripod. And then, for us to have stopped at the exact spot where we started our patrol, we were doing a reconnaissance force at the ridge line, just—it was a little eerie. But then again, on this whole trip, we've had little coincidences like that, that are just almost beyond belief."

He had been moved by the ceremony, he said. He had mourned with the Hoangs. But part of him was not there. Scales had begun to fall from his memory. Being there clarified everything. "I feel like all this is happening and I'm looking around and I'm here, but I'm not here either. I can almost feel myself climbing back up the ridge line. At one point after the major part of the ceremony was done and the film crew that was with us had finished what they were trying to film, I kind of wandered off from the group a little bit and just stood there for a minute and just remembered all kinds of details, just little things. I remembered going up the ridge line, remembered the troops cursing at me, almost on the verge of mutiny because it was—you saw, the ridge line, it's a daunting task. Being up there was—I haven't finished thinking that through yet. That's going to have to take some quiet time in similar mountains back in North Carolina when I get back home."

"I noticed when you walked away from the group at the ceremony that what you did was take close-up photographs of the flowers," I said.

"I tried to distract myself. It didn't work. There's some beautiful little wildflowers there. And I'm a nature photographer, I take a lot of those kinds of pictures and I saw a couple that were just breathtakingly beautiful. So I took a few pictures of them. My head was full of wildlife, flashing-eyed deer, and I was hoping they would kind of go away. And they didn't. So I wound up just having to stand around a little bit and look at the area and piece the details back together and come to terms with it. It was good. It was good. See, part of the problem forty years later is you're never quite sure how much you made up in your mind and how much was real. All of a sudden, a lot of what I'd remembered had concrete footing again. I remember the helicopter ride. I remember them setting us down beside the road which didn't make sense because we weren't that far that we couldn't have been trucked out, so why they took us out with helicopters, I don't know. I guess we were in a hurry to get somebody out there. Now I had had a strange feeling when we got to that bend in the road and, and that concrete stuff was there, to prevent a landslide on that real steep turn. That concrete stuff was there even then. We almost decided to go up the steps and the concrete, but that would've put us almost where the steep parts were. So we went further down. Quite a ways down as a matter of fact, a couple of clicks. But looking there and I turn around and look back, and I remember when we got up top—the view is breathtaking, looking across the valley there, and I think all of us [in the patrol] took a few minutes to turn around and look at where we just walked up. You drive up in the road, it doesn't seem like much. But you take a 70 pound pack and walk up that asphalt highway, which at the time I don't even think was asphalt I think it was still—in fact I'm sure it was still dirt back then. . . . I remembered. When you remember back, unfortunately, the things that pop into your head first are shooting Dam, and the guy that drowned because I was a stupid idiot and browbeat him into crossing a river that he shouldn't have. . . . And you don't want to remember those. So you do everything you can not to remember them. And when I was out there that day, that's kind of what happened. I couldn't avoid it anymore. It all just flooded me. I remembered. I think I probably remembered everyone I lost when I was over there."[8]

When I told the Hoangs what Homer had said, Luong bowed his head and gripped his forehead, hard, his fingers digging in, his eyes tightly shut. Dieu stared, shaking his head. Cat and Tuoi began to weep. It was not the funereal wail I was getting used to from Cat. He and his sister just sat still, tears running

down their cheeks. They were not shattered. They were weeping at the *rightness* of it all. The serenity. They thought of the
camera light exploding at the communal center when I'd come
there with the documents in 2005. They thought of the failed
batteries, of the heavy camera smashed out of use on the knoll.
They remembered how when they had gone, futilely, to the
cemetery in 2002 and had given up on finding Dam's grave,
their jeep had died and had not started again until they had
prayed to his soul and told him they would come back and find
him and bring him home. What had happened now, what Homer
told them, had reaffirmed to them, as it had to Homer, that
Dam was what Phan Thanh Hao had called him. A sacred soul.

"I think Dam is a lot more powerful than I ever realized,"
Homer said later. "I think he's been guiding this whole thing.
From the day that I shot him. I think his very personality, the
fact that he was so meticulous in his dress, the fact that he won
awards, like every year, for years before I met him for his unpar-
alleled performance as a medic. Just everything about Dam,
from his very birth, had an aura to it. Of greatness. That hit me
when I looked into his eyes on that trip. I remember at the ceremony at the family's house, and again up in Mang Yang Pass, the
ceremony, how I couldn't keep my eyes off of his photograph.
Every time I see that photograph my eyes just go straight to his,
and it's like he's still alive. And they're the same eyes that I
looked into. I was only about thirty feet away. I ran over to kick
his weapon out of the way. So when I first looked into his eyes,
they were still alive. They were living eyes. I watched the life
disappear. If you've ever seen someone die, you know what I'm
talking about. There's that moment when the shine isn't there
anymore. The light. The light disappears from their eyes. So I
saw that. What I see in the photograph is not that. What I see in
the photograph is the living eyes. Technically, it's not there, you
don't see that in the photograph. When I look into the photographs of Dam, that's what I see. I see that sparkle. I see that,

that vibrancy. It's a kind of a comforting feeling. It's like he's saying, it's okay, I'm still here. I'm still doing things, even though
I'm not physically on this planet anymore. Through you, I'm
still accomplishing things. And that's very gratifying. I think
that's what this whole trip has been about. I'm Dam's servant.
I'm doing his work for him. I think he's touched a lot of souls,
and will touch a lot more. Even after death. And what greater
epitaph can a man have? So I'm proud to be some small part
of this."

As the train pulled into Vinh, I looked through the window.
And laughed. Tien was standing on the platform, an overnight
bag by her side. a case of Hanoi beer in her hands. She hadn't
been on the train five minutes when she pointed out of the window, at a small pond on the other side of the tracks.
   "When I was a girl I saw an American plane crash, right
there. The pilot parachuted down nearby. But he was dead."
   That night, drinking the beer with her and Quan, I told her
Homer's story, and about the way the Hoangs said they had
found items in Dam's grave that proved the location. I asked her
what she thought.
   She popped another tab, took a slug, and shrugged, then
smiled and gave the perfect Vietnamese non-answer. I wasn't
there, she said.

Could I be as certain as Homer that we'd been at the place
where he had ascended to shoot Dam? As certain as Tien about
the glimpsed wreckage of her youth? I thought again of O'Brien's
"The Man I Killed," and how it had informed this journey, Tim
creating and confronting in story what he needed to create and
confront, a specific face and a specific place to contain the bor-
derless agony of "faceless responsibility and faceless grief" that
he felt two decades after the war. Homer did not need to imagine Dam's face; it had burned into the contours of his own grief.
Its living eyes. But he needed to go to that place. And perhaps

he had. It didn't matter to me. The truth was the pain this good man had chosen to inflict upon himself.

Later, at the end of the journey, in the house Duc had built in Tam Dao, the house where he would finally bring his sister's and his father's ashes, the house looking over the slopes of other mountains whose trails he and Homer and I wandered under bamboo to hidden waterfalls, I e-mailed a description of what had happened to George Evans, who had wanted to be with us. He replied:

> Okay brothers (and a new sister now I assume), maybe this will catch you still in the mountains, my spirit there, and my body aching to follow. . . . I'm thinking of old Basho, whose poems I would come across on the roads, carved into road markers, stones, when I was wandering in Japan, in remote places, and how they would peg the moment of the place, capture it in a few words, lock the spirit in stone, the souls of the place, whether one believes in spirits or souls or not. Doesn't matter—it's there. And of course Homer came to that place again. Of course. Nothing about this whole adventure is hard to believe, except that we are all still alive to the world, are ones who can see it, have somehow tended to our memories and life forces in such a way to be able to remain open to it all, receptive, and have this chance to escape being simply skeptical about what the world presents us with, and not run from it. Homer brought this to us. After all his wandering in time. And he was supposed to.
>
> I have nothing to say about destiny that would make any sense, because what we believe about it (or not) is always too personal to express. But I believe I'm on that mountain with you. Just as I believe that after all these years Billy's picture came to me yesterday—in his prime and near the moment of his death— as part of this story, because he is part of the story, a counterpart to Dam, similar in many ways, lost in the same way, surviving in the same way, refusing to give up the world through us. And so we have to do these things. I attach the photo—it seems right.

You'll remember the story, Wayne, of how his sister found me last year after years of my not being able to find her, and she sent photos, which were destroyed when my computer crashed a few months back. I asked her to send them again, but she only sent me this one, yesterday—which I'd never seen—because it was the only one she could send. The only one that would be sent. You'll recognize him. And if you're still there, he'll be in the mountains with you. A good man. A very good man. A brother.

That I was swept into this story by Wayne and Homer, and that they are sitting there with my friend Duc, our friend, mountains away, Duc who I could have missed meeting by minutes if things hadn't been exactly the way they were, and all of us . . . well: There. It. Is. As they say. And it's my destiny now, even if it never was before. So I'm there even though I'm not. And Homer, yes, went back to the spot that changed his life forever, even if he never intended to—I'm certain it was the spot, because he said so, because a man from his world would remember a tree, a rock, the shape of a hill, the twist of a road. And a heart left behind decades ago. No regrets; only: live!

Thank him for me.

Love to all, George

What did I believe? I had asked myself, after my conversation with Tien. It was in this place I killed him, Homer had said. These are his bones. This is his grave, the Hoangs had said. Was it all true?

Of course it was.

# CHAPTER THIRTY-FOUR

# Thai Giang

Tien said that she wanted to go to the funeral for two reasons. "First, I want to see all of you again."

She drank her beer.

"Second, in case there are any people in the village who might want to harm Homer." Her reputation and her connections with Party officials would help her protect him, she said.

This was the first time the possibility of any hostility on the part of the residents of Thai Giang had been mentioned, since Thai and Khue's trepidations. I found it a little worrisome. But it also forced me to remember what I had started taking for granted: the way a man who had killed one of their own had been embraced by the family.

It was an acceptance they demonstrated again when we pulled into the Nam Dinh train station that night. We were to stay at a hotel there and then drive out at six in the morning to the village. But this night, the rest of the family was to meet us at the station and escort Dam's remains home. We would like, Luong said, Homer to carry Dam off the train and bring him to the car.

Fifteen minutes before we arrived, we stacked our bags in the corridor and were looking nervously out the windows. The shower-head carton had now been draped again in the red national flag; there was no longer a need to conceal the contents from the railroad employees or our fellow passengers. Dieu handed the box to Homer. When the train stopped, we stepped down into the humid heat of the night, Tien, Jessica, and I before Homer, so that we could bring his suitcase with us and watch him descend. He stood for a moment framed in the doorway, holding his burden, and then came down the steps.

We walked behind him to the exit that opened to the public-access area of the station, a small, quiet procession that prefigured the funeral that would occur the next day. The young women who take ticket stubs at the exit stared at Homer for a second, then took a step back. We could hear the other family members outside, weeping in anticipation. As we walked out to them, I wondered how we looked to the other people in the station. They were staring at Homer, a foreigner holding a box covered with the Vietnamese flag, surrounded by weeping Vietnamese. They understood what this was, but not who he was, and those who would guess would probably dismiss their own speculations as unlikely.

We left for Thai Giang at 5:30 the next morning, Mrs. Tien traveling with us. The television crew had gone back to Hanoi to get a new camera; they would come later to the village. It was only about twenty kilometers from Nam Dinh. It had been less than a week since Homer had first come here, but seemed much longer. He watched the landscape again transform from urban to countryside, until we were again surrounded by rice fields, the green, green stalks swathed by dawn breezes, going on forever.

The village had gathered already. The long courtyard next to the People's Committee office had been roofed with a blue tent. Hundreds of people were sitting or standing on both sides of the yard, some against the walls, some in the rows of chairs

on the left, including soldiers, old and young, in green fatigues or dress uniforms. Off to the side a band, its members
dressed in shining white uniforms and garrison hats, played traditional Vietnamese instruments: a *dan bao* monochord harp; a
moon-shaped *dan nguyet*, lute, with its accompanying *phách*,
the bamboo struck to mark the rhythm; a *trong chau* drum; a
sixteen-stringed *dan tranh* zither; and a *sao*, flute. At the end of
the courtyard, the altar had been set up, with Dam's picture on
it, and behind it the casket, a heavy, ceramic box, still flag-
draped, with the bones in it. To the altar's left was a speaker's
podium with a microphone. Dieu and Luong came to greet us,
and then led Homer, Jessica, Quan, and me to sit on small blue
plastic chairs, very near the altar. Doug hovered in the background, with Jessica's camcorder. Homer looked at Dam's photo.
I saw people in the crowd behind us stare at him, and then turn
and whisper to each other, and then stare even more. He was
here. The man who had killed Dam. His eyes were again fastened to Dam's in the photograph. It was very hot and humid already, and the body heat of all the people, caught under the
tent, pressed on our skins as if the air itself had turned to flesh.
Tien, I saw, was shaking hands with some army officers. More of
the Hoang family than I had ever seen before—the entire clan—
were sitting on the ground beside the altar and casket, praying
and crying—Pham Thi Minh, Dam's widow, among them—
or standing off to the sides, some behind our chairs, pushed
against us. There were many young people among them, new
generations. All of the Hoangs were wearing black and had
white headbands wrapped around their foreheads. One slim,
very beautiful young woman—Quynh, Dieu's daughter, a literature student at Hanoi University, I found out later—had beads
spelling out the word "Versace" embroidered on her blouse.

Now, as the band played, small family groups, couples, or
groups of friends walked, one group at a time, up the center of
the courtyard, between the rows of people. A father, mother, and
daughter. Two old women. A family of six, with small children.

Two old women. One person in each cluster bore a tray with a bottle, some fruit, and an envelope on it. As they reached the altar, which had a small bamboo mat in front of it, they slipped off their shoes or sandals, placed the tray on the altar, and handed the envelope to the girl in the Versace shirt. They lit incense sticks, placed them in the small bed of sand in front of Dam's photo, and brought their palms together and prayed, their joined index fingers striking their foreheads three times as they bowed. The next group repeated the same ritual, and the next, and the next.

The heat increased. We sat dazed, by the journey, the pressing heat, the sound of the monochord harp, the constant beat of the drums, the realization of where we were and what we were doing there. A general made a long speech at the podium. The processions began again. An older group of officers, in formal, dress uniforms. Five young soldiers, in clean olive-green fatigues, formed a line in front of the altar and saluted, one by one. And then, not directly afterward, but soon enough to create the counterpoint, the vision of transformation, came the real deal, five older men, the veterans, Quan whispered, who had enlisted with Dam. They walked to the altar, their faces lined and worn and tough, but their gait and posture relaxed, come to welcome their old comrade home—his photo still holding him, as the young soldiers who preceded them had, in the image of their eternal and lost youth.

There were more speeches. Luong, the oldest brother, the head of the family now, moved behind the altar. As he spoke, people became quiet. His voice, breaking with emotion at times, went into a kind of chant. I could hear, among the other words I recognized, our own, American, names, knit again into the story as they had been during the ceremony on the side of the mountain where Dam was killed and where we had, for a few moments, brought his bones to rest. Luong was again telling the story of how Dam was lost and how he had been found. The story of who had been lost and who had been saved.

When he was finished, Dieu took his place. Later, his daughter Quynh translated and sent me parts of his speech:

Forty-four years ago, my brother answered the call of the Nation to join the Army and went to Southern Viet Nam to fight against the Americans.

Ten years later, in 1974, we were given the bad news that our Dam gave up his life in the battle of the South. The memorial service was held by the Commune's Party with just the paper of death notice—without any of his belongings.

In April 2002, 33 years after his death, my family, with his comrades' help, went to the Pleiku forest in the hope that we could find him, but we had to come back without him because we didn't have enough information.

Thirty-six years later, in 2005, our tears continued when his belongings were sent back by the man who killed him in the war.

Today, he comes back for the third time, after 39 years, but it's the most perfect time. We are happy and proud to welcome his return.

We would like to thank the Commune's People and Party— who made our brother Hoang Ngoc Dam a brave soldier.

Our thanks are also sent to the Party and the Vietnamese Government who helped the American soldier bring my brother back to the fatherland.

We are grateful to spirits in the forests and rivers who revealed my brother's way to come home.

Thank you for your attention and for sharing in the ceremony today.

Thank you Minh Chuyen and the men from the Viet Nam Television films who followed us to the former battleground in order to record the journey.

Many thanks to the media who have helped us for many years to broadcast important information so that we could find our brothers remains.

Thanks to our friends the American war veterans, for your
goodwill in giving us information and giving his belongings
back, as well as going with us to the former battlefield to pick up
my brother.

Thank you to an American mother—Mr. Homer's mother,
who helped her son to preserve my brother's belongings over the
last thirty years.

Mr. Homer, we know that you are one of the American war
veterans who have admitted the mistake of coming to war in our
nation. You have tormented yourself over the things you did in
the war. Our brother's spirit and our whole family forgive you
and regard you as a friend. It's our Vietnamese traditional altru-
ism and humanism.[9]

When Dieu finished, he asked us, the three Americans, to
come to the altar. We walked to the mat in front of it and took
our place in the ritual, one by one. As I stepped up I looked into
Dam's eyes, as I knew Homer was still doing, and whispered my
apologies to him, for coming to his country when and as I did,
as well as my apologies to all the dead, Vietnamese and American, for the shortcomings of my own spared life, and for its joys
also, for everything they had never tasted: the love I'd held in
my arms, the son that I'd seen come into the world, and even
the thickening of grief in my throat and chest in front of this
photograph, which I could feel because I was alive. And I said
to Dam, a sacred soul, please bless and forgive this fine man
next to me who took your life, but who is your brave and good
brother, come to bring you and all of us to peace.

Now it is time to bring Dam to his grave. The young soldiers,
their olive fatigues as clean as the ones Homer saw Dam wearing
on the day of their accidental encounter, pith helmets on their
heads, are called up as casket bearers, and then Homer is called
up also. He takes one corner, and the six of them, the American
veteran and the five young Vietnamese soldiers, lift and carry

Dam's heavy casket to the funeral wagon. It is wooden, painted red and gold, and decorated with gold dragons, and six pushing stakes sticking out along its sides. Homer puts his hands on the stake at the front left corner of the cart and begins to push. We are out on the main road that goes through the village now: a small palanquin holding Dam's altar and photo, then the casket and its cart, and then hundreds of people, the entire village, walking slowly behind, at the pace of the cart. Dieu, the grim, undemonstrative veteran, whose demeanor had always been the opposite of Cat's volatile exuberance, his quickness to laugh or cry or hug, suddenly puts his arm over my shoulders, his face strained with emotion. He is the one member of the family who has seemed the most standoffish, sure of himself, sure of his enemies, proud and without regrets for the past. He looks into my eyes now and embraces me, his eyes filling, the marchers breaking around us, and somehow this gesture, from this man, means the most to me. Then he pushes me to the other side of the funeral wagon, the front corner opposite Homer. The soldier there steps away and Dieu puts my hands on the wooden stake.

There is a lag, and then I push against the weight of it, and we go forward. Are these truly Dam's remains I'm pulling? One way or another, of course they are, I tell myself, the weight of this soldier coming home. The war we are all burying here. The heat is physical and fleshy again; it presses like hands at my temples. My eyes burn from the sweat trickling into them. Heat waves lift off the paddies, distorting the air. Someone tilts a water bottle into my mouth. I am grateful I thought to wear a hat, but Homer has none. Suddenly the writer and documentary director, Minh Chuyen, places a floppy green jungle hat on Homer's head. Behind us, an old woman dashes up next to Jessica and opens an umbrella over her head, shielding her from the sun.

What several of my friends feared, a scream of rage at our presence, followed by a shower of stones, has not happened. Instead I am being cut open by myriad acts of kindness. I search the eyes of the people lining the side of the road, and see only curiosity or compassion or understanding.

We are out of the village now. We can see the cemetery, still far up the road. It is in the middle of the rice fields that are all around us now. Tears are filling Homer's eyes. He is looking, he will tell me, at the fields and thinking of the fields of his own boyhood, and he is thinking, these are the fields that the man he had killed rose to every morning and walked into in the dawn, and whose earth and water and rice he had felt cupped in his live hands.

We arrive at the gate in the waist-high wall around the graves. The tombs in the first section of the cemetery are all symmetrical; it is only after this enclosed area that the individualized family tombs rise in irregular clusters, like a small village, larger or smaller because of wealth or poverty, prestige or anonymity. But here, in the first section, all the graves are of the same height and of the same reddish stone. These are the soldiers' graves, those returned out of the 200 lost from the village, and that now include Dam. Some are inscribed with names, and the rest are unmarked except for the words War Martyr. I had always found that phrase pretentious or false: martyrs are pure victims; soldiers kill. But it seems appropriate now, an accurate way to name all the fallen soldiers of the war, and many more who still walk the earth husked and hollowed.

We stand in front at the opening Dam's family has made in the earth to take him back, the tombstone above it inscribed now with his name and those words, *Liet Sy,* War Martyr. The altar, Dam's photograph still on it, is placed next to the grave. Two men lower the heavy casket into the hole, using two wires slung underneath. The wire cuts into their palms, and the casket lists and lies tilted in the grave when they finally get it down. "There is never a neat ending here, is there?" Jessica whispers, and I see that she now understands.

The two men holding the wires manage to straighten the casket. We kneel at the graveside, and again I shield Luong's match as he lights more incense. He hands the joss sticks to us, and we bury their ends in the ground in front of the altar, the earth resisting and then parting for them. A moment later, Luong hands Homer and me chunks of that earth to throw into the grave. Homer's fingers work the ball of dirt, crumbling it, giving it back, and later he says to me that it is the feel of that earth in his hands, Dam's earth, that he will always take with him on his skin, replacing the red Pleiku mud. I say my farewell to Dam, a final one now, and think of the grace notes of this day. The grace and courage of a soldier who brought back the body and the soul of the man he had killed to that man's family and town and earth, taking onto himself their own rending grief. The grace and mercy of a family and a village that take that soldier to their hearts, that allow their gratitude at the ending he brings their story to outweigh their need to hate him for the death that began it.

I remember again what Phan Thanh Hao had said when we brought Dam's documents to the village, three years before: "In Viet Nam, you know, we have a certain spiritual relation that we call karma. . . . We think that Dam was a sacred soul. He was so sacred that he could gather us together: the ones who have fought, and the ones who were thirsty for peace. He was so sacred to gather all of us here, to do this thing, to meet today. So that is what we believe."

I look at Homer. He is staring again at Dam's photograph in front of the tombstone now, held by Dam's eyes. Dieu's daughter goes over to him, puts a hand on his shoulder, and whispers, we forgive you. Later, when I ask him how her words affected him, he says, "The only person that can forgive me is Dam. He's the one I took everything from. And I do think he will. He was a good man. Probably a better man than I am. So I do think he will forgive me. But I won't feel forgiven until I hear that from his own lips. And I look forward to that. I told my wife that when I die, if I don't die suddenly, if I have lingering death, where I have the time to think about mortality and life and death and what I have and haven't accomplished, that I'll think about my mom and dad, and my sisters—brothers and sisters, and—and my wife, and her family, but I sincerely think that my last thoughts as I pass out of this world will be Dam. I don't think it'll be a negative thought. I think it'll be a euphoric feeling. A going forward to meet friends. I think I have a guide on the other side that's going to help me along. I certainly hope so. I would like to know him. I really would like to know him."

I think of the scenario I had fantasized when we first saw Dam's altar. How each soldier must forever carry one of the dead he made back to the family. How he must bear the weight of that body and the weight of their grief. But looking at my friend now, the earth of Dam's grave still on his hands, I know that he is not who should be here, helping to bury the remains of the man he killed. I know who should be here, bearing the weight of this grief all around us, and I know that will never happen.

# Down at the End
# of a Dark Road

I visited Betty Steedly in South Carolina shortly after we returned, Homer traveling down to join us. Standing near the grave of the first Captain Steedly, just inside the edge of the Lemon Swamp, he told me that the experience in Viet Nam had been transformative for him. "I'm doing better than I have in forty years. I cannot begin to express how much this trip has changed me. It was miraculous. I've opened up to people, actually engaged in conversations," he said, grinning. He seemed a man at peace with himself.

I felt good about his reaction, and still do. Yet any sense of completion I might have had was shattered a few weeks after I returned, when my wife and I learned that the fiancé of our across-the-street neighbor's twenty-year-old daughter, Lauren Smith, had been killed by an IED in Afghanistan. Ryan Bauman and Lauren were to have been married in January 2009; he had already completed a year in Iraq before being sent to Afghanistan. Ryan died bravely, insisting on reclaiming the point position in a patrol after his Humvee had been struck by an IED the week before and he'd been taken off that duty. When he saw the IED, he swerved so that he took its full blast, saving the others in the vehicle. He was the fourth person from our county to die in the new wars; two others had died in Iraq. They were mentioned in the eulogy our senator gave at Ryan's funeral, and their names are inscribed—as Ryan's is now—on the county's memorial, the new casualties below the thirteen names listed on the plaque for the Viet Nam war, the seven for Korea, and the sixty-two for World War II.

But the fourth casualty, James Dean—always called by his nickname, Jamie—was not mentioned, nor is his name inscribed in granite. He came from an old county family; among the names of the World War II dead is a John Dean. Jamie had been killed not overseas, but in front of the farmhouse where he grew up. After coming back from a tour in Afghanistan in 2005, Dean learned that he had been reactivated to go to Iraq. Since his return, he had been under treatment at the VA for PTSD. "The patient states he feels very nervous, has a hard time sleeping, feels nauseous in the a.m., and loses his temper a lot, 'real bad,'" reported a Veterans Administration evaluation. "Was nearby an explosion that destroyed a Humvee with four GIs killed in front of his eyes."[1] The family, particularly his mother, had previously tried to get him to talk about his service, but all he would say was, "You don't want to know, Ma." The day he received his orders, he called his sister and told her he "just couldn't do it anymore," and that he was sitting with a shotgun in his lap.[2] His sister, worried sick, called the police and asked for help. The men sent to save Dean from committing suicide surrounded the family house: local sheriff's deputies, state police, and armored cars from three counties converged on the property. Overhead helicopters made the *whop whop* sounds familiar to all Viet Nam War movies. Feeling under attack, Dean told everyone to go away and fired several erratic shots from the window; in return, the house was bombarded with tear gas shells. The siege went on for sixteen hours. At dawn an armored personnel carrier drove up to Dean's door; he stepped outside with his shotgun and was killed by a police sniper, a bullet fired into his heart.

Richard D. Fritz, the state attorney, criticizing the police, called Dean's death the result of a "paramilitary operation . . . directed at an individual down at the end of a dark road, holed up in his father's house, with no hostages."[3] Fritz is correct. But it is equally correct to acknowledge that Jamie Dean died as a result of wounds received in combat, the same wounds that crippled Homer's life for so many years.

And so it continues. "Maybe someday humanity will gain the wisdom to settle conflicts without sending its youth to kill strangers," Homer had written to the Hoang family, but that hope remains as mercilessly distant as ever. In the meantime, there are thousands of Homers streaming back to us again from a carelessly and cavalierly entered conflict. I do not wish here to reinforce the stereotype of the hair-trigger, psychotic vet that may have been the bogeyman in the minds of the police who came down that dark road to protect the community from what the community had created to protect itself, the golem they envisioned that poor damaged farm boy to be. But neither can we allow denial of the mental and spiritual wounds that can freeze the lives of those who have seen and dealt death in our name to preclude giving veterans a level of support that goes beyond the attaboy of medals, bumper stickers, and looped ribbon decals. The human price of war has to be paid, and it has to be acknowledged. The coffins of the hundreds who have committed suicide are slipped undraped and unrecognized into the earth, as the damaged, in their thousands, are supposed to slip quietly out of our sight, except for a few spunky, uplifting examples.

Dr. Katherine Scheirman, a retired colonel and former chief of air force medical operations in Europe who ran the unit charged with evacuating wounded soldiers to the United States, was ordered at one point not to place the wounded, "if their wounds showed," on commercial flights so as "not to upset the American people."[4]

We don't want them sitting next to us. We are afraid that they will turn to us and begin to speak. The final comparison with the Viet Nam War lies in our refusal to truly listen to their stories, the stories of the damage we don't want to see scribed in their flesh and in their souls. The stories of the cost.

Ryan Bauman's funeral brought out hundreds of people; along with sailors and marines in uniform from the nearby base. They stood beside the road as the procession made its way north to Arlington, the line of cars followed by a contingent of motorcycle riders, many of them Viet Nam veterans, with the Missing in Action/Prisoner of War flags on their Harleys becoming their own self-defining ensign. The huge turnout, the community's words of support, and their mass act of witness were a comfort, I'm sure, for Lauren and for Ryan's parents—even though Lauren, as a fiancée, would not receive a flag nor any acknowledgment. But the hard part would come in the time that followed, when the realization of who had been subtracted from their lives was something they would have to bear individually, in the loneliness of long nights and empty dawns. "These are things I never wanted to talk about with my twenty-year-old daughter," her father, a former marine helicopter pilot, said to me. "Wars have their endings inside families," wrote Cynthia Enloe.[5]

The procession for Ryan's funeral, stretching on seemingly for miles, brought me back to Thai Giang, forming an endless ouroboros in my mind, one procession linking into the other, circling the earth: the community eternally gathering around the family, bringing home its sacrificial child.

The initial draft of the book you have just read was finished in late July 2008. Shortly after, I received e-mails from Viet Nam about the documentary that Minh Chuyen had filmed about the experience. He called it *Linh hon Viet Cong* (*The Soul of a Viet Cong*), which seemed an odd title to me, given that Dam had been a People's Army regular. But Minh Chuyen, a PAVN veteran himself, knew that to people in his country, most of them born after the war, the history of the war was blurry, and in the popular mind Viet Cong had become a term that stood for anyone who fought against the Americans and the Saigon government.

In any case, as had happened with Dr. Dang Thuy Tram's diary, the film, when it was aired on the main television channel, struck a chord in the public imagination. Hundreds of people called the network, asking that the film be rebroadcast. It was, on July 27, 2008, which is a holiday to commemorate wounded soldiers, something like our Memorial Day.

I had a chance to download and see the film a few weeks later, with Wick and Ho Nguyen, both of whom helped translate the running narrative. Although Minh Chuyen had captured the basic story, he had also omitted and changed certain facts, asserting, for example, that the ceremony we performed at the Mang Yang Pass was near the cemetery, and that Homer had helped search for the grave itself. The tweaks—done, I assumed, for what Minh saw as a way to heighten the drama—seemed unnecessary to me. The truth was dramatic enough—but at least, I told myself, the spirit of what happened was captured in the film, and that was what moved viewers.

On August 23, however, several articles appeared in Vietnamese newspapers, questioning discrepancies between the sites named in the film and the sites actually shown. One article also questioned why the filmmaker had not filmed the exhumation and the articles in the grave that proved the medium had correctly identified Dam's resting place.

The Hoangs left it up to Dieu to reply. His response was published under the last article just mentioned. The family, he owned up, did not have the permission—as they told us they already had when they called us in Pleiku—to exhume the remains, but had decided to go into the cemetery anyway and had hired people to help them dig up the grave. To protect those people, and because they did not have permission, the director had been forced to shoot in a different location and name it as the location of Dam's grave. "We secretly dug [the grave] up," Dieu admitted. "We came to ask for help from the Gia Lai provincial military headquarters and the Martyr and Society Service of the town, but they refused to help. Since we couldn't get permission, we had to hire men to dig it secretly. Director Minh Chuyen later had to arrange a shooting not inside the cemetery because of that. The most important thing is we finally got the remains of my brother."[6] They were sorry they and the filmmaker had had to deceive people, Dieu acknowledged. But otherwise, they were unapologetic. In another newspaper, Dieu was quoted as saying, "We have looked for Dam's remains since 2002, and I swear before my brother's spirit that we have taken him back home to let him rest with his ancestors."[7]

I remembered how quickly the situation had changed while we were waiting in Pleiku, how relieved Homer, Jessica, and I had been that the family had received permission, my amazement that it was all working out. But—as Jessica had observed when the casket slipped as it was being lowered—like all true Viet Nam War stories, this one had ended ambiguously. Had they actually retrieved the correct remains? It had never mattered to me. It still didn't. They had buried what could be buried; if it wasn't Dam, then some other unknown from the North had been brought home. What has stayed in my mind is the family's compassion to Homer, and their need to dig up the past in order to rebury it properly, with wisdom and compassion and proper commemoration. And perhaps what we put into the earth again *were* Dam's remains—what I'd seen in the Mang Yang Pass, I'd seen with my own eyes; what I'd felt in Thai Giang, I'd felt in my own heart. I remembered what George had written to me: "*Nothing about this whole adventure is hard to believe, except that we are all still alive to the world, are ones who can see it, have somehow tended to our memories and life forces in such a way to be able to remain open to it all, receptive, and have this chance to escape being simply skeptical about what the world presents us with, and not run from it.*"

The Hoangs, I realized, had protected us by keeping us away from the cemetery—and made sure at the same time that we would not interfere by objecting to what they would do there. One way or another, they were going to retrieve Dam's remains. They were still convinced that was what they had done.

The Hoangs had gotten their own ending. They had done what they felt they had to do.

And so had Homer.

# ACKNOWLEDGMENTS

My deep gratitude to all those who helped me write this book, first and especially to Homer Steedly and Tibby Dozier Steedly, Betty Steedly, the Hoang family: Hoang Huy Luong, Hoang Thi Tham, Hoang Dang Cat, Hoang Thi Tuoi; brother-in-law Hoang Minh Dieu, and his daughter Pham Thi Huong Quynh; Dam's widow, Pham Thi Minh, and his comrade-in-arms Pham Quang Huy, all of whom opened up their lives and trusted me with their stories. Many thanks to Phan Thanh Hao; she not only wrote the article that resulted in the return of the documents, but without her help, knowledge, insights, and hospitality, this book would have been impossible to write; to Ho Anh Thai and Le Minh Khue for their friendship and continual inspiration; to Y Ban for getting the articles published and coming with us on that first trip to Thai Giang; to Nguyen Qui Duc for his bottomless support, steadfast friendship, and generous heart; to Nguyen Thi Tien for her passion and determination; to Doug Reese for logistical miracles, and to Bill Deeter, who helped us understand so much; to tireless interpreters Le Thi Minh Hanh, Vu Bich Thuy, and Doan Anh Quan; to Nam Son and his family for their warm hospitality in Saigon; and to the People's and Veteran's Committees in Thai Giang Commune.

Great gratitude goes also to all the supporters of this book in the United States: George Evans for his insistence I write it after I expressed my initial reluctance, and for his support after I took up the task; Daisy Zamora, for her poet's heart; my tireless agent, Phyllis Westberg, for making it possible to do this at all; Ruth Baldwin and Nation Books for their faith and vision, and Randy Fertel, for introducing me to that publishing team, and for all I have learned from our conversations and the teaching we did together. To Ho

Nguyen, with me spiritually if not physically on this journey from the moment we first saw Dam's documents; to Michael Glaser for a good, merciless first read; and to Lucille Clifton for a life-saving talk after it was done. To Wick Tourison for his insights and his lifelong courage to insist upon the truth. To Marc Steiner and Valerie Williams, who opened many doors for me and walked through many more with me, and Jessica Phillips, a fine journalist and travel companion; to Roger Horn, for all his help and long friendship; to Edna Troiano for understanding what was truly important; to Neal Dwyer, who helped make the connections; to Tom Lacombe, who began it all with a single e-mail, and for his book *Light Ruck*, which helped me understand the war in the Central Highlands; and to Mike Archer, John Bauer, Ron Carey, James W. DeRoos, and Jack Hawkins, who generously shared their stories and allowed me to include them. To marine buddies: P.I. Jim Robbins, who tracked me down, then helped me track down Homer's own comrades-in-arms, and John Borman for clearing that jammed machine gun and for demonstrating after the war what grace, generosity, and redemptive power can exist within the warrior's heart. To the memory of George's friend Billy Dick; to the memory of Mike Archer's friend Tom Mahoney, who died near Khe Sanh, and to the memory of Mike's other friend "Doc" Robert Topmiller, a great spirit and peacemaker who took his own life forty years after he left Khe Sanh, the war reaching over those years to snatch him back; to the memory of Ron Grey; to the memory of James Stanley Bernard Childers, who died in my place, and to the spirit and memory of Hoang Ngoc Dam and all those who died on all sides of that war: may their sacrifice truly not be in vain. Finally, to all the writers, poets, and filmmakers who have come from the wars and who have borne witness and allowed us the means to mourn and the means to learn from our mourning, and to the memory of Sandy Taylor, who enabled and encouraged so many of us.

Above all, thank you to my wife, Ohnmar, for her love and support and patience, and to my son, Adam, for the same, and for the gift of his trust and his own great courage.

# PERMISSIONS

"The Face Beneath" by Lam Thi My Da, in *Green Rice*, trans. Collins, Martha, and Thuy Dinh, Curbstone Press, 2005. Reprinted with the permission of Curbstone Press. Distributed by Consortium.

Extracts from *The Song of a Soldier's Wife,* by Dang Tran Con and Phan Huy Ich, trans. Huynh Sanh Thong, Lac Viet #3, Council for Southeast Asia Studies, Yale Center for International and Area Studies, 1986. Reprinted with the permission of Council for Southeast Asia Studies, Yale Center for International and Area Studies.

Extracts from "The Distant Stars," "A Day on the Road," "Fragile as a Sunray," "Tony D," and "A Small Tragedy," by Le Minh Khue in *The Stars, The Earth, The River: Fiction by Le Minh Khue*, trans. Dana Sachs and Bac Hoi Tran, Curbstone Press, 1997. Reprinted with the permission of Curbstone Press. Distributed by Consortium.

Extracts from "A Walk in the Garden of Heaven," by George Evans, in *The Other Side of Heaven: Fiction by Vietnamese and American Veterans,* Curbstone Press, 1995, and "Two Girls," in *The New World,* Curbstone Press, 2002. Reprinted with the permission of Curbstone Press. Distributed by Consortium.

Quotes, paraphrases, and adaptations from the "flashbacks" section of the Web site www.swampfox.info adapted and reprinted with the permission of Homer R. Steedly Jr.

Extracts from *A Patch of Ground: Khe Sanh Remembered,* by Michael Archer, Hellgate Press, 2004. Reprinted with the permission of Hellgate Press.

Interviews from the radio series *Shared Weight,* producers Steiner, Mark, Steve Elliott, and Wayne Karlin, 2005, reprinted with the permission of the Center for Emerging Media, Baltimore, Maryland.

Quotations and paraphrased material from "The Tragedy of Company A, 3/8 Infantry" on the Web site www.forum.militaryltd .com/vietnam/m19464-tragedy-co-3–8-infantry.htm by John Bauer, reprinted with the permission of the author.

Quotations and paraphrased material from *The War Above the Trees: Operation Wayne Grey,* by Ron Carey, Trafford Press, 2004, reprinted with the permission of the author.

Some parts of this book were adapted from my article "Wandering Souls" published in *War, Literature and the Arts: An International Journal of the Humanities* (2006) vol. 18, numbers 1 & 2, Dept. of English, USAF Academy, Colorado Springs, 203–221, and in *Manoa: Maps of Reconciliation: Literature and the Ethical Imagination* (Spring 2007) vol. 19:2, University of Hawaii Press, Honolulu, 108–125.

# NOTES

## CHAPTER ONE: AN ENCOUNTER IN PLEIKU

1. "Episode 1: Wandering Souls," of *Shared Weight: 30 Years After the Fall of Saigon* (Radio Program, Center for Emerging Media, produced by Wayne Karlin, Marc Steiner, and Steve Elliott), first broadcast on WYPR Baltimore, May 30, 2006, subsequently on WAMU Washington, D.C., KQED San Francisco, WNYC New York, and elsewhere; interviews in Thai Giang village conducted and translated by Le Thi Minh Hanh, July 2006; and Homer Steedly, interviews and e-mail exchanges with author July 17, 2005, July 16 and July 28, 2008.

2. It was a phrase he knew from "surrender cards," which were scattered over the jungle by American aircraft on psyops (psychological operations) missions. The phrase literally means "come over," or "return," and was aimed at enticing Southern Viet Cong troops to "return" to the Saigon government's side. The use of the word may have been incomprehensible to Dam, except in the context of Homer's actions.

3. "Episode 1: Wandering Souls"; and Steedly, interviews and e-mails.

## CHAPTER TWO: EYES LIKE A MEAN ANIMAL'S

4. Tim O'Brien, "The Man I Killed," in *The Things They Carried* (New York: Penguin, 1990), 137.

5. Ibid., 201.

6. Some parts of this chapter, in a different form, were presented by the author at the conference "Thirty-Years After: Literature and Film of the Vietnam War," University of Hawaii, November 9, 2005. Other sections, also in different form, were first published as "Internal Exile and Communal Memory: Conversations with Three Writers Born of War," *Witness* 20 (2006): 155–156.

7. Dr. Jonathan Shay, in a somewhat different but related take, states that "Restoring honor to the enemy is an essential step in recovery from PTSD . . . the veteran's self-respect never fully recovers so long as he is unable to see the enemy as worthy." *Achilles in Vietnam: Combat Trauma and the Undoing of Character* (New York: Scribner, 1995), 115.

8. Michael Archer, *A Patch of Ground: Khe Sanh Remembered* (Central Point, OR: Hellgate Press, 2005), 171; and Michael Archer, e-mail messages to author, July 10–August 21, 2007.

9. Lam Thi My Da, "The Face Beneath," in *Green Rice*, trans. Martha Collins and Thuy Dinh (Willimantic, CT: Curbstone Press, 2005), 12–13.

10. O'Brien, "The Man I Killed," 201.

## PART ONE: THE WAR
## CHAPTER THREE: BAMBERG

1. http://carolana.com/SC/Towns/Bamberg_SC.html and www.oldplaces
.org/bamberg/towns.html.

2. All quotes and information from Homer Steedly in this chapter are
from e-mail interviews with author, March 3, 2008; conversations with author in Viet Nam, May 22–31, 2008; and interviews with author in Bamberg and Columbia, S.C., July 17–18, 2008.

3. http://www.nps.gov/history/nr/twhp/wwwlps/lessons/94rivers/94setting
.htm.

4. All quotes and information are from Betty Steedly, interview with author, Bamberg, July 18, 2008.

5. http://www.epodunk.com/cgi-bin/genInfo.php?locIndex=13047#Esse.

6. Robert Hayden, extract from "Those Winter Sundays," in *Angle of Ascent: New and Collected Poems* (New York: Liveright, 1966).

## CHAPTER FOUR: THAI GIANG

7. Dang Tran Con and Phan Huy Ich, *The Song of a Soldier's Wife,* trans.
Huyn Sanh Thong, Lac Viet Series no. 3 (New Haven, CT: Council on Southeast Asia Studies, Yale Center for International and Area Studies, 1986), 3.

8. I use the term "village" because it has the broadest and deepest social
and historical connotations, though in modern Vietnamese parlance, Thai
Giang is called a commune. Dam came from Doai Hamlet, a subdivision of
Thai Giang.

9. William Duiker, *Ho Chi Minh* (New York: Hyperion, 2000), 294–295.
Duiker notes: "As the number of dead mounted, bodies began to appear
along the highways, and hungry peasants wandered aimlessly, begging for
food or gathered near granaries zealously guarded by Japanese troops."

10. My Ha and Thu Phuong, "Famine Fed Farmers' Fight for Freedom,"
*Viet Nam News,* May 21, 2005.

11. Pham Quang Huy, interview with author in Thai Binh, December 26,
2007. Translated by Nguyen Qui Duc.

12. All quotes are from Hoang family, interviews with author in Thai Giang
Village, December 26, 2007. Translated by Nguyen Qui Duc.

13. "All men are created equal. The Creator has given us certain invio-
lable rights: the right to Life, the right to be Free, and the right to achieve
Happiness." Marilyn Young writes of how Ho checked his translation with
an American OSS officer who was one of his advisors, and clarified his
speech to the crowd by saying, "These immortal words are taken from the
American Declaration of Independence." Marilyn Young, *The Vietnam
Wars, 1945–1990* (New York: Harper, 1991), 10–11.

14. See Duiker, *Ho Chi Minh,* 465; and Neil Sheehan, *A Bright, Shining Lie:
John Paul Vann and America in Vietnam* (New York: Random House, 1988),

136–137. Sheehan describes how such warnings were often instigated by Lansdale, who "took measures to see that those Catholics who were unde-cided had their minds made up for them," including hiring famous as-trologers to print leaflets warning of disasters in the North. Lansdale's plan, "Operation Exodus," enabled much of the movement to the South as well, providing American naval transport and French air transport for refugees. Duiker notes: "Eventually a total of over 800,000 Vietnamese left the North, many of them Roman Catholics who were warned by their priests, 'the Virgin Mary has moved to the South. Shouldn't you?'"

15. Killen Konrad, *A Profile of the PAVN Soldier in South Vietnam,* RAND Corporation Study (RM 5013-1-ISA/ARPA) (Santa Monica, CA: RAND Cor-poration, 1966), 17, quoted in Michael Lanning and Dan Cragg, *Inside the VC and NVA* (New York: Ballantine Books, 1992), 70.

16. Sheehan, *Bright, Shining Lie,* 173. "Truong Chinh, the secretary-general of the Party, inflicted a horror on the country by letting the land-reform campaign get out of hand in his zealotry. The terror caused the death of thousands of small land-owners. . . . Catholics who had not fled to the South . . . had been singled out for vengeance by Chinh's land-reform cadres."

17. Duiker, *Ho Chi Minh,* 474–483. Duiker notes Ho Chi Minh's reluc-tance to begin the campaign, bowing finally to his own militants and pres-sure from Chinese advisors.

18. For an account of the Humanist Literature Movement in the North, see Barbara Crossette, "What the Poets Thought: Antiwar Sentiment in North Vietnam (Reconsiderations)," *World Policy Journal,* March 22, 2003.

19. RAND Vietnam Interviews, *Active Influence Within the Viet Cong and North Vietnamese Army,* Series AG (R-1024-ARPA-AD741301), No. 612 (Santa Monica, CA: RAND Corporation, March 1972), 10, quoted in Lan-ning and Cragg, *Inside the VC,* 39.

20. See Sheehan, *Bright, Shining Lie,* 159–160, who notes that such fig-ures limn the Vietnamese adulation of the "mandarin-warrior," a key figure in a history marked by warfare against Chinese invaders.

21. Bao Ninh, *The Sorrow of War* (New York: Riverhead, 1995), 119.

## CHAPTER FIVE: MAP SHIFTS

22. Information on Calley's background is from Michael Bilton and Kevin Sim, *Four Hours in My Lai* (New York: Viking Penguin, 1993); and Homer Steedly, e-mail interview with author, March 8, 2008.

23. For example, in *The Military Half* (the title itself referring to the dis-connect between political goals and military strategies in Viet Nam), Jonathan Schell notes that from 1965 to 1967, operations by American, Republic of Vietnam, and Korean forces in the heavily populated Quang Ngai Province (where My Lai is located) had destroyed approximately 70

percent of the villages in the province—the population whose hearts and minds we were trying to win. Schell, *The Military Half* (republished in *The Real War*, New York: Da Capo Press, 2000), 198.

24. Sheehan, *Bright, Shining Lie,* 383.

25. Bilton and Sim, *Four Hours in My Lai.* There is controversy about whether the commander of the task force that destroyed My Lai, Lieutenant Colonel Frank Barker, ordered his men to kill all the men, women, and children in the village, though the report of the Peers Commission, which investigated the massacre, concluded that his remarks during his briefing "created the potential . . . for the interpretation of his orders as authority to fire, without restriction, on all persons found within the target area" (96). The men of Charlie Company, briefed by their commanding officer, Captain Ernest Medina, felt the message was unambiguous. "Many of the senior NCO's left the meeting convinced that the order was to kill everyone. Henry Stanley—who resisted the order—remembers 'We all agreed that Captain Medina meant for us to kill every man, woman, and child in the village'" (99).

26. Ibid., 122.

27. Jonathan Shay, *Achilles in Vietnam: Combat Trauma and the Undoing of Character* (New York: Scribner, 1995), 31–32.

## CHAPTER SIX: "OF THE TWO OF US, WHO IS MORE SORROWFUL?"

28. All quotes and background information on Dam's life in this chapter are from the Hoang family, interviews with author in Thai Giang, December 26, 2007.

29. Dang Tran Con. This translation is by Ho Anh Thai, from an e-mail to author July 31, 2008.

30. Dang Tran Con and Phan Huy Ich, *The Song of a Soldier's Wife,* Huyn Sanh Thong trans., 5.

31. Information from interviews done for this book by Pham Thi Huong Quynh, the daughter of Dam's brother-in-law Dieu. Quynh states that there are 200 "war martyrs" from Thai Giang, 45 from the French war, 142 from the American war, and 13 from the border fighting with China in 1979. She notes that there are 37 graves in the war martyr section of the village cemetery, although some are inscribed with names but contain no bodies, "and vice versa."

## CHAPTER SEVEN: "YOU WISH YOUR BUTTONS WERE FLATTER"

32. All information about Homer's war experiences comes from personal interviews by Wayne Karlin and Marc Steiner in Pisgah Falls, North Carolina, July 17, 2005, later incorporated into "Episode 1: Wandering Souls,"

of *Shared Weight: 30 Years After the Fall of Saigon* (Radio Program, Center for Emerging Media, produced by Wayne Karlin, Marc Steiner, and Steve Elliot), first broadcast on WYPR Baltimore, May 30, 2006; and material quoted or paraphrased from Homer's Web site (www.swampfox.info).

33. Descriptions of the Plei Trap are from Tom Lacombe, *Light Ruck* (Fort Valley, VA: Loft Press, 2002); and Ron Carey, *The War Above the Trees* (Victoria, BC: Trafford, 2004).

34. Col. Hale H. Knight, *Combat Operations After Action Report for Operation Wayne Grey*: Sec. 15.b, Department of the Army, Headquarters, 1st Brigade, 4th Infantry Division, APO 96262 (Kontum, Vietnam), April 30, 1969, http://www.ivydragoons.org/AfterActionReports.htm.

## CHAPTER EIGHT: THE TRAIL

35. Lanning and Cragg, *Inside the VC*, 102–103.

36. All personal material on Dam in this chapter is from Pham Quang Huy and Hoang family, interviews with author at Thai Binh and Thai Giang, December 26, 2007.

37. Harold G. Moore and Joseph L. Galloway, *We Were Soldiers Once . . . and Young* (New York: Ballantine, 1992), 46–47.

38. Amherst: University of Massachusetts Press, 1994, 5.

39. Lanning and Cragg, *Inside the VC*, 75; and author's conversations with Le Minh Khue over a period of fifteen years.

## CHAPTER NINE: ONE WEEK

40. Carey, *War Above the Trees*, 46.

41. Lacombe, *Light Ruck*, 60.

42. The stories in this section are all taken from Homer's accounts in the "flashbacks" section of his Web site (www.swampfox.info). With his permission, I have paraphrased them to match the tone of the rest of the book and also to include some of the facts and emotions that Homer added to these accounts during our conversations.

## CHAPTER TEN: "MY BROTHER AND I WILL MEET EACH OTHER"

43. The names and locations of the places where Dam served in Gia Lai have been difficult to pin down, partially because many of the names used during the war have been changed. Different and at times contradictory names and locations were provided by the Hoang family during our interviews. The ones I've put here seem to be the most consistent, and were obtained during my interview with the family on December 26, 2007; Phan Thanh Hao's questions to the family, the answers to which were e-mailed to me on June 13, 2008; and Doug Reese's follow-up interview with the Hoang family, e-mailed to me on January 13, 2009.

44. Capt. Arthur Ahearn, "Viet Cong Medicine," *Military Medicine* (March 1966): 221, quoted in Lanning and Cragg, *Inside the VC,* 165–166.

45. Lanning and Cragg, *Inside the VC,* 46.

46. Ibid., 39.

47. The issue of Chinese troops or advisors in South Viet Nam is still contested. According to Lanning and Cragg, in 1989 the China News Service revealed that China had sent 320,000 troops to serve in North Viet Nam; how many actually went south with PAVN troops is unknown.

## CHAPTER ELEVEN: CAMP ENARI AND THE PLEI TRAP

48. www.swampfox.info/flashbacks; and Homer Steedly, interviews and e-mail exchanges with author, March 3, 2008, July 17–18, 2008, for background and information on Homer's duties and activities.

49. Knight, *Combat Operations After Action Report.* The 1st Brigade of the 4th Infantry Division was the central unit involved in Operation Wayne Grey. Its main body consisted of three infantry battalions: the 1st Battalion of the 8th Infantry Regiment (Homer's outfit, the 1/8/4), the 3rd Battalion of the 8th, the 3rd Battalion of the 12th (Tom Lacombe's), a brigade headquarters, and various attached and/or supporting elements from other regiments: artillery, air support, reconnaissance, etc. Pilot Jack Hawkins and crew chief Ron Carey, for example, were in the 119th Assault Helicopter Company of the 52nd Combat Aviation Battalion, two of those supporting elements. Each infantry battalion had five companies: a headquarters company and four infantry companies, each called by either a letter (A,B, C, D) or by its call sign in the military phonetic alphabet (Alpha, Bravo, Charlie, Delta). A company would consist of roughly 160 men, though most were rarely at full strength. Most of the soldiers in the 4th Division were draftees.

50. Lacombe, *Light Ruck,* 61–62.

51. Ibid., 62.

52. Carey, *War Above the Trees,* 62.

53. Knight, *Combat Operations After Action Report.*

54. John F. Bauer, "*Revisiting the Casualty Numbers: the Tragedy of Co A, 3/8th Infantry,*" http://www.ivydragoons.org/Files/Hill%20947%20Alpha%20Story_JBauer.html.

55. On March 31, 2005, George Callan's son—also named George—e-mailed this message to Homer after reading about his father on Homer's Web site:

> Dear Mr. Steedly, Hello again. I want to thank you for the time that you spent discussing your service and the interaction you had with my father in early 1969. I have spent the large majority of my life wondering about Vietnam and thanks to the 4th

ID website, and to men like you, I have been able to learn a great deal about my father and the place where he died. I have been educated about the Central Highlands, Plei Trap, and triple canopy growth that made it dark enough to need a flashlight during the day. I am still reading through your website and it has just demanded my attention like no other. The daily responsibilities and challenges faced by combat infantrymen during Vietnam serve to inspire me whenever I feel that my own life is becoming difficult. The fact that my father died there serving his country, and attempting to recover the M60 that went down when the point man was hit, always reminds me that I owe my best to whatever I am facing in my life. If you know any others who served with my dad and would be willing to talk about it, I would appreciate it. I have a 3 year old daughter who will need to know who her grandfather was and why she never met him. . . . God bless you Homer. You have helped me to know more about my dad and his last months of life. I cannot thank you enough for sharing your time and memories.

## CHAPTER TWELVE: A MEETING ENGAGEMENT

56. James DeRoos, telephone interview with author, January 19, 2009. DeRoos did not remember the exact details, but recalled the patrol and the fact that men were wounded, a fact also mentioned in the 1-8 Battalion *After Action Report* regarding operation Wayne Grey for March 17–18: "Company B continued Fire Support Base 20 security mission with local security, patrols and 2 platoon-sized ambushes vicinity YB 868068 and YB 851079. . . . 18 March 1969: . . . Air Support: Cider 22 employed air strike vicinity YB 720053 to YB 730049 for purpose of cutting road in that vicinity. One Medevac was employed with Company B for two WIA."

57. www.swampfox.info/flashbacks; and author and Jessica Phillips interview, May 27, 2008. On his Web site, Homer writes that he does not remember what wound the second man received, and in his initial memories, after thirty-five years, he was not certain of the sequence of events on the patrols. But in our interview, which took place near the areas where these actions occurred, many memories came back to him, including the detail about the tourniquet. Homer's quotes and other details about his encounter with Hoang Ngoc Dam in this chapter come from that interview and my own conversations with him in Viet Nam, May 22–31, 2008.

58. www.swampfox.info/flashbacks.

59. Ibid.; Carey, *War Above the Trees,* 48–49; and Jack Hawkins, e-mail message to author, February 24, 2008.

60. Homer's letter home at the time described the events with typical understatement:

> Dear Mom and Dad, As you have already guessed, things are really happening over here. 3/8 had a company nearly wiped out a few weeks ago. We have had several contacts ourselves, but nothing real big. I had to shoot an NVA major. I took his identification papers and will send them home sometime soon. Please put them up somewhere for me. He was real young for a major. That same payday I almost got shot by a kid who went crazy and started shooting at everyone. I was walking down the road when he opened up on me. The MP's finally got him, but he had already killed his pay officer and wounded the 1st Sergeant. That couple of days have been my worst yet. I'm still XO, but I soon hope to get a chance at being Company Commander. If I do get a company, I will probably extend for a while to get in as much command time as possible. I have also started a correspondence course in Physics to get back in the track for college. The army is selecting OCS graduates, who haven't finished college, to go to school full time with regular Army pay until they get their degree, and I hope I get selected. I think I have a real good chance. Got the bluing and steel wool, and chow, thanks a bunch. I also got the recording: sure was good to hear from everybody again. I have some work to get done now, so bye, Love, Homer.

http://www.swampfox.info/Letters_Home/18MAR69.html. Homer later explained that he wasn't sure why he thought Dam was a major.

61. Interview with author and Phillips, May 27, 2008.

## CHAPTER THIRTEEN: "I WILL PROBABLY NOT MAKE IT OFF THIS HILL ALIVE"

62. Knight, *Combat Operations After Action Report*.

63. www.swampfox.infor/flashbacks; and Steedly, interviews and e-mail exchanges with author, July 17–18, 2008, for all information on Task Force Alpha, unless otherwise indicated.

64. www.swampfox.info/flashbacks; James DeRoos telephone conversations with author, January 30, 2009.

65. James DeRoos, telephone conversations with author, January 19, January 22, and January 30, 2009; James DeRoos, letter to author, January 28, 2009; and Department of the Army, Headquarters, 4th Infantry Division General Orders 5233, 7 August 1969, awarding the Silver Star to Captain James W. DeRoos. DeRoos retired from the army in 1971, after serving with Special Forces in Cambodia, and spent three decades as a high school history teacher, retiring in 2008.

66. Carey, *War Above the Trees*, 253–254; Headquarters, 4th Infantry Division General Orders 5843, describing the award of the Bronze Star medal for heroism given to Capt. DeRoos for that action; and Hawkins, e-mail message to author, February 24, 2008. Hawkins, the pilot who helped rescue Homer, now flies helicopters in the Antarctic for the U.S. government. He writes of the Task Force Alpha LZ:

> The trees were in the neighborhood of 50 feet and were pretty dense except where the top of the hill was. I think that also helped us as [the NVA] had less opportunity to get a lead on us. The LZ was an oval that was cut out, and I remember one tree that was always in the way in the direction I came in. After getting to the LZ, I would want to get away from the top of the trees and get into the "hole" as quickly as possible. That one tree kept me above the tree line longer than I liked. I did not see any American positions, in that when I would go in, I would do the best to block everything out except flying the helicopter as fast and hard as I could. If I remember right, they had some sandbags set out that we landed on. There was a stump about 15 to 20 yards in front of the way I normally landed (I think I wound up in the LZ facing south), but I remember seeing a trooper shooting his M-16 up into the trees. There was also a mortar round that had gone off either on the sandbag pad or right in front of it. The trees around it were pretty shattered up. I think there was a dead snag in the direction that I went out on the last flight. To be honest, I never cared enough to stay on the ground to scope out the LZ!

67. Carey, *War Above the Trees*, 260.
68. Robert M. Granger, e-mail, March 29, 2009.
69. Ibid.

## CHAPTER FOURTEEN: DEATH DANCE

70. According to Neal Sheehan, by 1966 Marine General Victor Krulak had realized the futility of fighting a war of attrition. "The Vietnamese Communists had at their disposal . . . a probably military manpower pool of 2.5 million men. If one accepted the [then] current kill ratio of one American or Saigon soldier for 2.6 Viet Cong or North Vietnamese—an exchange of corpses that Krulak thought might be 'optimistic'. . . . 10,000 Americans and 165,000 Saigon soldier would have to die [in 1965] in order 'to reduce the enemy [manpower] pool by only a modest 20 per cent.'" Bright, *Shining Lie*, 630.

71. www.swampfox.infor/flashbacks; and Steedly, interviews and e-mail exchanges with author, for all information on Steedly's second tour, unless otherwise indicated.

72. Homer Steedly, e-mail to author, July 29, 2008.

73. Homer Steedly, interview with author and Jessica Phillips, May 26, 2008.

## PART TWO: HOMECOMINGS
## CHAPTER FIFTEEN: TIGER

1. Michael Norman, *These Good Men* (New York: Simon & Schuster, 1989), 131–133.

2. Information in this chapter is from Homer Steedly, interviews and e-mail exchanges with author, July 17, 2005, March 3, 2008, May 21–31 2008. Some of the combat memories draw on information from the swampfox Web site and our conversations about those incidents. Several passages were taken from the author's article "Wandering Souls," in *War, Literature & the Arts: An International Journal* 18, nos. 1 & 2 (U.S. Air Force Academy, Boulder, CO, Winter 2006): 203–221; and in *Manoa: Maps of Reconciliation: Literature and the Ethical Imagination* 19, no. 2 (University of Hawaii Press, Honolulu, Winter 2007): 108–125.

## CHAPTER SIXTEEN: THE SORROW OF WAR

3. Pham Quang Huy, Hoang Minh Dieu, interview with author in Thai Binh, December 26, 2007. Translated by Nguyen Qui Duc.

4. Bill Deeter, MIA Research Specialist, U.S. Defense Attaché Office, Hanoi, e-mail message, June 5, 2008:

> On 31 May 1967 PFC Brian K. McGar, PFC Joseph E. Fitzgerald, rifleman, SGT John A. Jakovac, Ammo Bearer, CPL Charles G. Rogerson, and SP4 Carl D. Flowers were members of a long range reconnaissance patrol deployed at BS 735 453 in Quang Ngai Province, RVN. The patrol was instructed to move to the base of Hill 310 and to check out an area along a hedgerow where several VC had been seen and fired upon by gunships earlier that day. Then, at night, the patrol was to move to the top of Hill 310 to establish an observation point.
>
> Early that afternoon, a report was received that the patrol had established a position at BS 717 454 and reported everything was normal. At 2030 hours the patrol reported that they were going to proceed to the top of the hill to establish the observation point. Radio contact with the patrol was lost sometime after this, as the patrol failed to make a scheduled report at 2145.
>
> The following morning search elements began sweeping the area in which the patrol was last known to be located (BS 718 450). During the search, bodies of two patrol members were dis-

covered in a fresh grave. They were CPL Regerson and SP4 Flowers. In the area near the grave, the search element also found an expended NAK-47, 5.56 and 7.62 MM brass as well as hand grenade fragments. In addition, blood trails were discovered leading from the area. An intense search was conducted for three days following the incident and at various times from 2 June 1967 until 12 June 1967 without success.

From 7 Jan to 23 Jan 94, RE1 conducted a joint excavation near Pho Phung Village, Duc Pho District, Quang Ngai Province. The site is located at Grid Coordinate 48PBS7145645563. Portions of all major long bones, for each of the three individuals, were recovered. In addition, portions of crania, humerii, foot bone fragments, as well as 2 calcaneouses (heel bone), 2 mandibular fragments (one with teeth), 3 pelvic fragments; 86 teeth were also recovered, of which 30 have dental restorations. Some U.S. materials not associated with this case, such as bomb fragments, CS canisters, and unknown aircraft wreckage, were found during the excavation process. The site was officially closed by the CILHI Team Leader and anthropologist on 23 Jan 94.

5. Barbara Crossette, "What the Poets Thought," *World Policy Journal* 20, no. 1 (March 22, 2003): 69.

6. Xuan Thieu, "Please Don't Knock on My Door," in *The Other Side of Heaven: Postwar Fiction by Vietnamese and American Writers,* ed. Wayne Karlin, Le Minh Khue, and Truong Vu, 137–154. Translated by Bac Hoai Tran and Dana Sachs (Willimantic, CT: Curbstone, 1995).

7. Bao Ninh, *The Sorrow of War.* Translated by Phan Thanh Hao (New York: Riverhead, 1996), 42–43.

8. "Episode 2: Artists Born of War," of *Shared Weight: 30 Years After the Fall of Saigon* (Radio Program, Center for Emerging Media, produced by Marc Steiner and Steve Elliott), first broadcast on WYPR Baltimore, May 31, 2006. All interviews in this chapter are by the author and Marc Steiner, trans. Vu Bich Thuy.

9. Bao Ninh, *Sorrow of War*, 133, 135.

10. Ibid., 30.

11. Ibid., 91.

12. Ibid., 230.

## CHAPTER SEVENTEEN: TIBBY

13. According to *Webster's New World Dictionary of the Vietnam War*, edited by Marc Leepson with Helen Hannaford (New York, Simon & Schuster Macmillan, 1999, 134–135) "Fragging peaked in 1970–71, a period of widespread demoralization among U.S. troops. According to the

Pentagon, 788 probable explosive-device fragging assaults took place in Vietnam between 1969 and 1972, resulting in 86 dead and 714 wounded. Many more suspected fraggings were not investigated for lack of evidence."

14. Jonathan Shay, *Achilles in Vietnam: Combat Trauma and the Undoing of Character* (New York: Scribner, New York, 1995), 6.

15. Jonathan Shay, *Odysseus in America: Combat Trauma and the Trials of Homecoming* (New York: Scribner, 2003), 4.

16. Robert Stone, *Dog Soldiers* (New York: Ballantine Books, 1975), 57.

17. Robert J. Lifton, *Home from the War: Vietnam Veterans: Neither Victims nor Executioners* (New York: Simon & Schuster, 1973), 40–41.

18. Philip J. Caputo, *A Rumor of War* (New York: Holt, 1996), prologue, xiv.

19. Homer Steedly, e-mail interview with author, March 20, 2008. All quotations from Homer Steedly in this chapter are from that interview.

20. Shay, *Odysseus*, 56.

21. Joan Fiset and Don Johnson, "The Elders' Thoughts," in *Sunken Dirt Where Our Foxhole Was* (Seattle: Vet Center, 1998).

22. Elizabeth Steedly, e-mail interview with author, April 8, 2008. All quotes and biographical information in this chapter are from this interview.

23. www.scguard.com/museum/index.html; and "This Is Your Life Mr. National Guard," a booklet prepared for the general's retirement on January 19, 1959.

### CHAPTER EIGHTEEN: THE SONG OF A SOLDIER'S WIFE

24. Le Minh Khue, "Literature and the Fate of Women" (address delivered at the 2007 Asian-African Festival of Literature, Jeonju, Korea, September 25, 2007). Translated by Le Minh Phuoc and Wayne Karlin.

25. Pham Thi Minh, interview with author, May 28, 2005, Thai Giang Village, translated by Le Thi Minh Hanh, and included in "Episode 1: Wandering Souls" of *Shared Weight*, WYPR Baltimore, May 30, 2006.

26. Da Ngan, interview with author, May 31, 2005, interpreted by Ho Anh Thai, and included in "Episode 2: Artists Born of War."

27. Ho Anh Thai, *The Women on the Island*. Translated by Phan Than Hao, Celeste Bachi, and Wayne Karlin (Seattle: University of Washington Press, 2000), 94–95.

28. See John Balaban's translation of the poet's work in *Spring Essence: The Poetry of Ho Xuan Huong* (Port Townsend, WA: Copper Canyon Press, 2000). Interestingly, Ho Xuan Huong is an ancestor of Ho Anh Thai.

29. Dang Tran Con and Phan Huy Ich, *The Song of a Soldier's Wife*, 13.

30. Neil L. Jamieson, *Understanding Vietnam* (Berkeley: University of California Press, 1993), 18.

31. The American soldier was Fred Whitehurst, a military interrogator. According to Seth Mydans in the *New York Times*, as he was about to burn the diary, his interpreter, Nguyen Trung Hieu, who was reading it, said, "'Don't burn this one, Fred, it already has fire in it.'"

> The journey of the diary itself has given it a special postwar symbolism for people here [in Viet Nam]. It was returned to the doctor's family just last year by a former American soldier who recovered it after she died on the battlefield in 1970. The writer, Dang Thuy Tram, was killed at the age of 27 in an American assault after she had served in a war-zone clinic for more than three years. Among the intertwining passions she expressed were her longing for a lost lover and her longing to join the Communist Party. This combination of revolutionary fervor with the vulnerabilities and self-doubts of a too-sensitive young woman might be called ideology with a human face, reminding readers that it was people like them, trapped in a moment of history, who died on their behalf. "Later, if you are ever able to live in the beautiful sunshine with the flowers of Socialism," wrote Dr. Tram, addressing herself, "remember the sacrifices of those who gave their blood for the common goal."
>
> Seth Mydans, "Doctor Killed in U.S. Attack Makes War Real," *New York Times*, June 6, 2006.

32. Le Minh Khue, "The Distant Stars," in *The Stars, the Earth, the River: Fiction by Le Minh Khue* (Willimantic, CT: Curbstone, 1997), 4.

33. Le Minh Khue, "Literature and Premonition" (keynote address at Baeong-ju Lee International Literary Festival, March 31, 2008). Translated by Le Minh Phuoc and Wayne Karlin. *The Stars, the Earth, the River* was given the festival's first ever Best Book Award on this occasion.

34. Le Minh Khue, "Fragile as a Sunray," in *The Stars, The Earth, The River,* 67.

35. Le Minh Khue, "Literature and the Fate of Women."

36. Le Minh Khue, interview with author, May 31, 2005, in "Shared Weight, Episode 2: Artists Born of War."

37. Dana Sachs, "Small Tragedies and Distant Stars: Le Minh Khue's Language of Lost Ideals," in *The Art of the Short Story,* ed. Wendy Martin (Boston: Houghton-Mifflin, 2006).

38. Le Minh Khue, "Tony D," in *The Stars, The Earth, The River,* 125.

39. Michael Norman, *These Good Men* (New York: Simon & Schuster, 1989), 133.

40. Bao Ninh, *The Sorrow of War,* 42.

41. Le Minh Khue, interview with author, May 31, 2005, in "Episode 2: Artists Born of War."

## CHAPTER NINETEEN: THE ATTIC
42. Tibby Steedly, e-mail interview with author, April 8, 2008.
43. "Episode 1: Wandering Souls."
44. Ibid.
45. Tim O'Brien, interview with author, November 11, 2005, in "Episode 2: Artists Born of War."
46. Joseph Campbell, with Bill Moyers, in *The Power of Myth with Bill Moyers*, ed. Betty Sue Flowers (New York: Doubleday, 1988), 157–158.
47. Philip Caputo, *A Rumor of War*, 355.
48. Judith Lewis Herman, M.D., *Trauma and Recovery: The Aftermath of Violence—from Domestic Abuse to Political Terror* (New York: HarperCollins, 1992).
49. Jonathan Shay, *Achilles in Vietnam*, 4.
50. Some parts of this chapter have been adapted from Wayne Karlin, "Internal Exile and Communal Memory," in *Witness*, Vol. 20 (2006), Oakland Community College, Detroit, 148–166.
51. www.swampfox.info.
52. "Episode 1: Wandering Souls."
53. Homer and Tibby Steedly, interview with author, April 8, 2008.
54. Ibid.
55. Tom Lacombe, presentation of his book *Light Ruck* at the Virginia Festival of the Book, November 16, 2005.

## PART THREE: WANDERING SOULS
## CHAPTER TWENTY: THE MISSING
1. George Evans, "Section 5, A Walk in the Garden of Heaven," *New Letters: A Magazine of Writing & Art* 61, no. 1 (1994): 102.
2. Van Le, "Quang Tri" (trans. Nguyen Ba Chung and Bruce Weigl), in *Mountain River: 1948–1993*, ed. Kevin Bowen, Nguyen Ba Chung, and Bruce Weigl, 139 (Amherst: University of Massachusetts Press, 1998).
3. See information on casualty figures from Dieu's daughter Pham Thi Huong Quynh in chapter 6. Thai Giang also had nine "heroic mothers," that is, mothers who had lost three or more sons in the American War.
4. Hoang family and Pham Quang Huy, interview with author, Thai Giang, December 26, 2007. Translated by Nguyen Qui Duc.
5. Ibid.
6. "Episode 1: Wandering Souls," of *Shared Weight: 30 Years After the Fall of Saigon* (Radio Program, Center for Emerging Media, produced by Wayne Karlin, Marc Steiner, and Steve Elliott), first broadcast on WYPR Baltimore,

May 30, 2006; and interviews in Thai Giang village conducted and translated by Le Thi Minh Hanh, July 2006.

7. Hoang family and Huy interview, December 26, 2007.

8. The figure 300,000 is cited by numerous sources, though its statistical origins remain unclear. A few examples:

- Record, Jeffrey. *The Wrong War* (Annapolis, MD: Naval Institute Press, 1998), 182: "In 1995, Hanoi itself officially admitted communist losses of 1,100,000 dead and another 300,000 missing in action."

- Rydstrom, Helle. *Embodying Morality* (Honolulu: University of Hawaii Press, 2003), 182: "Furthermore, in 1993, about 300,000 Vietnamese soldiers were missing in action. By March 1997, the missing in action had increased by another 100,000. The Vietnamese government's intention of identifying the remains of all deceased Vietnamese soldiers is, according to official sources, extremely difficult because of a lack of information and changes in terrain."

- Churchill, Ward. *On the Justice of Roosting Chickens* (Oakland, CA: AK Press, 2003), 150: "[Kissinger on January 23, 1973, at the Paris Peace Accords] also announces that no reparations will be paid until every American serviceman missing in action during the war has been accounted for by the Hanoi government (no suggestion is made that the U.S. might account for any of the 200,000–300,000 Vietnamese soldiers missing at this point.)"

- Kwon, Heonik. *Ghosts of War in Vietnam* (New York: Cambridge University Press, 2008), 48. Kwon does not delve into statistical reasoning behind the 300,000 missing but offers up a possible source with a footnote citing Bao Ninh's *The Sorrow of War*, pp. 79–80.

- Holst-Warhaft, Gail. *The Cue for Passion* (New Haven CT: Harvard University Press, 2000), 96: "Like the Americans, the Vietnamese counted as 'missing in action' those soldiers whose remains were not discovered . . . The Vietnamese count their MIAs at somewhere about 300,000 . . . "

In addition, 300,000 is the official number quoted by the Vietnamese Embassy in the United States; however, there is no explanation offered of the methods used to obtain that figure. If each village in the North had the same proportionate losses and MIAs as Thai Giang—142 lost in the American war, out of which 37 bodies were returned—the overall figure does not seem exaggerated, and in fact may be underestimated.

9. "A Prayer for the Dying: How Americans Absorbed the Loss of 620,000 Lives During the Civil War," *Washington Post*, February 24, 2008, Book World T-3.

10. Kwon, *Ghosts of War,* suggests that the Vietnamese government's policy of doi moi (renovation)—the regulated market economy initiated in the 1980s in response to desperate poverty, runaway inflation, and resistance

to collectivization—and the era of relative prosperity that followed, "included a growing political tolerance towards communal and associational activities including religious worship" (29) that led to a revival of traditional beliefs and their connected rituals—including rituals to bring home the remains of the hundreds of thousands of missing soldiers and bring their wandering spirits to rest. Kwon maintains that the political apparatus, recognizing the strength of the need to commemorate the dead, utilized it to create a sense of national memory and identity based on the remembrance of the war as it was incorporated into the lives of individual families. The government cooperated and indeed worked with traditional ritualists and mediums, and so "[t]he search for missing soldiers and the ensuing rituals of home reburial turned the population into a long file of marchers behind the state officials . . . these events . . . dramatized the agency of the state as the sole legitimate undertaker to orchestrate the vital transformation of mass war death" (49). Kwon is not questioning here the sincerity of the state or of the families or suggesting that the revival and incorporation of these rituals is a cynical manipulation. His explanation does help explain why the Hoangs, a northern, "orthodox" family with a deepseated ideological belief in communism and an equally deep-seated belief in the faith and rituals prevalent in rural Vietnam, were able to feel secure and indeed socially encouraged in their search for Dam's remains.

11. Porter Mokie, Vietnam Veterans of America, http://www.vva.org/accomplishments.html.

12. Sedgwick Tourison III, interviews and detailed e-mail exchanges with author, May 1–3, 2008. Wick's experience with the manipulation of intelligence for political expedience went back to the excuse for the escalation of the Viet Nam War, the Gulf of Tonkin incident. On August 2, 1965, the American destroyer USS *Maddox* was attacked by North Vietnamese PT boats. A reported second attack on August 4 was found to have been faked. "I interrogated the commander: We captured him in July 1966, after another raid. He told me and my partner that the second attack never happened, that it was an excuse concocted by Lyndon Johnson to start bombing North Viet Nam, and to start the ground war in Viet Nam, which he did. I asked the captain, his name was Senior Captain Tran Bao, to prove what he said. And he did, to both of us—he laid it out logically and thoroughly how it could not have happened: how many boats they had, how many were disabled, how the torpedoes that would have been needed had been depleted. We sent the de-briefing to the higher command, and received a blistering message telling us to not send any more debriefings on the incident."

13. Sedgwick Tourison III, interview with author, February 19, 2008.

14. Nguyen Thi Tien, e-mail to author, June 13, 2008.

15. Philip Caputo, *A Rumor of War*, 123–124.

16. Nguyen Thi Tien, *Stories of the Searcher*, trans. Ho Nguyen (Hanoi: Van Hoc Publishing, 2005), 7–8.

17. Ho Anh Thai, "A Fragment of a Man" in *Behind the Red Mist: Fiction by Ho Anh Thai*, translated by Nguyen Qui Duc (Willimantic, CT: Curbstone, 1998), 1–23.

18. Nguyen Thi Tien, e-mail to author, June 13, 2008.

19. All of Nguyen Thi Tien's quotations, unless otherwise indicated, are from her interview with the author and Phan Thanh Hao, Hanoi, January 2, 2008.

## CHAPTER TWENTY-ONE: THE ALTAR

20. Doug Reese, interview with author and Jessica Phillips, Viet Nam, May 25, 2008.

21. Parts of this chapter adapted from Wayne Karlin, "Wandering Souls," in *War, Literature & the Arts* and in *Manoa: Maps of Reconciliation*.

22. Episode 1: Wandering Souls."

23. Ibid.

24. Ibid.

25. Ibid.

26. Ibid.

## CHAPTER TWENTY-THREE: THE DOCUMENTS

27. All translations by Ho Nguyen.

## CHAPTER TWENTY-FOUR: TRANSIT

28. "Episode 1: Wandering Souls" and "Episode 2: Artists Born of War" of *Shared Weight*.

29. All quotes and background information about Woody Curry are from "Episode 3: Woody's Journey," of *Shared Weight* (interviews by Valerie Williams and Marc Steiner).

30. Elmer Pence (41st CAC veteran), e-mail to author, December 14, 2008.

31. "Revelation in The Mother Lode," in *Sudden Dreams: New & Selected Poems by George Evans* (Minneapolis, MN: Coffee House, 1991), 55–56.

## CHAPTER TWENTY-FIVE: THE RETURN

32. "Episode 1: Wandering Souls." Parts of this chapter were adopted from the author's "Wandering Souls" in *War, Literature and the Arts: An International Journal of the Humanities* (2006), and in *Manoa: Maps of Reconciliation: Literature and the Ethical Imagination* (Spring 2007).

33. "Episode 2: Artists Born of War."

34. "Episode 1: Wandering Souls."

35. George Evans, "Two Girls," in *The New World* (Willimantic, CT: Curbstone Press, 2002), 25.

36. George Evans, e-mail interview with author, May 19, 2008.

37. Ibid.

38. "Episode 1: Wandering Souls."

39. Ibid.

## PART FOUR: INTERLUDE
### CHAPTER TWENTY-SIX: THE PISGAH NATIONAL FOREST

1. Elizabeth Steedly, e-mail interview with author, April 8, 2008. Homer's remarks about the connections between the Central Highlands and the Pisgah are from our conversations in Viet Nam, May 20–30, 2008.

### CHAPTER TWENTY-SEVEN: THE CUC PHUONG NATIONAL PARK

2. Their saga is recounted in Duc's memoir, *Where the Ashes Are: The Odyssey of a Vietnamese Family* (Reading, MA: Addison-Wesley, 1995).

3. Hoang family interview, December 26, 2007.

## PART FIVE: HOMECOMING
### CHAPTER TWENTY-EIGHT: THAI GIANG

1. Tibby Steedly, telephone interview with author, April 7, 2009.

2. This conversation took place in the Café Cong and is taken from my notes. Later Homer went into more detail, and some of his quotations from that interview are spliced into the dialogue here. Homer Steedly, interviews with Jessica Phillips, May 27, 2008.

3. Her full name is Phan Thi Bich Hang. According to AFP's Frank Zeller (www.news.swaf.org, June 26, 2007, and conversation with Zeller in Hanoi, May 27, 2008), she is one of the ten most famous mediums in Viet Nam. Her reputation was secured when she was consulted by former deputy prime minister Vu Vang Dung to find the remains of his sister, killed by the French in 1950. Hang told him that his sister's spirit described being tortured by the French, details that were only contained in a confidential report the former deputy prime minister had in his possession. The reputable mediums are contacted (in a prosaic manner) through the Science Technology Union for Informatics Application, located in Hanoi. They operate as Ms. Bich Hang operated throughout our trip, not by going with the family seeking remains, but by staying in touch by cell phone and describing where the family must go and what they must do. I was not sure if the translation of "zombie" was correct, but when I asked for a meaning of the word, I was told, "a dead person who still goes around," which indeed seems to fit the word.

## CHAPTER TWENTY-NINE: VINH

4. Homer Steedly, interview with author and Jessica Phillips, May 26, 2008.

5. Ibid.

## CHAPTER THIRTY: PLEIKU

6. Stanley Karnow, *Vietnam: A History* (New York: Viking, 1983), 412–413, 641.

## CHAPTER THIRTY-TWO: THE MANG YANG PASS

7. Harold G. Moore and Joseph L. Galloway, *We Were Soldiers Once . . . and Young* (New York: Ballantine, 1992), 46–47. For a more detailed account, see Bernard Fall, *Street Without Joy* (New York: Schocken Books, 1961).

## CHAPTER THIRTY-THREE: THE HAI VAN PASS

8. The quotes in this chapter are from my notes on the trip and Homer Steedly, interview with author and Jessica Phillips, May 27, 2008.

## CHAPTER THIRTY-FOUR: THAI GIANG

9. Hoang Minh Dieu, e-mail to author, August 8, 2008. Translated by Pham Thi Huong Quynh (Dieu's daughter).

## EPILOGUE:
## DOWN AT THE END OF A DARK ROAD

1. Quoted in Dan Barry, "Asked to Serve Again, A Soldier Goes Down Fighting," *New York Times On-line*, May 29, 2007.

2. Ibid.

3. Ibid.

4. Kathy Dobie, "Denial in the Corps," *The Nation On-line*, February 18, 2008.

5. Cynthia Enloe, "Women After Wars: Puzzles and Warnings from Vietnam," in *The Curious Feminist* (Berkeley: University of California Press, 2004), 204.

6. Dinh Thang, "Mot nu a su that . . . o dau?" *Tuoi Tre On Line*, August 24, 2008, http://www.tuoitre.com.vn/Tianyon/Index.aspx?ArticleID= 275057&ChannelID=10.

7. "Dao dien Minh Chuyen noi gi?" *Tien Phong*, August 23, 2008, 9.

# INDEX